THEATRE FOR THE PEOPLE

Flensburg

Schleswig

Rendsburg   Kiel

Cuxhaven

Lübeck

Wilhelmshaven   Bremerhaven   Hamburg

Wiesmoor

Oldenburg   Lüneburg

Bremen

Uelzen

Nienburg   Celle

Osnabrück   Minden   Hannover   Helmstedt

Georgsm.hütte   Braunschweig

Münster   Bielefeld   Hameln   Hildesheim

Goslar

Hamm   Paderborn
Essen   Gelsenkirchen
Mülheim   Castrop-Rauxel
Duisburg   Dortmund   Göttingen
Düsseldorf   Velbert   Witten
Bochum   Hagen
Wuppertal
Solingen   Remscheid   Korbach

Kassel

Köln

Bonn   Marburg

Gießen

Koblenz   Friedberg

Frankfurt

Wiesbaden   Hanau   Hof

Mainz   Großauheim

Darmstadt   Aschaffenburg

Trier   Bamberg   Bayreuth

Worms   Eberbach   Würzburg   Erlangen

Kaiserslautern   Fürth

Heidelberg

Saarbrücken   Amberg

Heilbronn

Karlsruhe

Pforzheim   Ludwigsburg   Regensburg

Baden-Baden   Stuttgart

Eßlingen   Göppingen   Ingolstadt

Tübingen   Landshut

Reutlingen

Ulm   Augsburg

Freiburg   München

Tuttlingen   Memmingen

Konstanz

Berlin

The German Volksbühne
associations today

● Places with resident
  companies

○ Places visited by
  touring companies

CECIL W. DAVIES

THEATRE FOR THE PEOPLE
The story of the Volksbühne

MANCHESTER UNIVERSITY PRESS

Published 1977 by Manchester University Press,
Oxford Road, Manchester M13 9PL

ISBN 0 7190 0666 X

Printed in Great Britain by
Lowe & Brydone Printers Ltd, Thetford, Norfolk

CONTENTS

FRONTISPIECE Map of the German Volksbühne
associations today   page   ii

PREFACE   vii

PROLOGUE Before 1890. The prehistory of the Volksbühne   1

ACT I 1890-1914. From Brauhaus to Bülowplatz
1 The first decade   13
2 Into the twentieth century   55

FIRST INTERMISSION 1914-1918. War and revolution   86

ACT II 1918-1933. The Berlin Volksbühne in the Weimar
               Republic
1 To 1923   88
2 The Piscator affair   95

SECOND INTERMISSION The Nazis. 'Night over Germany'   113

ACT III The Volksbühne since 1945 and outside Berlin
1 In Berlin   117
2 Developments outside Berlin   139

PRINCIPAL SOURCES   145

NOTES   149

APPENDICES
A The Articles of Association of the Freie Volksbühne   157
B Membership statistics   159
C The sixteen districts of the Federation in 1930   165
D The Christian 'Volksbühne' movement   165
E Other audience organisations   168

INDEX   171

PREFACE

The Volksbühne movement is Germany's unique contribution to the
history of the theatre and its audience. It is arguable that it could not
have arisen in any other country, and certainly attempts to transplant
it have never met with more than partial success. The tradition of
theatre as a moral institution with an educational function, running
from Lessing through Schiller and Hauptmann to Brecht, is its foundation. Because of this tradition nineteenth-century German working-class
movements could naturally and unselfconsciously use drama as a
medium for social education and propaganda, and could regard the
Naturalism of Ibsen and Hauptmann as organically related to the aims
of social revolution. A comparable movement in England led to the
founding of the Workers' Educational Association: evening classes were
an appropriate expression of working-class aspirations; theatre was
not.

The Volksbühne could also only grow in a country where regular
rather than occasional theatre attendance was regarded as normal. In
England the nearest parallel is perhaps the regular cinema-going of the
1920s and 1930s; but a German movement that offered its members not
only the most significant plays, but offered them on a regular monthly
basis, could gain thousands of members in pre-1914 Berlin, and develop
into a mass movement in the politically more favourable climate of the
Weimar Republic.

Such a movement is bound to be the object of attacks, and the
Volksbühne has been attacked throughout its existence — from the right,
because of its Social Democratic associations; from the left, because
it has never subordinated the human values of art to party political aims;
from theatre directors who have believed that the Volksbühne inhibits
experiment, and from dissatisfied members who thought it offered too

many serious or experimental plays. It has been attacked by commercial interests who saw it as a competitor, and by politicians and
taxpayers who have resented subsidies its theatres have received.
Some accuse it of being a mere cheap ticket organisation, a theatrical
soup-kitchen; others of diverting the theatre to political ends. The
Nazis dissolved it and burnt most of its records; the Communists of
East Germany tried to bend it to their purposes — and eventually also
dissolved it.

It is true that Volksbühne members and officials can be compla-
cent; in some cities the Volksbühne rests on its laurels; in some it
has lost initiative to Christian or commercial rivals; sometimes its
programmes are not sufficiently adventurous; sometimes is advertising
campaigns are dull and old-fashioned. Its healthy tradition of democracy and self-government can lead to delays and inefficiency; its
unwillingness to abandon old ways (for example the ticket lottery in the
foyer) can lose it membership.

But it remains the envy of other nations — especially of the theatres
of other nations. It provides a firm basis for seasonal programme
planning; it encourages revivals of the classics and the production of
new plays of contemporary significance. It has never concerned itself
with experimental forms, but with human and social content, and its
rank-and-file membership tends not to support experimental theatre
for its own sake. Although theatre directors sometimes resent its
block bookings in times of prosperity, only the Volksbühne and comparable organisations have kept the German theatres open in times of
economic difficulty.

This book is written from the point of view that the positive
contribution of the Volksbühne (and those of its younger rivals and
imitators) to the German theatre has far outweighed, and still out-
weighs, any ill effects it has had. Its existence creates a regular and
informed theatre public — not an audience of prodigies, but one better
educated, more critical and better prepared for the theatrical experience than would otherwise exist.

The story of the Volksbühne has never before been told within a
single book. Vast quantities of highly indigestible material exist on
the Berlin Volksbühne, and innumerable brochures and articles relate
to particular places or aspects outside the capital. Some references
to the early days of the movement, and perhaps some account of
Piscator's relationship to the Volksbühne are usual in most books on
the German theatre. Here the attempt is made to tell the whole story
consecutively and reasonably completely in the hope that the true worth
and importance of the movement will thereby emerge. Even here, to
keep the book within reasonable compass in a time of financial strin-
gency, the story of the movement outside Berlin is outlined only very
briefly.

To write on the Volksbühne inevitably involves trespass out of the realms of theatre and drama into those of political and social history. In these the author claims no expertise and must apologise if in attempting to relate his subject to its necessary background he sometimes makes statements which to the political or social historian are naïve, unbalanced or unclear. Perhaps the interdisciplinary character of the subject has deterred other and wiser men from writing this book; doubtless others, perhaps in Germany, will later improve upon it. Meanwhile it is offered as an opportunity for English-speaking readers, and especially students of German theatre and drama, to learn about the Volksbühne and judge it for themselves.

PROLOGUE

Before 1890   The prehistory of the Volksbühne

Let us begin with an impression of the Berlin Volksbühne in 1930:

> Even if he is not very observant, the traveller who comes from
> the east and enters Berlin at night sees a strange picture. The
> weary engine moves painfully over the railway track which ploughs
> like a furrow through the midst of the mighty city, and somewhere,
> far outside, comes to an end on lifeless lines. The cosmopolis
> hammers at the stranger with merciless blows. First it destroys
> an illusion — on this short journey it does not shine in its Sunday
> best: it lays all its features bare: floods of light alternate with
> murky terraced streets; interminably empty black walls lead to
> the overhead railway; the eye takes a long, endless, sobering look
> at eternally identical rows of windows, yards, alleys and dark
> canyon-like streets. Thus the monster, Berlin, offers its visiting
> card: impersonal, factual, busy, almost cynical and brutal. But
> suddenly a sharp gap opens to the observer for a few seconds in
> the black walls; in huge illuminated letters a word shines out like
> magic, only to sink again into the grey of the grey walls. What
> was it? — Volksbühne? — Yes. Somewhere the great building of
> the Theatre on the Bülowplatz breaks into a scarcely cheerful row
> of houses in the busiest part of the capital. In flaming letters of
> light it stamps one word upon the dark night of its surroundings,
> the word that, over the years one might say was transformed
> from a proper noun to the concept of Culture.
>
> When this shining beacon in 'Berlin C' is extinguished and the
> bright day dawns, the other inscription on that great building be-
> comes visible, like an answer. It reads: Art for the People. [1]

Founded in 1890, the Freie Volksbühne was the first and is still the
largest of the audience organisations that are a characteristic feature
of German theatre-going. It was a child of its time, born of a marriage
between political and artistic movements, socialism and naturalism.

Bruno Wille's announcement and appeal for support for the new body, published in Berlin on 23 March 1890, began:

> The Theatre should be a source of high artistic gratification, moral uplift and a powerful stimulus to thinking about the great topics of the day. But it is debased to the level of drawing-room wit, society small-talk and penny-dreadfuls, the circus and comic papers. The stage is subjugated to capitalism, and the taste of the masses of all ranks of society has been corrupted primarily by certain economic conditions.
>
> Nevertheless, under the influence of sincerely struggling poets, journalists and speakers, a section of our people has freed itself from this corruption. Writers like Tolstoy and Dostoyevsky, Zola, Ibsen and Kielland as well as a number of German 'Realists' have found a sounding-board in the working people of Berlin. [2]

To understand how Wille's appeal came to be couched in such terms, and why it met with an enthusiastic response one must try to appreciate the political, social and cultural context in which it was written and read.

In the mid nineteenth century over two-thirds of the population of Germany was rural. In the following sixty years (to 1910), while the population as a whole did not quite double itself, the urban population quadrupled. The Silesian weavers whose abortive revolt in 1844 was the subject of Hauptmann's Die Weber (The Weavers), were handloom workers in a cottage industry; by the time the play was written (1891) there were over 150,000 factory workers in Berlin alone. During the same period Germany was transformed from a politically impotent group of states to a powerful Empire dominated by Bismarck under the hegemony of Prussia. But this 'united' Germany was socially divided, and the rapidly expanding urban proletariat developed into a political and social power that even Bismarck was unable to check.

The political and economic aspirations of the new working class were expressed through the movement known as Social Democracy. Before 1848 it was extremely difficult for the workers to achieve any political organisation at all. Nevertheless, even as early as 1834 German emigrés founded in Paris a 'League of Outlaws' (Bund der Geächteten). Four years later came a similar body, more firmly grounded in the working class, the 'League of the Just' (Bund der Gerechten). At the beginning of 1846, Marx and Engels founded a 'Communist Correspondence Committee' (Kommunistische Korrespondenzkomitee) in Brussels; then, prompted by the London section of the League of the Just, they founded in 1847 the League of Communists (Bund der Kommunisten), the first revolutionary workers' party, and in February 1848 issued the Communist Manifesto.

The principal founder of the German Social Democratic Movement
in Germany itself, however, was not Marx or Engels — exiles in England, whose names were known to comparatively few German workers —
but Ferdinand Lassalle, a child prodigy, son of a Jewish silk merchant.
Born in Breslau in 1825, Lassalle was intended for commerce but after
a year at the Trade School in Leipzig (1840-41) he changed course,
studying in Breslau and Berlin, visiting Paris and becoming a convinced
Hegelian. He published a number of books and pamphlets of which the
most important and scholarly, the System of Acquired Rights (1861),
anticipated some of the basic ideas of Marx's Capital (1867). In 1862
he became a political agitator among the German workers, advocating
a system of state socialism in his working-class programme. In May
1863 in Leipzig he founded the General German Workers' Association
(Allgemeiner Deutscher Arbeiterverein: ADAV) which he led dictatori-
ally, à fact which naturally had a detrimental effect on its politics and
internal democracy. Lassalle was killed in a duel in Switzerland on
the last day of August 1864. Almost religiously honoured by his
followers, a bon vivant of social democracy, he was an opportunist who
had gone so far as to offer Bismarck his support in smashing the Prussian Constitution if Bismarck in return curbed the power of the capital-
ists and provided measures of social security: Bismarck was not
impressed, remarking, 'What could the wretched man offer me? '

Lassalle's ADAV had a wide basis upon which to work. In the late
fifties, especially after the economic crisis of 1857, workers' associations multiplied rapidly and by 1860 there were over eight hundred
workers' associations and workers' educational associations in
Germany. In fact a majority of these held aloof from the ADAV and
formed themselves a few weeks after its foundation into the Union of
German Workers' Associations (Verband — originally Vereinstag — der
deutschen Arbeitervereine: VDAV) under liberal middle-class
leadership. In 1868 the middle-class elements were forced into resignation and in 1869 at Eisenach the remaining members and member
bodies joined with opposition members of the ADAV and the German
section of the International Working Men's Association (Internationale
Arbeiterassoziation), led by Marx and Engels, to form the Social
Democratic Workers' Party (Sozialdemokratische Arbeiterpartei),
which thus became the first revolutionary and primarily Marxist party
in Germany. In article II, paragraph 6 of its constitution the new
party declared:

> Taking into consideration that the liberation of labour is neither a
> local nor a national but a social problem, which comprehends all
> countries in which modern Society exists, the Social Democratic
> Workers' Party regards itself, as far as the laws covering associ-
> ations permit, as a branch of the International Working Men's

Association [First International] identifying itself with its en-
deavours. [3]

In thus declaring an international loyalty to class before loyalty to
State the party was challenging conservative and national forces. [4]
Its programme, too, was likely to disturb Bismarck. It included
demands for adult male suffrage, direct legislation 'through the
people', separation of Church and State, school and Church, compul-
sory free education. The economic collapse (1873) with widespread
unemployment and lowering of wages that followed the temporary war
boom of 1870-71 seemed to confirm Marxist theory in practice. The
party grew. It was indeed the first German political party to develop
a real party organisation, and towards the end of the seventies its
membership had reached half a million. Bismarck, who understood
no policy in such a situation except suppression, brought his proposed
anti-socialist legislation before the Reichstag in May 1878. It was
thrown out; but after the July elections in which the Conservatives
gained seats, the anti-socialist law (Sozialistengesetz) was passed in
September. The passing of this law (which was renewed until 1890)
was the most important event in the development of German Social
Democracy. Theoretically it should have resulted in the elimination
of the Social Democratic Party, which it declared illegal. Many leading
social democrats were expelled from the capital, party property was
seized and its press suppressed. Yet,

> Bismarck treated the Social Democrats in a curiously old-fashioned,
> high-principled way. Men are bound by their generation, and Bis-
> marck, despite his Realpolitik, had much more resemblance to
> Gladstone than to Hitler ... this persecution bore the unmistakable
> stamp of the liberal era; Social Democrats were still allowed to be
> candidates at the elections and to sit in the Reichstag; the number
> of members of the party increased steadily, and in all about 1,500
> persons were imprisoned (an average of a little over a hundred a
> year). [5]

In fact, there was just enough persecution to stimulate growth and the
development of a good, tight, organisation; the Social Democratic vote
doubled in twelve years. By 1890 the Social Democratic Party was the
strongest in Berlin. Far from weakening its stance during the period
of illegality the party had adopted a more distinctly Marxist position.

To evade the anti-socialist law, and at the same time to collect
money to help those suffering under it, many societies whose true
intentions were kept secret were founded upon various pretexts. They
multiplied particularly in the last years of the anti-socialist law. Their
names were harmless-sounding, often absurd: The Camel Club,
Goblin's Grotto, Miller and Mayor, Sowtooth, Blue Onion, Old Aunt.

Many were, or claimed to be, literary or debating societies. Some indeed, changed in character, and the interest in literature which had been a mask became a reality, for the legislation that prevented the workers from organising themselves politically also prevented their cultural and educational development. The motives that led the workers to want culture and education were mixed. On the one hand culture was seen as bourgeois privilege of which the worker was deprived; on the other hand education was seen as an instrument for promoting the idea of socialism. In any case, the cultural and educational aspects were as old as the movement itself. As we have already seen, many of the workers' associations that went to form the Social Democratic Party were themselves educational. The importance of drama, too, had been recognised from the very beginning. Engels himself hastily wrote a one-act play (now lost) for a festival of the Brussels German Workers' Association (Brüsseler Deutscher Arbeiterverein) in 1847. Its subject was maladministration in a small German State and the downfall of the prince through a popular revolution. It was rehearsed in a few days and performed by members of the Workers' Association and their supporters. Lassalle too, in 1856-58, wrote a tragedy, Franz von Sickingen. Its subject was the Peasants' Revolt — for Lassalle, in common with many others, saw parallels between its failure and that of the March Revolution. Lassalle saw in each a 'tragic collision' between the 'Idea' and the 'necessity for compromise', between 'revolutionary ends' and 'diplomatic means'. He considered that false revolutionary tactics had brought about failure, both in the Peasants' Revolt and in 1848-49. After its publication in 1859 Lassalle sent copies with long covering letters explaining his tragic idea to Marx and Engels, both of whom answered him at length with keen but friendly criticism. It is true that when Lassalle wrote again to Marx countering his criticisms, Marx's only reaction was in a short letter to Engels: 'Incredible, that a man at this time and in these circumstances of world history not only finds time to write such stuff, but demands our time to read it.' [6] But the fact remains that for Lassalle, Marx and Engels a play could be relevant to the political struggle in which they were engaged.

An historical play such as Franz von Sickingen was, however, not typical of the drama of the social democratic movement. The plays performed by the workers' groups on small, often improvised stages were not plays, like Goethe's Götz von Berlichingen and Schiller's Die Räuber (The Robbers), in which exceptional individuals help the poor from outside. The great individual had no place in them. The new Socialist hero derived from the collective idea; the message was the power of solidarity; and the joy of acting was inseparable from the will to reveal the class struggle. The plays took many forms and included much comedy and satire. During the sixties there were all kinds of one-act agitation pieces, election farces, festival items, <u>tableaux vivants</u>, and full-length plays, especially strike-plays. Whatever the form and however amateur the players, the workers' theatre dealt with the great social and national questions whose solution was necessary to the workers' well-being. Had the middle and upper classes known what was going on in the workers' clubs the opposition would have been as strong as it later was to Hauptmann's <u>Die Weber</u>. And in some ways the performances in these clubs anticipated the naturalist movement.

Just as the workers' clubs themselves had to hide under innocuous names under the anti-socialist law (1878-90) so too the revolutionary plays had to be disguised. No longer was the hero's name Roth (Red), Fels (Rock), Stein (Stone), or Frei (Free). During these twelve years historical subjects in which, as in Lassalle's play, parallels could be seen with contemporary events, but which at the same time might avoid the attentions of the police did become typical. [7] Nor did the socialist amateurs confine themselves to propagandist plays. A few of the groups, if they were good enough, played classics, but on the whole the rest of the material was 'harmless rubbish'. It is a great mistake to idealise the nineteenth-century German workers. On the whole they preferred popular farces to Ibsen and Zola.

The German stage generally was suffering in the eighties from a feeling of stagnation, and the most lively and progressive movements in production and in dramatic writing were failing to penetrate the official theatres. Yet in this period, before cinema and radio existed and before sport had become mass entertainment, the theatre was at the centre of interest in matters of entertainment and 'improvement'. In the seventies there had been considerable theatrical success, and the opening of the Bayreuth Opera in 1876 had induced a feeling that a new era was about to begin. Therefore there was in the late seventies and the eighties a multiplication of theatrical enterprises in the capital. Alongside the two 'Royal' theatres a whole circle of others competed for the public. The reputation of the Deutsches Theater founded by Adolf L'Arronge in 1883 was very high, perhaps even higher than that of the Royal Theatres. In 1888 Oscar Blumenthal founded the Lessing Theater and in 1889 Ludwig Barnay created the Berliner Theater out of an operetta-house. It was thought of as a People's Theatre when founded and its prices were somewhat lower than most, though its audience was still middle-class, not working-class. There were also the Wallner Theater, the Residenz Theater, the Belle-Alliance Theater, the Zentral Theater and the Ostend Theater. But still a lack of life was felt. To the political censorship, which banned plays dealing with social problems, hunger, poverty and so on, was added the self-censorship of the theatre managements who, in a city of timid critics and a thoughtless public, put business before art in order to assure themselves of a regular audience. The repertoire consisted largely of Scribe, Sardou, Dumas fils, and the endless legion of well-meaning but powerless descendants of Schiller. There was no place for the real modern drama. Problems were avoided and theatres concentrated upon cheap effects, circus-like comic situations and showy settings. A high subsidy granted to the Königliches Schauspielhaus specifically for productions involving financial risk was used for productions involving none. Bruno Wille's castigation of the theatre as 'debased to the level of drawing-room wit, society small-talk and penny dreadfuls' and at the same time enslaved to economic conditions was fully justified. Even this theatre, for what it was worth as entertainment, was largely inaccessible to the working classes. The ten-hour working day was normal, and the battle against the twelve-hour day not completely won, but the theatre performances started at 7.30 p.m. or even earlier. The prices of most seats were beyond the means of men earning an average wage of 20 to 25 Marks per week. Though most theatres had a gallery at 1 Mark or 75 Pfennigs per seat, even this was high to working men, many of whom also felt humiliated at being segregated at a separate entrance from the well-heeled majority in the theatre.

Thus the deep divisions in German society were reflected in the theatre. Schiller had said, 'Wir Deutsche sind noch keine Nation' (We Germans are still not a nation) and the English historian Buckle said in his History of Civilisation in England (1857-61): 'There is no nation in Europe in which there is so great a distance between the highest and lowest minds' (sc. as in Germany). These divisions remained after the founding of the Empire in 1871 and were still there in 1890. In the theatre their existence was partly the cause and partly the effect of the non-existence of a national theatre and because there was no national theatre attempts were made throughout the nineteenth century to introduce the working class into the theatre. Such plans for reform were always linked with a political party, a profession or a specific world-view, and the distinction was always drawn between theatre as entertainment and theatre as education. Naturally, in the first half of the nineteenth century the phrase 'working class' only meant the lower middle classes (die kleinen Bürger), the so-called Third Estate, not the true proletariat, the Fourth Estate, which developed in the second half of the century.

In 1848 Landenberg, a government minister, introduced a National Theatre Law with the support of the Ministry of Culture. This led to many ideas for 'underprivileged' and 'educational' theatre. But Landenberg died and the idea was lost. In 1859 a petition was presented in Berlin for concessionary cheap seats for workers: 'For a really small admission charge, to present carefully rehearsed classical and

improving dramas, and thus to counteract the trivial-obscene tendency
in the people'. [8] The petition was refused. The Oberpräsidium
thought the people did not need theatre, and the Minister of the Interior,
Count Schwerin, thought it wrong to encourage the workers' 'passion
for pleasure' (Vergnügungssucht). Yet Schwerin himself authorised
three new 'Possentheater'!

As the working-class movement grew some conservatives saw that
theatre-going was part of the workers' standard of living. Theatre
then became a factor in social politics. It was thought that access to
the theatre would stop the workers thinking about socialism — a secular
'opium of the people'. Let the workers be given a share in the culture
of the higher classes and they will seek to alter but not to destroy it.
From interested motives some theatre managers hoped to improve the
state of the theatre by getting the poor as additional audience.

Other reformers were disinterested. Some idealists wanted a
revival of the ancients as a 'sublime example'; they wanted large
theatres, cheap seats and material suitable to the mass of the people,
so as to re-establish the ancient ideal of theatre. Even the Church
expressed the view that theatre was good for the cultural development
of the people, and an anonymous essay of 1890 under the title 'Theatre
and Church' claimed that the Church was not opposed to the theatre.

More practical was the action of Botho von Hülsen, Intendant of
the Königliches Theater, who in the late seventies halved his prices,
partly to get over the bad months of the year, partly to make theatre-
going possible to a broader mass of the people. The policy proved to
be good business and the theatre was sold out every evening instead of
being badly attended. It is a mystery why this experiment did not
develop further. Even this wider audience, however, was lower-
middle-class, not working-class.

In 1886 a new Director of the Ostend (East End) Theater, Kurz,
tried to establish a people's theatre with a 'literary programme'. He
gave over a hundred performances of Das Neue Gebot (The New Com-
mandment) by Ernst von Wildenbruch. [9] The experiment was
unsuccessful. The audience for the literary programme came to the
Ostend Theater from Berlin's West End. Like the workers, they
preferred new plays to classics. Under a new director the theatre
went in for spectacular 'Possen' with song and dance, and then the
audience came once more from the working-class districts. In 1888
Witte-Wild tried a similar experiment in the same theatre, but could
not hold out for long. He was also involved in the following year with
the schemes of Baron von Malzahn. In May 1889 Baron von Malzahn
delivered a speech in Berlin, 'The Founding of a German People's
Theatre, a national task' , which was also published as a pamphlet.

Though much of it was platitude the speech contained definite proposals for an experiment that involved constructing theatres using, for cheapness, iron, not stone, as building material. The first theatre was to be in Berlin. On the basis of this speech an attempt was made to found an Association for the Founding of People's Theatres (Verein zur Begründung von Volksbühnen). The matter was discussed with Ludwig Barnay, Director of the Berliner Theater and a General Meeting was held in October 1889 at which plans for a theatre seating three thousand were advanced. But nothing came of it. The plan failed partly through lack of resources, partly through the lack of any inherent idea that might have interested wider circles and attracted a membership.

In March 1890 an economist, Georg Adler, published an article, later reprinted in the Berliner Neueste Nachricht, opposing the building of People's Theatres as impracticable. They would need too much subsidy to raise through collections, and State help was unlikely. He proposed instead that the 'Court' theatres should, as a condition of their subsidy, have to put on a workers' performance once every eight days at which seats in the stalls would cost 50 Pfennigs, the circle less. Tickets were to be sold through the Workmen's Sick Pay Office and the plays were to be taken from the existing repertoire. There was little response: from the Kaiser, none. [10]

All these schemes failed because their founders did not themselves belong to the working people. As Otto Neumann-Hofer wrote in September 1890:

Are educated people in a position to create a workers' theatre? They may try. They will raise the money — no worker will go to the theatre.... The 'People' has confidence only in its own creation. [11]

The people would not be patronised, he went on. It must not be a question of 'spreading education' or 'teaching the ability to appreciate', but of sharing one's own artistic life. The attempt to found a people's theatre must come from the people themselves. In the end it did so, but in a very particular way.

The most important movements in the European theatre and drama of the eighties were those which are usually grouped under the broad heading of Naturalism. The seventies saw a great development in the German-speaking theatre of a meticulous historical accuracy in externals derived from Charles Kean's productions at the Princess Theatre, London, adopted by German directors. From our point of view this fashion would not have been of particular importance — and was in fact attacked by many young Naturalists — had it not also been associated with the Meiningen Court Theatre (Herzoglich-Meiningensches Hoftheater), the creation of the Duke George II of

Saxe-Meiningen, his actress wife and his Director Ludwig Chronegk
which through its tours between 1874 and 1890, extending from New
York to Moscow, exercised an extraordinary influence upon theatrical
production. The repertoire of the company was primarily serious and
classical. Ibsen's The Pretenders and Ghosts were exceptions and
their most popular productions were Julius Caesar and The Winter's
Tale, with German classics such as Schiller and Kleist. But the style
of the Meiningen company, with its attention to detail and its use of
ensemble playing instead of star acting, provided the ideal medium for
the production of the new naturalist drama in which ordinary men and
women are often represented as products of their environment and whose
actions are both interdependent and dependent upon external and social
forces. In France, André Antoine, who founded the Théâtre Libre in
1887 for the performance of naturalistic drama, was partly influenced
in his style by the Meiningen Players. In Germany it was Otto Brahm
who applied what he learnt from Chronegk to the production of the new
naturalistic drama.

1878, the year of the anti-socialist law, may also be regarded as
the birth year of the naturalistic movement in German literature. [12]
In that year Ibsen's Pillars of Society was given its first performance
in Germany, and, coincidentally, the first of many journals associated
with the brothers Heinrich and Julius Hart, the Deutsche Monatsblätter,
appeared. Ibsen did not immediately have a striking influence upon the
German Naturalists, whose model at first was Zola, and it was nearly
a decade later, in 1887, that the performance of Ghosts in Germany
firmly established his supremacy. Meanwhile many of the greatest
European plays of the naturalist movement were written: Ibsen's A
Doll's House (Nora in Germany), Ghosts, An Enemy of the People,
The Wild Duck and Rosmersholme; Strindberg's The Father; Tolstoy's
Power of Darkness. Of these only Nora had a German production
(1880) during that period though at the same time the most influential
critics, first the Hart brothers, later and even more importantly Otto
Brahm, were declaring these to be the most significant contemporary
plays.

Brahm and his friend Paul Schlenther together saw the 1878 production of Pillars of Society. In retrospect this seemed to Brahm to
mark the beginning of his enthusiasm for Ibsen. Writing in 1904, he
said:

> The first powerful theatrical impression which I experienced
> when I began to look at the world, the world of the theatre, with
> my own eyes, and which passionately involved my interest, — the
> first powerful impression of the production of a living dramatist
> came to me through Henrik Ibsen ... [after a reference to
> 1878].... From that hour we adhered to the new naturalistic art,
> and our aesthetic life had welcomed its content. [13]

Schlenther's recollection was different:

> When we first saw the Pillars of Society in Berlin in 1878, Brahm
> saw in this pioneering work not much more than in Björnson's
> Bankruptcy. When afterwards we discussed the performance we
> had experienced together, while I stressed the novelty of the piece,
> Brahm criticised its weakness, which today, spoilt by Ibsen him-
> self, everyone sees.

In an unpleasantly snobbish reference to Brahm's early career in a
bank, he added: 'To the man who had escaped from being a counter-
clerk, a knight's boot was still considered more poetic than a cheque
book'. [14] Even concerning A Doll's House in 1883, says Schlenther,
Brahm expressed himself with reservations. Whichever memory is
correct concerning Pillars of Society and A Doll's House, from the
time that Brahm read Ghosts in 1884 he became the German apostle of
Ibsen, and in the following years campaigned for him to be performed.
His work was eventually rewarded. In 1886 there were two private
performances of Ghosts, one in Augsburg on 14 April, described because of censorship problems as a 'dress rehearsal in camera for
invited guests', and one on 22 December at the Meiningen Court
Theatre. Then, less than a month later on 9 January 1887, the police
permitted a single performance of the play at the Residenz Theater,
Berlin. Brahm wrote this up enthusiastically in the Frankfurter
Zeitung, and in Die Nation, perceptively comparing its effect with that
of Sophocles' Oedipus Rex. He also used the occasion to announce an
aesthetic creed:

> In the whole wide world, among people and things, I see nothing,
> absolutely nothing, which cannot be submitted to artistic treatment:
> Everything lies there, openly and freely, the poet has only to lay
> hold upon it, unhindered by any barrier of theory. It is not the
> 'what' that is decisive but only the 'how'. [15]

This is very far from the counter-clerk's scorn of the cheque book.
The 1887 Ibsen performance was followed by others; An Enemy of the
People and Rosmersholme (1887); The Wild Duck, Lady Inger and A
Doll's House (1888); The Lady from the Sea, Pillars of Society and
Ghosts (again only one performance (1889)). A Berlin Ibsen Society
was formed which provided an enthusiastic nucleus of the audiences.
The time was ripe for the establishment of Brahm's own theatre
society: the Freie Bühne.

Although the dramatic groups within the Social Democratic party
did not perform the plays of the naturalistic school, the position was
different within the reading and discussion clubs. Here the works of
the Naturalists were read and discussed avidly. The members were
excited by the expressions of Darwinism and Determinism in works of

art. In this art they saw a genuine attempt to show life 'as it really is' both in matter and in manner. They saw this new 'real' art as something set against the unreality of bourgeois art. Its themes, if not socialist, were strongly social and were closely related to the theories of the influence of environment and of historical materialism which were the mode of thought of the Marxist left. Ignoring, or simply not perceiving, Tolstoy's religion and Ibsen's individualism (which Brahm saw and underlined), the workers claimed Naturalism as <u>their</u> art, as the new <u>Weltanschauung</u>. In this light such widely different works as <u>Crime and Punishment</u> and <u>A Doll's House</u> were read and fully discussed in the social democrat clubs. Of course, the men who formed these reading and discussion groups were themselves an élite within the working-class movement, but an intellectual élite which wanted to see the new poetic art become the art of the whole 'Fourth Estate': 'The old poetic art is dead, a new one is in embryo! May it find entrance into the heart of the proletariat!' [16] The principal practical step towards realising this ideal was the founding of the Freie Volksbühne.

ACT I

1890-1914   From Brauhaus to Bülowplatz

1 THE FIRST DECADE

i Otto Brahm and the Freie Bühne

Otto Brahm, the son of a small merchant called Abrahamsohn, was
born in Hamburg on 5 February 1856. After leaving school he spent
those three years in the bank to which Schlenther later made wry
reference, experience that taught him a business sense that was later
very valuable to him as a man of the theatre. The life of a student
followed, in Berlin, Heidelberg, Berlin again, Strassburg and Jena.
At Strassburg he formed his lifelong friendship with Professor Erich
Schmidt, and at Jena in 1879 he gained his doctorate with a dissertation on a specialised aspect of eighteenth-century German drama. The
firm literary foundation of his later theatrical career was laid.
Returning to Berlin he dedicated himself to writing, especially on
theatre, and became critic on the National-Zeitung and the Augsburger
Allgemeine Zeitung. Because of the current antisemitism Abrahamsohn
wrote at first under the pen-name Otto Anders but later altered his
name to Otto Brahm. Soon after, he became critic for private theatres
on the Vossische Zeitung. The paper's critic for the 'Royal' theatres
was Theodor Fontane, and the two critics became friends. Finally he
became critic of the free-thinking weekly, Die Nation, remaining with
it until 1889.

    In a decade he became Berlin's greatest theatre critic. As such
he 'learnt to see and feel theatrically', and later as a theatre leader he
fulfilled what as a critic he had demanded. His stance was on behalf of
contemporary dramatists, at first Ernst von Wildenbruch, Paul Heyse
and Otto Ludwig, later Anzengruber, Björnson and, above all, Ibsen.
But as well as championing contemporary dramatists, and severely
criticising the Deutsches Theater for excluding these and playing only

safe classics, Brahm as critic also prepared the way for a new art of
acting. Impressed and influenced though he was by Chronegk, he
stressed also the importance of the actor's being wholly and continually
absorbed and submerged in his role. He criticised many actors for
'playing cat and mouse' with the parts they acted, moving in and out of
character according to whether they were active in a scene or not. But
he emphasised that the individual actor must play within the framework
of the production as a whole. In the same article in which he criticised
the Deutsches Theater for its timorous repertoire during its first two
seasons, he praised its Chronegk-influenced style:

> Seldom has the most important problem of the actor's art been so
> happily solved as here: the problem of perceiving the spirit of a
> work of imagination and expressing it in the performance, the
> individual tone and mood which this work and no other has by
> nature.... Whoever wishes to raise a poet's creation to life on
> stage must be capable of perceiving the fundamental notes which
> give the work its mood and make them reverberate in the listener
> through the medium of his performers. [1]

Four years later, when he had founded the Freie Bühne, he declared:

> I have a pugnacious disposition and I work happily to carry through
> the new forms of poetic art in order to win back for the theatre,
> which threatens to lose touch with modern German life, its full
> significance for our intellectual life. [2]

It used to be said that Brahm's Freie Bühne was modelled upon
Antoine's Théâtre Libre, but this is not wholly true; the Freie Bühne
was no mere imitation of the Théâtre Libre. Nor did Antoine's company
visit Berlin in 1887 as was formerly thought. Its first foreign tour was
to Brussels in 1888, and the 1887 production of Ghosts in Berlin was
not, as was believed, by Antoine's theatre. The starting point of the
Berlin company was very different from that of the Parisian one.
Antoine did not have to cope with censorship problems — a major reason
for the need for a private, independent theatre in Germany. He established a private theatre so as not to compete with the commercial ones,
to avoid making enemies and to get kinder critiques. His plays were
deliberately chosen from those not performed elsewhere in Paris. As
these were largely the naturalistic plays it has even been suggested that
the Théâtre Libre became the home of naturalistic drama more by
accident than by design. Brahm, on the contrary, was the conscious
champion of Naturalism and required a private theatre club in order to
perform naturalistic plays which the censor would not pass.

The founding of the Freie Bühne was planned at a meeting held in
the Weinstube bei Kempinski on 5 March 1889. The actual invitation
was issued by Theodor Wolff and Maximilian Harden, but from the very

start Brahm was the leader of the discussion. Also present was
Brahm's friend Paul Schlenther, the inevitable Hart brothers and
another writer, Julius Stettenheim. Very sensibly the initiators had
also brought in a sympathetic publisher, Samuel Fischer, a lawyer,
Paul Jonas, and a theatre agent called Stockhausen. [3] One month
later, on 5 April 1889, the Theaterverein 'Freie Bühne' was founded.
The constitution provided for two categories of membership, active
and passive. The active membership consisted only of the ten founders;
the passive, all the rest. There was no pretence of democracy. The
ten had control of the society and were free to carry out their aim of
leading the theatre in a new direction. Even ten was too large a committee for practical day-to-day purposes and a smaller executive
committee (Vorstand) was created consisting of Brahm himself as
Chairman, Paul Jonas as vice-chairman and legal adviser, and Samuel
Fischer as treasurer. Within even this smaller committee Brahm had
almost dictatorial powers, including those of choosing both the plays
and the actors. He valued Fischer's artistic judgements, and, of
course, Fischer Verlag could publish the plays. It was a good executive, and though the other seven did unselfish work, it is noteworthy
that of the founders only these three were still members at the time of
the society's last production in 1909.

In the first instance all members paid an annual subscription to
cover the ten proposed performances. This assured the society of its
financial security in advance — again in contrast with Antoine, who
lacked this. In fact it was only in the first year that the full ten performances were given. The growth of passive membership was quite
rapid. By June 1889 there were 354 members, by the end of 1889 there
were over nine hundred, and by June 1890 there were over a thousand.
By then the subscriptions had brought in as much as 25,000 Marks. (The
average price of a seat at the beginning was 3.50 Marks, plus a subscription of 1 Mark.) The Freie Bühne quickly came to be regarded as
the most interesting association in the city and its members soon
included many theatre directors, writers, actors and actresses,
critics, and an array of professional people — professors, lawyers,
doctors, high-ranking civil servants and so on. Their names had
drawing power and no doubt some people joined later out of snobbery.

During the first months of its existence the new society had to cope
with its own growing pains and internal frictions, to choose a repertoire and to find a host theatre. Over disagreements as to actual plays
to be produced three active members soon resigned, Harden completely,
Wolff and Stockhausen to become ordinary members, and later enemies
of the Freie Bühne. They were replaced by the writers Ludwig Fulda,
Fritz Mauthner and, most importantly, Gerhart Hauptmann, then still
completely unknown to the public, changes which strengthened still

more the literary basis of the group. In June 1889 Fischer complained
that Brahm in some matter or other had gone over his head as treasurer. Brahm apologised. Later, when Brahm edited the society's
periodical, Fischer objected to Brahm's receiving an honorarium for
this work: Brahm gave up the editorship. Later, too, Stettenheim left
and Mauthner became estranged because of Brahm's arbitrariness and
inability to compromise. It is hardly surprising that frictions should
have arisen quite soon between Brahm and the Hart brothers. Their
concept of Naturalism was far more idealist than Brahm's, and their
use of the word was broad enough to include Goethe. Heinrich Hart
claimed later that he actually opposed the appointment of Brahm as
the society's virtual director in 1889, on the grounds that Brahm was
insufficiently an idealist. The Harts were very critical of Brahm as a
person, saying he was cold and uninspiring; they tried to alter the
constitution to give the passive members more power; they were
annoyed when Julius Hart's play Der Sumpf (The Swamp), which was
originally on the list of proposed productions, was turned down by
Brahm. In 1890 they were involved in the founding of the Deutsche
Bühne, on the same principle of ten performances a year — but of
plays by German authors only. They attacked the Freie Bühne publicly,
and Brahm replied with fierce irony. Thus in the very first year they
were both estranged, but did not officially resign until 14 April 1897.

Meanwhile, despite frictions, the work proceeded. All active
members chose plays to submit to Brahm — and Hauptmann of course,
was actually writing. Schlenther helped in due course with the selection of artists; all did routine chores. Fontane, though only a 'passive'
member, was a valuable promoter of the Freie Bühne in his writings.
The problem of a host theatre seemed to be solved in June when an
arrangement was almost concluded with Lautenberg at the Residenz
Theater, but it fell through, and in July a contract was signed with
Blumenthal at the Lessing Theater which, in spite of frictions, gave
the society a home for its first season. Nor was it perfectly simple
for the Freie Bühne to obtain its actors. Other theatres feared its
rivalry, even though it was merely a Sunday afternoon society; they
thought its founders were seeking private profit and that they were
corruptible. So many of the best players were banned by their managements from playing for the Freie Bühne and for the first production
some of the leading actors had to be brought from Breslau and Vienna.
There were other problems, too. Many of the passive members had no
real interest, and there was anxiety as to how large the actual audience
would be. Inevitably many an unacknowledged genius brought his ancient manuscript and became the Society's enemy when it was turned
down, or when, having been praised by the Freie Bühne it was turned
down by other managements. But Brahm and his colleagues were not

to be discouraged: 'Freie Bahn der Freien Bühne! ' (Free way for
the free theatre!) Brahm concluded his article in Die Nation (5 October
1889) immediately after the opening production.

That production was, of course, of Ibsen's Ghosts. It was nominally directed by Hans Meery, but in fact Brahm gave such detailed
directions and supervised so closely that in effect he himself directed —
no wonder that in the Nation article he said it would be unbecoming for
him to enter upon a proper critique of it! To attempt to recapture the
quality of the performance we are dependent upon the critics partly
because of all prompt copies and the like from the entire output of the
Freie Bühne, only one production copy, two stage managers' books and
one actor's copy survive, together with some stage plans and some
letters. We know that the play was neither cut nor altered — which was
remarkable enough at that time. Fontane approved its choice, but
Landau did not feel it to be the real start of the activity of the new
society, more the epigraph to the book. But he praised the production
highly and compared it with the Meiningen players, referring to the
unity of style. This unity was evidently a characteristic of the production, every aspect of which was consistently real, whether the dark,
shadowy setting or the manner of acting. In all things there was plainness and simplicity, an avoidance of non-essentials and of exaggeration.
Silent expressiveness was a noteworthy feature. Frenzel noted the
Kunstpausen (artistic pauses) though he thought them too long. But
these pauses were one of the keys to a new stage style and allowed
time for the psychological effect of word and action to communicate
itself fully: this was nine years before Stanislavsky's historic production of Chekhov's Seagull in 1898 which is often popularly regarded as
having introduced 'the pause' into European acting. Naturally the
critics tended to compare the individual performances with those in the
production of 1887. Oswald, played by Emmerich Robert from the
Vienna Burgtheater, was the most highly praised. Fontane compared
him with Franz Wallner, the Oswald of 1887, saying that whereas
Wallner had merely presented an unfortunate, Robert gave a character
and a psychological study of neurosis. He evoked the audience's sympathy not simply with a 'sick man' but with a person (Mensch). The
person once more became the central point of the stage. At the end,
'The applause of the audience was strong and loud, despite hisses from
opponents of Ibsen. ' [4]

In this same review article Brahm took the opportunity of giving
further publicity to the proposed programme of the Freie Bühne, which
was to include, after Ghosts:

Gerhart Hauptmann: Vor Sonnenaufgang (Before Sunrise)
Edmond and Jules de Goncourt: Henriette Maréchal (1865)
Tolstoy: The Power of Darkness (1886)

Anzengruber: <u>Das vierte Gebot</u> (<u>The Fourth Commandment</u>)
Björnson: <u>The Glove</u> (1883)
Arthur Fitger: <u>Von Gottes Gnaden</u> (<u>By the Grace of God</u>)
Strindberg: <u>The Father</u>

Although three German authors were listed, Brahm had to defend himself immediately against accusations of a predilection for foreign
wretchedness. All these plays were in fact performed in the first
thirteen months of the society's existence, with the addition of:

Holz and Schlaf: <u>Die Familie Selicke</u> (<u>The Selicke Family</u>)
Alexander Kielland: <u>On the Way Home</u> (these two as a double bill)
Hauptmann: <u>Das Friedenfest</u> (<u>The Feast of Reconciliation</u>)

There was some justification for Landau's feeling that the production
of <u>Ghosts</u> was more an announcement of policy than a true beginning,
for it was the second production, on 28 October, of Hauptmann's <u>Vor
Sonnenaufgang</u> that Brahm himself felt to be a real 'new beginning'.

    Gerhart Hauptmann was not only the central figure of German
Naturalism, but is also a key figure in the history of the Freie Bühne
and the Freie Volksbühne. He was associated with a Berlin literary
society called <u>Durch</u> (<u>Through</u>), among whose members were Bruno
Wille and some of his friends. <u>Vor Sonnenaufgang</u>, his first play, had
already been published in the summer by C. F. Conrad, and controversy had raged. Brahm wrote about it in <u>Die Nation</u>. He was
impressed by 'the audacity and originality of the observation, the
complete aliveness of the characters, and the fearless consistency in
the shaping of gruesome and distressing material'. [5] The actual
performance was therefore eagerly awaited both by supporters and
opponents of the new Naturalism. In advance, the actors were harried
and threatened in anonymous letters. At the performance the hostile
first-nighters, their indignation fully roused through the weeks of
lively controversy, used all the well-known tricks of their kind, whist-
ling and jeering, to try to put the actors off their parts. The first act,
in its quite austere and simple naturalistic setting, passed off quietly
enough, but the setting of the second gave the cue for mounting noise.
The farmyard scene with its dwelling house, servants' quarters, fields,
the archway between the cattle stall and the hay-loft, the village inn,
vegetable garden, dove-cote, green fence with white points, oak tree
with surrounding bench led the critic Frenzel to comment sarcastically
that 'they forgot the dunghill with the crowing cock on it'. [6]

    ... and as fanatical admirers advanced against fanatical opponents,
    a battle developed of lungs and hands, of hissing and clapping,
    which was pursued with quite unusual violence and fluctuated

inconclusively from one side to the other, until a great love scene
in the fourth act made even the opposition applaud. [7]

The opposition was evidently awaiting the fifth act when, as they knew
from their reading, Marthe is in labour off stage, and Dr Schimmel-
pfennig constantly having to go off to attend to her; so, although Brahm
tactfully eliminated the off-stage 'cry of a woman in childbirth' which
Hauptmann prescribed in the stage directions, a certain Dr Isidor
Kastan, possibly pretending impatience at the birth's delay, stood up
in his seat, waving over his head a pair of obstetric forceps, as if he
intended to hurl them on stage, and shouted, 'Are we in a brothel,
then?' [8]

Kastan's moral objection was voiced more deliberately in
Frenzel's critique, where the play was described as 'an offence against
morals, sentiment and taste'. [9]

The great breakthrough of Naturalism into the German theatre had
taken place.

ii The founding of the Volksbühne

The programme of the Freie Bühne continued through the winter as
planned, and aroused the greatest interest even among non-members.
In particular the productions were discussed in a workers' debating
society founded during the period of the anti-socialist laws and given
the innocuous, rather absurd name, of Alte Tante (Old Aunt). Unable
to afford individual membership of the Freie Bühne, the club conceived
the idea of applying for corporate membership. One or two members
would attend the show and report upon it to the other fifteen or twenty
members. Apparently hesitant of making an official approach to Brahm
himself, they decided to send a delegation to an individual member —
not indeed, one of the ten 'active' members — whom they could trust,
to ask him to act for them. They chose a monumental mason, Schleupner, and a bookbinder, Willi Wach, to visit Dr Bruno Wille.

Bruno Wille, the son of an insurance inspector, was born in 1860
in Magdeburg. As a student in Bonn and Berlin, he first studied the-
ology, but finding this inconsistent with his philosophy of life, he
changed his studies, devoting himself to philosophy, with history,
mathematics, science and economics. But he never lost some of the
attitudes engendered by his theological beginnings; his mind always
moved in 'higher' regions, the world of ideas and dogma; he never
fought for anything in which he did not really believe; and he was ready
to turn against himself when convinced that a new course was right and
honourable. He had a strongly developed personality, many-sided,
rich in talents, imagination and fire, verging on the eccentric. Even
as a student he felt the injustice of his intellectual and artistic

privileges and came to see later that the workers' need for intellectual
and artistic things was as important as their physical needs. Writing
in 1893, he said:

> I am painfully aware that I personally cannot be free so long as
> human society is not free ... and what has led me on to the side
> of the materially deprived masses is not the sensual pleasure of
> tasting good food, of a full belly and idle body, but the recognition
> that the liberation of the people from political control and economic
> exploitation would bring immeasurable spiritual advantages. [10]

His socialism was never orthodox, therefore, and in some sense not
deeply rooted. He and his friends moved in the same circle of ideas
as the socialists (equality of women, environmental theory and so on)
which were also the themes that the Naturalists took up in writing.
His sympathy was with individuals rather than with the workers as a
body and he wanted to see the individualisation of the masses rather
than the stereotyping of individuals in a monolithic party. His aristocratic nature could not stand party discipline for long: he had to follow
his own convictions and made no secret of his undemocratic sentiments
even in the political field. In 1890 he and his friends were thinking and
acting socialistically: later on, socialism was replaced for him by
other interests — Zola and Ibsen made a deeper impression upon him
than Marx.

Intended by his parents to be a teacher, he became for a short time
a private tutor in Bucharest, but his dislike of teaching led him to take
the risk of earning his living as a freelance writer and lecturer — a
hard life. His articles were printed, however, and through his lectures
to workers' clubs he became known and liked by the working-class
people. Soon after having completed his studies he joined the circle
Durch where he met Leo Berg, the Harts, Arno Holz, Wilhelm
Bölsche, Gerhart Hauptmann and his brother Carl. He was the ideal
person to form the bridge between the literary and political movements
of his day.

Taking with them another bookbinder, the young Heinrich Wibker,
Schleupner and Wach visited Bruno Wille on a Sunday. Together with
his friend and fellow-lodger Wilhelm Bölsche and a few other friends
they walked with him to Friedrichshagen and strolled on past the
Müggelsee to Wilhelmshagen, while the three workmen explained their
proposals to Wille. Wille thought the idea of corporate membership of
the Freie Bühne to be impracticable, but he promised to think the
matter over: he said that a way must be found to give the workers and
the poor entrée to the theatre, and especially to a theatre producing
the works of the young dramatists. Wille's mind moved quickly.
Naturally enough Brahm's society offered itself as a prototype, and he

conceived the idea of setting up a Freie Volksbühne, alongside the
Freie Bühne. One evening in a Lokal on the Alexanderplatz he asked
his friend Julius Türk, 'Do you think one could found a Freie Bühne
for the workers?' Soon after the Sunday afternoon walk, the Berliner
Volksblatt, the organ of the Berlin social democrats, published, on 23
March 1890, Wille's Aufruf zur Gründung einer Freien Volks-Bühne
(Appeal for the founding of an Independent People's Theatre). The
appeal began as we have seen with a triple declaration of faith as to
the true nature of theatre: it should be 'a source of high artistic
gratification', a source of 'moral uplift' and 'a powerful stimulus to
thinking about the great topics of the day'. It is a declaration that has
remained the fundamental ideal and Credo of the movement from that
day to this, but it contained in embryo all the major internal conflicts
in the future history of the Volksbühne — conflicts between art and
politics, conflicts between propaganda and the improvement of the
individual. Wille then unequivocally laid the blame for the trivialisa-
tion of contemporary theatre at the door of capitalism, which he blamed
not only for the commercialisation of the theatre itself but primarily
for the corruption of public taste. The appeal continued with a reference to writers — and not only dramatists — who had freed themselves
from this corruption and 'found a sounding-board in the working people
of Berlin'. The list of examples is limited neither to writers of the
left nor to Naturalists in any doctrinaire sense: Tolstoy and Dostoyevsky, Émile Zola, Ibsen and Ibsen's younger fellow-countryman
Alexander Kielland (1849-1906), and a general reference to 'several
German "realists"'. Wille went on:

> It is a necessity for this section of the population which has been
> converted to good taste not only to read the plays of their choice
> but also to see them produced. Public performances of plays in
> which the revolutionary spirit lives are frustrated either by
> capitalism, for which they do not prove to be good box-office, or
> by the political censor.

These difficulties could be evaded in club performances:

> These obstacles do not exist for a closed society. It is therefore
> possible for the Freie Bühne to arrange the production of plays
> having the tendencies referred to.

But membership of the Freie Bühne was too expensive for working
people: '... therefore the founding of a Freie Volks-Bühne seems to
me to be appropriate.' There followed Wille's practical proposals,
which were extremely well thought out. Whatever later changes
occurred, he was undoubtedly on the right lines:

1. Following the example of the Freie Bühne, the new association
would consist of a 'leading group' and of its 'members'.

2. The leaders would choose the plays and the players.

3. For a quarterly subscription members would get seats for three performances.

4. One performance would take place each month, on a Sunday.

5. The subscriptions would aim to cover only the rent of the theatre and honoraria for the players.

6. The subscriptions would be as low as possible: it was hoped that the cheap seats would be obtained for 1.50 Marks quarterly — that is for three performances at 50 Pfennigs each.

Those interested were invited, without commitment, to send their names and addresses on postcards to Wille, with a note of the sub-scription they thought they could afford. From the response the founders would know roughly how many members they could count upon and therefore know how low the subscription could be. 'If sufficient addresses arrive an undertaking is assured that can contribute some-thing to the intellectual uplift of the people.' [11] In conclusion Wille promised that the outcome of the appeal would be published, through newspapers and associations.

There was in fact a very good response. Young enthusiasts col-lected signatures (several could be put on one postcard) and soon Wille had several hundred names. Altogether about a thousand responded. The appeal had been well formulated. While making clear that the new organisation would consist of supporters of Naturalism and of socialism, neither of these was narrowly defined, and all party-political reference avoided. While this may have been partly in view of the still valid anti-socialist laws and a wish to avoid initial conflict with authority, the appeal was also an expression of Wille's own beliefs. He asserted a couple of years later that he had not published the appeal

> in order to advance socio-political propaganda and to subordinate
> art to such 'agitational' ends, but to bring together two things
> dear to his heart, people and art, so that they might mutually
> ennoble each other. [12]

He saw the proletariat as being educated by an élite of its own number, which the Freie Volksbühne would serve.

Before calling a public meeting, Wille gathered a group of col-leagues for the enterprise. One, of course, was Wilhelm Bölsche. Bölsche was Wille's age; he had published two novels, but had made no money, though he was better off than Wille and remained dependent upon his father, editor of the Kölnische Zeitung. Like Wille he was not a party man. Another was Julius Türk, also a friend and fellow-

lodger. Born in 1865 at Lautenburg, Türk moved with his parents to
Berlin at the age of six and attended the Gymnasium zum Grauen
Kloster. But just before he entered the fifth form, the second from
the top, he ran away to become an actor. He joined a travelling troupe
and finally got an engagement at Sonnenburg; but the theatre closed
down, and he was forced to return to Berlin, where, through the influence of his brother, later Professor Dr Moritz Türk, he became a
book-keeper in a well-known wholesale business. He still read and
wrote plays. He became a social democratic agitator and speaker,
lecturing on art, drama and the theatre as well as on the French
Revolution, Siberia and social and political questions. A far more
deeply convinced socialist than Wille, he became after the lapse of the
anti-socialist law an enthusiastic member of the legal Social Democratic Party. Türk was a hearty, fundamentally good-natured man,
though he easily sulked. He was a man of many parts, though of one
ambition — to succeed in the theatre. Perhaps, however, he was too
many-sided to excel in any one thing, and it was his fate always to be
in close contact with the great men of the naturalist and the socialist
movements, all of whom were considered his superiors in their
special ways. Thus a tragic fate seemed to pursue him — until his
ultimate suicide. At this time, however, he had his close friendship
with Wille: the two gave each other financial help, and spoke together
at meetings. Like Bölsche he was an eminently suitable partner for
Wille in the new scheme. The third primarily literary colleague whom
Wille selected was Julius Hart, a socialist by feeling, always ready to
raise the banner of revolt against narrowness, prejudice, darkness
and abuse of power.

To these literary friends, Wille added three more who seemed to
him to be leading spokesmen of the workers' movement. Curt Baake
at the age of twenty-six had already been for five years editor of the
Berlin party paper Das Volksblatt. He was clever, a good speaker and
exceptional tactician: and he was keen on the theatre. His contemporary Dr Conrad Schmidt edited the Volkstribüne, and was an enthusiast
for Naturalism. One man represented the manual workers themselves,
Carl Wildberger, a master upholsterer. He was 'one on his own', a
giant in stature, liked a drink, a daredevil. A good-natured, helpful
man, he was body and soul in politics, and a good speaker. It was
typical of him that he used to read aloud to his workers in the workshop
books that he thought worth while, including plays of the young realists.

One of the most important modifications to Wille's original plan
was suggested by another friend of his and Türk's, Paul Richter, a
wine merchant. Wille had originally thought of graduated seat prices
[13] but the others wanted to abolish distinctions based upon cash.
How was it possible to have a single price and yet avoid injustice to

those in poorer seats? Richter solved this by proposing that a lottery
for seats be held.

On 20 July Wille proposed to his colleagues a series of plays for
the new society. They were:

Power of Darkness (Tolstoy)
Pillars of Society (Ibsen)
A Doll's House (Ibsen)
Ghosts (Ibsen)
Dantons Tod (Danton's Death) (Büchner)
Robespierre (Griepenkerl)
Vor Sonnenaufgang (Hauptmann)
Die Familie Selicke (Holz and Schlaf)
Der Sumpf (Julius Hart)
Brot (Bread) (Conrad Alberti)

Six of these had already been performed by the Freie Bühne, but not
Robespierre, Dantons Tod, Der Sumpf and Brot. The list apparently
included also a play by Bleibtreu.

Less than a fortnight later, on a hot summer afternoon, 29 July
1890, the inaugural meeting took place in the Böhmisches Brauhaus.
There were almost two thousand present, and the room was really too
full: tables had to be removed and some people had to stand.

A group to conduct the meeting was elected by acclamation, and
Wille delivered his opening speech whose theme 'Die Kunst dem Volke'
(Art for the People) has been the 'motto' of the Volksbühne ever since.
Wille said that this demand had excited the best minds of ancient
Greece and of the German classical period; that working people were
no longer satisfied with the treasures of art that already existed; that
the new organisation aimed at raising the way of life of the people.
Critical of the existing theatrical situation, and casting scorn on the
profit motive, Wille declared that it was not possible to wait until the
workers had power, but that organised self-help was needed, now. His
detailed proposals followed. He was emphatic, surprisingly, that the
choice of plays must be left to the 'judgement, taste and intelligence of
the majority of the members', but that most would be plays arising out
of the struggle for truth. He named not only naturalist plays and the
others in the list of 20 July, but also plays of Goethe and Schiller. He
refuted the accusation that this would create a 'Social Democratic
Theatre': it would serve no party, and there was no need for its members to adhere to the Social Democratic Party. To this extent the
Freie Volksbühne would be no different from the Freie Bühne, with
which under some circumstances a joint trust might be formed. Like
the Freie Bühne, it would use professional artists. But all seats would be
the same price, and the seats would be allocated by a lottery. The

minimum charge would be 50 Pfennigs, but anyone who could afford to
pay more was expected to do so. For the secure establishment of the
society enough members were needed to form two sections, so that
there could be two performances of each play. Actors were available.
Wille added that one could assume that if the Freie Volksbühne in Berlin
were successful, other towns would follow the lead. After pointing out
that there would be no profit to the founders and that there was no
literary clique behind this, wanting to produce their own works, Wille
concluded with an appeal for a large membership as the surest way of
confounding the scorn of critics and opponents.

A lively discussion followed, primarily between the writer Conrad
Alberti-Sittenfeld and Curt Baake. Baake finally rebuffed Alberti, who
was a poor speaker though he had recently published a book on the 'art
of speaking'. He was not lacking in a sense of humour, however, and
a few days later he sent a copy of his book, with a dedication, to Baake.

Two motions were finally carried unanimously. The first was: 'The
meeting declares itself in agreement with the speaker's proposals as
to the need for a Freie Volksbühne Association, and resolves to found
such an association.' [14] The second appointed a commission to draw
up a constitution. The commissioners were Bruno Wille, Wilhelm
Bölsche, Julius Türk, Curt Baake, Conrad Schmidt, Carl Wildberger
and, notably, Otto Brahm. A third motion which was carried with four
dissenting votes, agreed to a retiring collection in aid of the Hamburg
building workers, who were on strike at the time.

The commission started work at once, though not without conflicts.
Only a few days before the public meeting Bruno Wille had published an
article in the Sächsische Arbeiterzeitung (23 July 1890) in which he
said that the anti-socialist laws had 'corrupted' the Social Democratic
party. He did not mean that individuals had been corrupted, nor did he
mean bribery — he used the word philosophically or figuratively — but
the literal and more derogatory interpretation was possible. In other
ways, too, Wille's individualism opposed itself to the party attitudes.
He was not appointed secretary of the commission and there was considerable friction. Baake as a friend of Wille's tried to keep the peace
by suggesting other leadership, but Wille would not agree. Eventually
the members resolved their differences, or rather agreed to ignore
them, and set to work. After one good week's effort the constitution
was ready. [15] It was well conceived, and though changes, mostly
minor, were later made from time to time, it provided an excellent
basis for the new association. The twenty-five clauses covered a broad
policy statement: method of enrolment; arrangements for general
meetings (two a year) and extraordinary general meetings; election of
officers; composition and responsibilities of committees; the amount
of the entrance fee and monthly subscriptions; details of payment,

stamping of cards and so on; responsibilities of the treasurer and
auditors; minimum number of performances (one for every member,
monthly from October to March); equal opportunities for all sections;
the conduct of the lottery by the 'organisers' (Ordner); the dates of the
association's working year (1 September to 31 August); conditions
under which the constitution could be changed; and the method of dissolution.

The officers elected at the August general meeting were to be a
chairman, treasurer, secretary, six members of the board of management (Ausschuss), the organisers and three auditors. The chairman,
treasurer and secretary were to form the executive (Vorstand). This
executive had wide powers, including choice of producers, actors and
lecturers. If the Association's assets were adequate the executive
could conclude firm contracts with the acting company. The Board of
Management, consisting of the executive plus the six other members,
would choose the plays and the subjects of lectures and recitals and
decide all questions affecting the Association's literary standards.
Bruno Wille disapproved of this more democratic aspect of the constitution, and the elections at general meetings, and he warned the others
against this form of organisation. But he was forced against his convictions to yield to the majority, who felt the need to satisfy the
workers, and so he lost control from the very beginning; and although
Brahm had considerable influence on the 'artistic' paragraphs of the
constitution, the Freie Bühne was not the model for the form of the
new association.

The machinery through which one acquired membership of the
Association and a seat in the performance was described in some
detail. Membership cost 1 Mark and lapsed if the monthly subscription
was not paid by the seventh of the month. The monthly subscription
was 50 Pfennigs (minimum) from October to March and 25 Pfennigs
(minimum) for the rest of the year. It was the treasurer's responsibility to set up agency offices in all parts of the city according to need,
whose proprietors would receive enrolments and subscriptions. (In
practice these agencies were tobacconists' shops and the like.) A
membership card, valid only for that member, was to be issued on
payment of the enrolment fee, and subsequently monthly subscriptions
could be paid at any agency: a receipt was to be gummed on the card
opposite the appropriate month. Only the fully paid up member had a
right to attend performances or general meetings. At the theatre all
arrangements were conducted by the honorary 'organisers' who were
to choose from their own number a chairman (Obmann) and two committee members (Beisitzer). These three put the tickets in the urns
in the foyer, and also decided which seats were to be excluded from
the lottery if there were too few members to fill them all. The lottery

was to begin at least one hour before the performance. Each member, having had the validity of his membership card checked at the entrance, was to go up to the lottery tables on which the urns with the tickets stood, each overseen by an organiser, and draw out a ticket giving the actual number of the seat.

The second public meeting took place on 8 August again in the Böhmisches Brauhaus, and again with about two thousand present. Wille, Wildberger, Baake, Brahm and Hedwig Gröber were called to lead the discussion, while Türk gave the opening report. With regard to plays, he emphasised that the association did not exist simply to produce German plays, nor was it interested in operettas or farces. 'True poetry' must be the watchword. The Commission had considered the original list of plays and now proposed the following opening plays: Dantons Tod; Power of Darkness; Thérèse Raquin; Vor Sonnenaufgang; Ghosts; An Enemy of the People; Die Familie Selicke. [16]

Once more there were lively debates and twice the disturbance was so great that the police threatened to close the meeting. The first important point of dispute was on the first clause of the constitution. This read:

> The Freie Volksbühne Association sets itself the task of bringing before the people poetry in its modern sense, and particularly to present, read in public and explain through lectures up-to-date works executed with truthfulness. [17]

Some members wanted one word altering so that the clause would refer to poetry in its 'popular' (volkstümlich) sense instead of in its modern sense. The amendment, which was defeated, showed that the policy statement was too much weighted on the cultural side, rather than the socio-political, to satisfy everyone. Another more practical amendment, that the closing date for monthly subscriptions should be later than the seventh of the month — the fifteenth or eighteenth — was also defeated. There was also a considerable discussion as to how to attract young people into the association. In the elections that followed, Wille became chairman, Wildberger treasurer and Türk secretary, these three thus constituting the executive committee. There was much opposition to Brahm's being elected to the board of management: he was suspect in the eyes of many of the workers as not being closely enough attached to the left. He was defended by Baake, and eventually both Brahm and Baake were elected, together with Bölsche, Julius Hart, Conrad Schmidt (all 'intellectuals') and one 'worker', Richard Baginski, a shoemaker. The three auditors were workers (the leader of the shop assistants, the organiser of the metal workers and a printer), as were all the honorary organisers. Most of the elections were almost unanimous, at most there were a dozen dissidents. A further collection for the Hamburg strikers was forbidden by the police, so one was made for Freie Volksbühne funds. The new association, with six or seven hundred members, was founded.

iii The first two years

The first two years of the life of the Freie Volksbühne were unique in its history and possessed characteristics which never exactly recurred in later periods. During these years the organisation managed to contain within itself the conflicting personalities and divergent aims which ultimately and, it now seems inevitably, led to the great schism of 1892: and those very conflicts and divergences, though they produced in the end intolerable tensions and tore the movement in two, nevertheless actually enriched the achievement of the young organisation in its initial stages. A body which united — with however much friction — apostles of a literary movement and leaders of a political, and which could contain even for a short time in its executive committee both the despotic idealist Wille and the ambitious maverick Türk, was bound to exhibit more life, though stormy life, than one with a single artistic or political aim and no more than one powerful leading personality.

After the meeting of 8 August the committee wasted no time. First it was necessary to find a theatre. An idea of sharing a regisseur and actors with the Freie Bühne proved impracticable. Indeed, Wille's calculations at this time even seemed to suggest that the whole conception was after all impracticable. As Türk said: 'The Association was founded, but poverty-stricken. It possessed no theatre, no actors, no scenery, no director and no money.' [18] Brahm had believed that many theatres would welcome the new association, but whether through the influence of the press, the fear of socialism, the plays proposed or the money offered, 'they declined, silently and politely. The child must be put into the street.' [19] Eventually the association was reduced to the Ostend Theater. This theatre, seating 1,200, had been opened in 1877 with ambitious plans for a classical programme, but the public had not supported it and its artistic personnel had gradually disbanded. Even an attempt to bring in an audience through a sensational play failed. Then, as we have seen, Kurz in 1886 and Witte-Wild in 1888 had tried unsuccessfully to develop serious programmes. Then Max Samst took over the theatre, with E. Friedrich as his partner. Samst had long defended the existence of this theatre and he now sought, by making big concessions to popular taste, to build up his audience. He put on many local and topical farces, with song and dance, sensational pieces, dramatisations of popular novels and occasional classics. He was an energetic theatre director. Often there were (after the coming of the Freie Volksbühne) three performances on a Sunday of three different plays — sometimes all directed by him. The executive saw some productions there and were not impressed. Beggars, however, could

not be choosers, so on 1 September 1890, hardly more than three
weeks after the founding, an agreement with Samst was signed. According to its terms the association hired the theatre, with lighting and
personnel for certain Sunday afternoons at 350 Marks a performance,
but it retained the right to bring in its own director and to use outside
artists for important parts, at its own cost. The director was Cord
Hachmann, a pupil of Brahm's, who remained the Freie Volksbühne
director until the autumn of 1891, when he went to America. Samst,
of course, could only gain by the arrangement and hoped that the
new Sunday afternoon audience would also come on Sunday evenings.

Even the six weeks or so that had to elapse between the signing of
the agreement and the first actual production, were not wasted. Apart
from the practical work of establishing agencies (nineteen at first,
later twenty-six), printing membership cards and so on, a recital of
'freedom poems' was given at the Sans Souci Concert Hall on 17 September before an audience of two thousand and a week later there was
a lecture by Dr Conrad Schmidt (repeated on 3 October), 'Naturalism
and the worker'. Two days before the first performance, Wilhelm
Bölsche delivered an introductory lecture on the play to be performed
and the next day (18 October) an important article by Wille appeared in
the Magazin für Literatur, in which he described how the Freie Volksbühne had arisen out of the struggle to awaken the intellectual hunger
of the workers, and how the Freie Bühne had provided the model and
inspiration for the new body.

The first Freie Volksbühne performance began three quarters of
an hour late, in an unheated Ostend Theater on Sunday afternoon, 19
October 1890, the play being Ibsen's Pillars of Society. It was obviously an excellent choice of play for the occasion. Being one of Ibsen's
realistic dramas it pleased the supporters of the naturalistic movement, and being his simplest, most transparent piece of social criticism
it pleased the socialists and was easily comprehensible to an audience
unaccustomed to theatre-going and so naïvely delighted by the occasion
that there were no complaints even about the cold or the delay. The
play was preceded by a Prologue in verse, written and spoken by the
poet Richard Dehmel, then a young man of twenty-seven.

The thousand or so original members of the Freie Volksbühne heard
the play with 'devout seriousness', with 'intense, intelligent attention'.
Otto Erich Hartleben, who made these comments, also said that they
had understood Ibsen in their hearts, that they were able to surrender
themselves to him because they 'brought their own revolutionary
seriousness to meet the seriousness of the revolutionary poet'. [20]

The second production, less than a month later (9 November)
revealed other aspects of this new theatre audience. The play was Vor

Sonnenaufgang. For some reason or other, although Dehmel gave a
recital on 7 November, two days before the performance, the 'introductory' lecture by Wille was not given until 14 November, five days
after it, so that the audience came to the play without special preparation, and knowing only what they had heard and read previously. The
play as a whole was vigorously applauded, but Hartleben was somewhat
disillusioned by certain specific reactions. Often, he wrote, there was
laughter in the wrong places; the tendencious tirades of Loth, made
more conspicuous by the very poor actor who took the part, filled the
audience with enthusiasm, while they did not react at all to poetic
subtleties, and broke into 'unseemly merriment' at the sight of Krause,
the drunken peasant. The Volkstribüne disagreed with Hartleben
editorially, saying that not all the positive reactions arose from the
tirades, that indeed not one of these had been followed by a burst of
applause, and that the reaction to the drunk could be explained psycho-
logically. Not that the paper was wholly satisfied with the behaviour
of the audience: 'a certain tense feeling of apprehension was lacking'.
Two members of the Association also wrote letters which were published. They said that Hartleben was right in part — some of the
audience had behaved as he described; but they insisted that the
majority possessed the kind of understanding needed to appreciate this
kind of play. These were clear, logical letters that can probably be
accepted as giving a balanced view.

Between this production and the next there were arranged, apart
from a further recital by Dehmel, three lectures on the Berlin working
class and the Freie Volksbühne, given by Bölsche, Türk and Dr Franz
Lüttgenau, and on Saturday 13 December Wille gave an introductory
lecture on Ibsen's Enemy of the People, which was performed the next
day. Membership, through energetic recruitment, had now risen to
about sixteen hundred and a second section had been formed. In mid-
January, because the fees had been lowered, the membership stood at
about eighteen hundred. This month Otto Brahm gave two introductory
lectures on Schiller's Kabale und Liebe (Intrigue and Love), which was
then given two performances, one for each section.

On 8 February at the invitation of Oscar Blumenthal, the first
section was enabled to see a special performance of Sudermann's Die
Ehre (Honour) at the Lessing Theater. It was evidently this performance to which Sudermann also invited Ibsen. Ibsen was deeply impressed by the attentiveness and responsiveness of the Freie Volksbühne
audience and kept repeating 'Das sind Hörer! Das sind Hörer! ' (What
an audience!)

This was the one play (and the performance was offered to the
association free) over which the Freie Volksbühne did not exercise its
own choice. In one sense the choice in these early days was easy — the

whole range of drama was available, because it was being offered to a
new audience. Because the performances were private, there was no
need to consider possible clashes with other theatres — nor did the
association think it necessary to pay full royalties. Nevertheless, lack
of money limited the number of able players who could be engaged,
educational considerations were always borne in mind, and the leaders
had a natural desire to break new ground. In spite of a close sense of
kinship with the Freie Bühne, only four of the twenty plays produced in
the first two years had previously been produced by that association.
[21] Pissemski's Der Leibeigene (The Serf) had actually been turned
down by the Freie Bühne (perhaps Brahm thought it more suitable for
a working-class audience) and it became the Freie Volksbühne's first
world première. The second was Kein Hüsung by Fritz Reuter, adapted
by Jahnke and Schirmer. This caused some arguments, as Jahnke
added a fourth act which really contradicted the rest of the play. Eventually this was dropped. Kein Hüsung was preceded by Fulda's Das
verlorene Paradies (Paradise Lost), the first production to be performed for three sections (March–April, 1891) and was followed by a
single performance of Schiller's Die Räuber for the second section
only. An almost absurd search for a comedy suitable for this earnest
association led to the choice of Anzengruber's Doppelselbstmord
(Double Suicide) to end the first playing year.

Meanwhile the introductory lectures had continued regularly with
occasional evenings of recitations, while on 1, 2 and 3 May 1891 a
special May Festival had been held in the Ostend Theater. This clearly
had the character of a socialist junketing. There was a prologue by
Karl Henckell, a programme of singing and oratory, and a melodrama
by Wille, Durch Kampf zur Freiheit (Through Struggle to Freedom), of
which it is said that it would have been better omitted. Its subject,
however, is of interest: it was about the Silesian weavers. At the end
all joined in singing the May Festival Marseillaise by Wurm.

During that first playing year 3,948 people altogether had been
members of the association, but never more than 2,500 at the same
time. Indeed at the end of the working year the membership was only
1,873, so that over 50 per cent, some 2,075, must have left during the
year: and they left not only towards summer, but even after the second
performance. Another 1,774 joined in the second year, throughout
which the average membership was something under 3,000, in three
sections, and it sank at the end of the playing year to 2,567. So about
30 per cent left during the second year. This large turnover in membership greatly reduced the educational value of the association's
productions and lectures.

The agreement with the Ostend Theater did not long stand up to the
tests of practicability. Troubles constantly arose over such matters as
the availability of the theatre for rehearsal — no doubt Samst with his
slapdash approach thought the rehearsal requirements of the association

excessive; and in any case rehearsals produced no income. The actors
at the Ostend Theater were so badly paid that it seemed a betrayal of
the ideals of the Freie Volksbühne to allow them to be so exploited, for
salaries of 2 Marks to 5 Marks per day. The Freie Volksbühne itself
therefore paid the actors an extra gratuity. This seems to have aver-
aged about 5 Marks per performance for each actor — but only the total
expenditure is known, and the size of the part may have been taken into
account. Three of the best actors of the Ostend Theater were not on
permanent contracts, and these had to be taken on individually and paid
special honoraria. In the spring of 1891 Samst offered to reduce the
rent to 200 Marks per performance, provided that productions continued
throughout the summer. The Freie Volksbühne offered 150 Marks — the
additional 50 Marks being for the benefit of the actors. The matter was
apparently concluded and the association committed, when the theatre
management declared there had been a 'misunderstanding', and asked
for the original rent of 350 Marks. Wildberger as Treasurer was
furious and there were polemical exchanges in the press. The upshot
was that in July, at the end of the season, the Freie Volksbühne left
the Ostend Theater — though it returned on 6 September for a single
anniversary performance of Vor Sonnenaufgang.

During the theatrical close season an Open Air Festival (Waldfest)
was held on Sunday 9 August at the Müggelschlösschen at Friedsrichs-
hagen. The plans included a concert at 11.0 a.m. by the Friedsrichs-
hagen Kurkapelle, and in the afternoon competitions for women and
children, a Punch and Judy show, Moritat singing, a men-only show,
surprise-theatre, and book raffle. In the evening there was to be a
torchlight procession and firework display, also a Wasserapotheose
and community singing of the Workers' Marseillaise and other songs.
In the event it rained that day until 4 p.m.; but after that it cleared up
and so many people streamed out of the city that there was a shortage
of tables and chairs. Altogether some eight thousand or ten thousand
people were attracted to the festival, and the atmosphere was good:
people took home a very good impression. The Wasserapotheose was
poetically described in the Volksblatt:

> Near the shore a skiff moved slowly along in which stood a lady in
> appropriate costume and pose, holding a great banner in her hand
> and lit by red Bengal Lights, while the band played appropriate
> tunes. [22]

When the thousands of working-class people joined in the Workers'
Marseillaise, other visitors to the Müggelschlösschen struck up Die
Wacht am Rhein, but this caused only merriment and no bad feeling.

For the second season the Freie Volksbühne moved to the Belle-
Alliance Theatre in the south of the city. It was a larger theatre than

the Ostend, seating 1,400, and more expensive to hire. It was not
a leading theatre, but of better reputation than the Ostend, and its
actors were paid four or five times as much. There were difficulties,
but there were fewer guest artists to pay. Hachmann at this time going
to America, George Stollberg was appointed as his successor. Stollberg was a competent director, but of no great originality. Once more
an Ibsen play, The League of Youth, was selected to strike the right
note at the start of the season, which also included Ghosts, A Doll's
House and Zola's Thérèse Raquin. Contemporary social drama was
represented by Ludwig Fulda's Die Sklavin (The Slavegirl) and the
world première of Max Halbe's Der Eisgang (The Ice-breaking).
Anzengruber's Der Pfarrer von Kirchfeld (The Pastor of Kirchfeld)
was no doubt included so that this serious play could build on the
success of Doppelselbstmord. The older plays were Gogol's Government Inspector, Otto Ludwig's Der Erbforster (The Hereditary
Forester, 1849) and Hebbel's domestic tragedy Maria Magdalena
(1844). After the end of the season a second Waldfest was held (14
August) at the Müggelschlösschen. A prize of 100 Marks had been
offered for a suitable play to be performed at this, but there were no
entries. Instead there was a morning concert, songs, Punch and Judy,
games for adults and children, swimming races, a comic regatta, a
water-farce, bowls and gymnastics, a fortune-teller, raree show,
gypsies, living pictures with Bengal Lights, torch-light procession,
fireworks display and a book raffle. Wille produced a special Wald-
festnummer of the periodical Freie Volksbühne for the occasion. This
periodical had been started early in 1892. At first the Berliner
Volkstribüne had offered space for printing introductions to plays, but
later partly because of the tensions between the association and the
Social Democratic Party, the Freie Volksbühne decided to have its
own periodical. It sold at 10 Pfennigs for sixteen pages and six numbers were issued under Wille's editorship, with introductions to plays
written by himself, Bölsche, Heinrich Hart and others. The periodical
reached more members than did the lectures, and in any case the
lectures ended with the introduction to A Doll's House on 15 January
1892, because of police objections.

From its very inauguration the Freie Volksbühne had to fight a
running battle with the authorities, represented by the police. The
police had no standing in cultural matters, but they could nevertheless
place many difficulties in the way of a society. They came to public
meetings and behaved rudely and provocatively. Even at the first
meeting of all they had insisted on a limitation of numbers, and at a
meeting in November the interference became really ludicrous. The
police lieutenant tried to have the gallery cleared. This 'gallery' was
only about three feet above floor level, but when the management of
the Böhmisches Brauhaus said that although hundreds of gatherings had

been held there, the police had never demanded this, the lieutenant
said that he did not regard the gallery as part of the hall. This remark
caused laughter, and the lieutenant, very formal in his helmet, threatened to dissolve the meeting. So Wille gave way. Later in the meeting
the lieutenant insisted on all speakers giving their names and addresses.
Then some ingenious sea-lawyer suggested that in fact the meeting was
not in session because the policeman had his helmet on. This time it
was the lieutenant who gave way: he removed his helmet.

Basically the police had two objections to the Association. The
first was that so many socialists were gathered together at its meetings
and performances. The second was irritation that the Association was
able to avoid the censor. As in Britain until the abolition of the powers
of the Lord Chamberlain, only the theatre was actually subject to
censorship as such. Article 27 of the Prussian constitution declared
that everyone was free 'to express his opinion through word, writing,
print and pictorial representation'. The Freie Bühne had been called
into being to evade censorship, and the Freie Volksbühne was clear
that it could only achieve its ends as an association (Verein). Under a
law of 1850, all Vereine were divided into three categories: (i) inoffensive, simple associations such as smoking clubs, and associations
purely for amusement, with no special social aims; (ii) associations
that aimed to influence events; (iii) political associations. The ambi-
guity of these definitions gave the police an open door for creating
difficulties. At first they entered the Freie Volksbühne under category
(i). In view of the declared policies of the association this was strange.
The association was 'a child of the working class movement'. [23] It
was natural that it should take up collections for strikers and join in
May Day demonstrations; and when eventually the police said that the
Freie Volksbühne aimed at 'influencing public affairs', Türk's response
was, 'Yes, we do wish to influence public affairs, and we're proud of
it.' On another occasion he recalled the opening sentence of Wille's
original appeal — the theatre should provide a strong stimulus to thinking about great topical questions. Türk was, indeed, more 'political'
than some of the committee and thought the Social Democratic party
ought to have more influence in the association. Even so, his notion of
'political theatre' was very unlike later conceptions — Piscator's, for
example, — and was probably far nearer that expressed in an article in
the Volkstribüne in 1890 (unsigned, but probably by Conrad Schmidt)
which said that the theatre should 'assist the liberation of mankind',
and distinguished between the functions of politics and art, saying that
that of politics was 'to fight for the rights of man', and that of art, 'to
ennoble feeling and will'.

On 20 April 1891 the police chief demanded from the association
certain information, such as lists of members' names and addresses,

a demand which by implication put the association in the second category. It was feared that it was only a step from this to the third category. Among other restrictions, women could not be members of associations entered under category (iii), so the fate of the Freie Volksbühne, which had many women members, would have been sealed. On legal advice, the association appealed against the chief of police. The case was heard on 30 June 1891. The police statement gave evidence as to why the Freie Volksbühne was a category (ii) Verein: its aim was to change the economic structure of society — Wille's original appeal was cited; Wille in an essay introducing Vor Sonnenaufgang had written: 'We live in a time before sunrise; in a transitional age; we still do not see the approaching sun; but we see how dawn begins to glow on the horizon'. He had also criticised society in his introduction to An Enemy of the People. Conrad Schmidt and Julius Türk were also quoted, as was the phrase, 'Poetry can inspire great deeds'. Reference was made to the May Festival, to collections taken at meetings in aid of the Social Democratic Party (though this had been without the knowledge of the executive) to the fact that many of the committee were Social Democrat agitators, and to the choice of plays. One could not say this was an 'inoffensive' association, rather it was a disguised political association. In fact they concluded that the association ought to be entered under category (iii)!

For the Freie Volksbühne Dr Wolfgang Heine said that the police had drawn a false conclusion. Popular education, he said, was a public event. Art aims at educating people. Therefore the Freie Volksbühne which aimed at educating people through art must aim at influencing public events, and so be entered under category (ii). He maintained that they did not argue from artistic premises to economic and political conclusions, but looked at artistic questions from a socialist standpoint. Therefore, they were not playing politics. After a two-hour discussion the District Commission decided on lifting the police order. The judgement said that although most members of the association were socialists, socialism was not a party but a philosophy — which could be expressed through art. The Freie Volksbühne cultivated this philosophy in the realm of art. There was a distinction between, for example, giving a lecture on socialism, and handling an artistic theme from a socialist viewpoint. On the other hand, it could be argued that art influences life and that therefore the Freie Volksbühne influenced public affairs through the power of a philosophy.

This judgement did not satisfy the police, but they realised that it was not going to be easy to prove their case. Police President von Richthofen [24] was an honest and certainly not unreasonable man. He genuinely saw the Freie Volksbühne as he said he did — as a dangerous body working directly towards revolution. He appealed to a higher

court, saying that for the converted, Social Democratic associations
arranged meetings with speakers on politics and economics. For the
uncommitted — which included many women and girls — a more indirect
approach was needed. They must gradually absorb the party spirit
through social cheer and pleasant conversation. To this end, he said,
workers' and children's festivals were arranged and associations
founded whose declared aims were simply amusement. Recently, in
the same way that an attempt had been made to draw together the
educational associations by founding a school for workers' education,
so too, federations of working-class singing-clubs and working-class
social clubs had been formed in order to consolidate their forces and
achieve some centralisation. He saw the founding of the Freie Volksbühne association just at this juncture as quite obviously intended
directly to further the Social Democrat cause. He asked how such
'propaganda', through 'producing poetry in its modern tendency' could
be understood otherwise than as an intention to fill the 'so-called
Proletariat' with a particular view of the social order, and to convince
them of the necessity of revolution. He did concede that up to the
present the plays presented did no more than portray shortcomings in
the existing social order through particularly shocking examples. But
he firmly maintained that such an education of a particular class of
people must have its influence upon public affairs, as it exercised a
decisive influence on each individual in relation to the way he fulfilled
his civic duties. Therefore, he concluded, an association having these
aims and working in this way, does exercise an influence upon public
affairs.

Von Richthofen was obviously justified in his opinion that the
association did influence public affairs and did intend to do so, at least
in so far as it wanted to strengthen its members' class-consciousness.
In saying that it was working directly for revolution, he was wrong,
though only to the extent that he credited the whole body with the
opinions of some of its members. He did not understand the conflict
between the 'revolutionary' and 'cultural' wings within the association,
but he doubtless did know of the attitude expressed by Bela Balázs:
They didn't want to change theatre-styles, but the world. [25]

The court gave judgement in favour of the Police President. The
judgement reads fairly enough, though it is so wordy and tortuous that
when Wille cited it in a periodical the following May he inserted after
the first sentence — of eighty-nine words: 'What a long sentence! ' It
was followed by a sentence of ninety-nine words. The court said, in
effect, that if sober discussions of social questions could spread and
confirm Social Democratic views in working-class circles, then
imaginative works showing the exploitation of the workers and appealing
to imagination and emotions would obviously do so in a far higher
degree. It admitted that even the Social Democrat founders might well

have seen as their immediate aim only the presentation of naturalistic plays primarily to the working class. But it suggested that perhaps people like Brahm and Hartleben were not quite clear as to the implication of what they were starting. Later, the judgement said, it was hardly credible that the leaders of the association were not aware that they were influencing public affairs or that they did not, at least as a distant aim, wish to do this. The plays were all chosen to show the 'hollowness and untenability' of the present condition of society and to arouse discontent in the working class. The introductory lectures to a number of plays were quoted, to show that the audience had been invited to see them in the light of Social Democratic ideas. The judgement, however, did not go along with the Police President's argument that the association was working directly for 'revolution', and entered it under category (ii). This judgement, given in January 1892, was really all the Freie Volksbühne wanted. It was no longer in danger either of being dissolved, or of being entered under category (iii). To avoid further trouble the lectures were dropped, their place being taken shortly afterwards by the periodical. The association was then left in peace for a long time, and even the political implications of the split later in the year did not arouse the police to action, as it was feared they might.

That fear arose because the split brought into sharp focus the ideological conflicts which underlay it and inevitably made patent the strong political motives of those opposing Wille. In some sense it can be argued [26] that both the Social Democratic Party and the movement that led to thoroughgoing Naturalism originated partly in historical materialism, and that although these are two clearly independent movements, one artistic, the other political, their paths crossed in 1890 and thus provided the unique opportunity for the founding of the Freie Volksbühne. The founders, on both sides, however, saw only the convergence and could not anticipate the almost immediate divergence. Von Richthofen's reference to the recent (1890) founding of the School for Workers' Education (Arbeiterbildungsschule) was by no means irrelevant. Although Wilhelm Liebknecht, and with him the Social Democratic leadership, had declared belief not in achieving power and freedom through knowledge but in achieving knowledge and education through power, the demand from the rank and file for immediate education so grew during the period of the anti-socialist laws that it could not be resisted by the leadership. The founding of the School for Workers' Education was one result of this. The struggle for participation in artistic experience was seen as part of the struggle for education.

Three years later (1893), Franz Mehring said that art is so inseparably a part of the life of a complete person that the more the socialist movement developed the workers into complete people, the greater was the demand for art. Thus the party leadership saw art as

a means of broadening the workers' education. Into this situation came,
from the artistic side, the naturalistic movement, which Dr Conrad
Schmidt referred to as 'Our Ally'. So it was not simply theatre, but
specifically naturalistic drama, that was seen by the active social
democrats as their fellow-fighter. It was therefore appropriate that
the working-class Freie Volksbühne should take as its prototype the
bourgeois Freie Bühne, itself founded primarily to produce the Naturalist drama. Kautsky, editor of Die Neue Zeit, who expressed this
opinion, added that if the Freie Volksbühne promoted plays that any
other theatre would put on and was distinguished only by its lower
prices, if it sank to being a 'dramatic soup-kitchen', it would lose all
cultural and historical significance. Nevertheless, it was the party
rank and file, not the party leadership, that took part in founding the
Freie Volksbühne. Even Franz Mehring showed no interest at this time.
The leadership simply remained silent. Some may have hoped for so
immediate a coming of the socialist state that they could regard the
association as preparing the proletariat for its new status. In any case
the anti-socialist laws were in operation until 1 October 1890, so that
in July and August Liebknecht dare not have gone to Berlin. Bebel was
speaking in Dresden on 10 August, two days after the founding meeting.
But even had they been in Berlin, these two men might well not have
seen the meeting as important enough to warrant their attending it.
Wille's personality had already alienated the party leadership.

Obviously the Freie Volksbühne movement could not have succeeded had the social-democratic leadership been actively opposed to it;
and in spite of the silence of the leaders, the central organ of the party
in the capital, the Berliner Volksblatt, under the editorship of Baake,
did support Wille and printed his initial appeal. The importance of
Baake's presence in the Freie Volksbühne at the time of its coming into
existence cannot be overrated.

Initially the conflict between Wille and the others was not an open
one. Although he wanted the spread of education for the development
of the individual, while the workers wanted it in preparation for the
coming take-over of power, it was easy for the two sides with naturalistic drama as their common ground not to see that they had different
aims. When Wille used the phrase 'through education to freedom', his
hearers could put a political interpretation upon it. Those with strong
political aims for the new movement did not emphasise them, as this
would have compromised its beginnings. Nevertheless, some things
said at that time make it clear that 'art' was unimportant to some of
the political wing. There were those who emphasised the importance
of the content of plays — they ought to show economic and class conflict.
The proletarian membership did not stress artistic qualities: they
thought in terms of 'education'. In fact even 'education' does not describe what the ordinary member wanted. He was not interested in

Naturalism but wanted the edification of seeing his own outlook confirmed on the stage, and in addition simple enjoyment.

The lifting of the anti-socialist law had far-reaching consequences
for the new movement. Because the changes that had been hoped for
did not come quickly enough many artists lost interest in politics. It
was at this time (and in part for this reason) that the naturalist movement began to be more concerned with the individual and less with the
mass. It was — though this was not yet obvious — the parting of the ways
for the Freie Volksbühne and the Social Democratic Party. Big differences emerged at the party conference held in Erfurt in October 1891.
Part of the opposition was turned out, and others, including Wille, left
voluntarily. This excluded opposition formed a new party, the Independent Social Democratic party, with its own periodical, Der Sozialist.
Wille was a member of this for a time, and then withdrew from politics
altogether. After this conference some of the party members tried to
collect a hundred signatures in order to call an extraordinary general
meeting of the Freie Volksbühne to oust Wille from the chairmanship;
but they were unsuccessful.

Meanwhile conflicts had occurred within the committee. The three
original members of the executive (Wille, chairman; Carl Wildberger,
treasurer; Julius Türk, secretary) should have been complementary to
each other; but in fact, frictions developed. Politically Türk was
opposed to his two colleagues, and was critical of their competence.
Franz Mehring said later that the chief merit had been not in having the
idea of the Freie Volksbühne, but in the detailed work that made its
realisation possible. Türk did most of this and gave all his strength to
the new organisation for a very modest salary. Wille did so little that
Baake wanted him to be made 'honorary chairman' and removed from
the leadership. Wille, for his own part, could not avoid suspecting that
Türk was carrying on intrigues with the aim of becoming the leading
figure of the organisation, and in particular of taking charge of the
actual productions.

Tension within the executive committee increased and in the spring
of 1891 Türk handed in his resignation as secretary. Probably to avoid
publicising the internal frictions he gave personal reasons for his
resignation. He was replaced by Otto Erich Hartleben, Türk remaining
an ordinary committee member. At the Erfurt Conference Türk alone
of Wille's circle did not secede with the 'independents', and from that
time regarded himself as a representative of the official party on the
Freie Volksbühne committee.

As the next annual general meeting approached in the summer of
1892, Türk wished to regain a position on the executive. Carl Wildberger needed a break from the treasurership, which carried an

honorarium. Apart from a desire to increase his own influence, Türk
also needed the money, so that when some members asked him to
accept nomination for the post, he accepted. The general meeting in
July 1982 was stormy. Wille and his supporters strongly opposed
Türk's nomination, but even in the face of this he was elected treasurer.
At the same time, an 'independent', a supporter of Wille, Bernhard
Kampffmeyer, was elected secretary; the situation was explosive.

Conflicts concerning theatre and politics, unimportant in themselves, but serious in the context, occurred almost immediately, in
August and September. The committee supported Wille, who accused
Türk of personal and political agitation against his leadership, saying
he would shortly offer proofs. It may be that Türk had already, as
Wille believed, plotted a major offensive against him, or he may have
decided on one at this point. On 21 September an appeal doubtless
initiated by Türk, though his name was not among the twenty-three
signatures, appeared in Vorwärts attacking Wille on several grounds.
Very few of the signatories held, or had held office in the association.
At a committee meeting two days later, Wille took Türk to task, but
Türk insisted on a general meeting. The full committee then decided
to publish a pamphlet explaining the whole position to the membership.
Türk, however, refused to put his side of the argument in the pamphlet.

Two thousand members of the Freie Volksbühne met in the Sans
Souci on 4 October 1892, for a tumultuous general meeting that lasted
until 2 a. m. First, Wille put the case against Türk. Türk responded
with a two-hour speech leading to a resolution that the committee
should accept his accusations. In the vote on this Türk's supporters
were in an obvious majority. Wille tried to speak out of turn. Tumult
arose and the meeting was adjourned. When it resumed, a new chairman was elected. Wildberger was called upon to justify his book-
keeping, which he did, not without attacking Türk, and he received
some support.

Then Paul Dupont, one of the twenty-three signatories, spoke. He
demanded the enlargement of the executive, saying that it needed fresh
blood and representatives of the proletariat. If the 'literary gentlemen'
didn't agree, well, the workers no longer needed them and could undertake the leadership alone. There were loud and general cries of 'Hear!
Hear!' The speech was seen by Wille and his friends as highly provocative and it played a large part in later conflicts. The discussion
continued, and about one o'clock Wille spoke again. Woe to the
association, he declared, if the writers were excluded from it. Then
he concentrated upon the need for complete political independence for
the association. Türk had endangered this, and were he given a free
hand the police would soon declare the association political and threaten
its whole existence. At this the noise became so great that Wille could
no longer make himself heard and the meeting had to be dissolved.

Although no decision had been reached it was clear that Wille's days in the association were numbered. His opponents, however, had difficulty in finding a suitable successor. Eventually Türk advertised a continuation of the adjourned meeting at the Sans Souci, while Wille advertised one for the same day at the Böhmisches Brauhaus. For a moment it seemed as though the split had already happened, but Türk gave way, and on 12 October the meeting was resumed again with almost two thousand members present. Wille continued his former speech with much interruption: one heckler was thrown out. Then, unexpectedly, Türk's supporters moved the closure. Wille protested that Kampffmeyer had as yet had no opportunity to speak. But the closure was carried. It was evident that the majority were determined at all costs to have a change of leadership. Being in a hopeless minority Wille and his friends gave up the fight. Amid loud cheers Wille, Kampffmeyer and most of the association's officials, together with two or three hundred supporters, left the room. Of Wille's friends only a small group around Wildberger remained. Wildberger, who announced triumphantly that a new association would now be formed elsewhere, still wanted to defend himself and attack Türk, and his trump card was that he still held the profits from the last open-air festival, which he refused to hand over. After long and bitter argument, Türk himself conceded that they must look to the present rather than the past. Business then continued. The constitution was altered so as to enlarge the executive to five members — a first and second chairman, a first and second secretary, and the treasurer. The old executive was declared to have resigned, but Türk of course was re-elected as treasurer. Two unremarkable men were elected secretaries. The second chairman was Paul Dupont, a representative of the working classes and leader of the stone-masons' union, but in no way a horny-handed proletarian. Despite his attack on the 'literary gentlemen' he was himself well read, a clever and subtle thinker, a skilful speaker and editor of the stone-masons' journal. For chairman no less a figure than that of Franz Mehring had been found.

After the election of officers it was agreed to raise a loan of two or three thousand marks.

Wildberger had good grounds for declaring that a new Volksbühne would be formed. Wille had already realised that if he were defeated he must found a new association, and now he, with some hundred and fifty or two hundred of those who had left with him, hurried to the Strausberger Strasse, where they crowded excitedly into the Fortuna Festsälen. Far from throwing up the sponge, everyone felt that this was the opportunity to found a body avoiding the mistakes of the first. Wille, Kampffmeyer and Wildberger (who came over after the end of the meeting at the Sans Souci) were asked to prepare a constitution.

When most had gone home, Wille and a close circle of friends, some
old, some new, sat until morning in a café, talking things over.

Three days later (15 October), the committee, with co-opted
friends, met and formally constituted the Neue Freie Volksbühne. This
time there was no one to thwart Wille's undemocratic ideas — ideas
which had been strengthened by his experiences in the Freie Volksbühne.
The constitution drawn up was non-democratic. For an organisation
intended to reflect the broad mass of workers it was extraordinary that
the draft showed clearly that its originators detested the very idea of
constitutional control. Its ideal was rather that of a free society of
equals. It revealed important assumptions about the association's work,
and particular evidence of Wille's mind — always bold, full of ideas,
spacious but unpractical. While keeping closely to the original formu-
lation of aims, Wille widened the intended field of operations:

> The association proposes to bring before its members elevating
> and liberating works of art of all kinds, especially theatrical per-
> formances, poetry and musical works, also when possible works
> of painting and sculpture, and to explain these through lectures and
> articles. [27]

There was to be an annual general meeting, but its powers were remarkably limited: it elected three auditors, and, with a three-quarters
majority it could object to particular members of the leadership — but
it could not elect them! The leadership consisted of twenty 'artistic
experts' (five of them musical), and twenty 'technical experts' (corresponding to the Ordner of the original Volksbühne, and responsible for
practical arrangements, especially the lottery for seats). Who selected
the original members of these two groups, or how, is not stated.
Evidently they were hand-picked by Wille and his closest associates.
Once in being, both bodies were self-perpetuating, having power to fill
gaps in their own number, and to co-opt advisers. The artistic experts
alone elected the chairman and secretary; the two groups of experts
voting together elected the treasurer: chairman, secretary and treasurer constituted the executive. An interesting concession to 'democracy'
was that any member could sit in on meetings of the technical experts —
but not of the artistic, where the real policy-making power lay. The
names of the original technical experts can only be guessed at — probably
many were Ordner who had seceded with Wille and knew the ropes:
indeed, we know that these seceding officials took with them the actual
urns and other impedimenta of the lottery, thus nearly wrecking the
seating arrangements at the first performance of the 'old' Volksbühne —
whose committee, presumably, did not discover the loss until the last
moment. And whatever theoretical objections may be felt to the undemocratic selection of the artistic experts, the original list is
certainly impressive, though many of the newcomers did little but lend

their names. [28] For the rest, the practical articles of the new
association were much the same as those of the old: registration fee of
at least 1 Mark; monthly subscription of at least 50 Pfennigs, the right
of the committee to raise these minima; payment through agencies
before the 15th of the month, Sunday afternoon performances, ten plays
a year; lottery for seats.

Sadly, if inevitably, the split was followed by bitter conflict between
the two organisations. The dispute over the festival profits held by
Wildberger actually led to legal action, though it never came to court,
and the ideological fight was continued by the leaders of both sides in
periodicals devoted to literature and social criticism.

Seen in the perspective of the later history of the two associations
the differences between them seem perhaps less important than the
resemblances. The literary element did not lose all influence in the
'old' association, nor was the leadership of the 'new' wholly cut off
from or uninfluenced by its working-class membership. But at the time
personal bitterness and political fanaticism emphasised the depth of the
rift, which was not formally and completely healed until 1920. Until
then the narrative of the vicissitudes and growth of the two so closely
related organisations must be pursued along parallel lines, first of all
to the next crisis of their history in 1895.

iv The Freie Volksbühne to 1895

What determined above all the history of the Freie Volksbühne during
the three years between the split and the association's temporary dissolution in 1895 was the appointment of Franz Mehring as chairman.
The appointment was remarkable, for Mehring had never been seen at
any previous assembly of Volksbühne members and had in fact been the
association's quite bitter enemy. It is therefore important to try to
understand why Wille's opponents chose Mehring as his successor, and
why he accepted the office.

Franz Mehring was born on 27 February 1846 in Schlawe, Pomerania. From his north German family and background he inherited a
melancholy disposition, combined with great depth, thoroughness and
devotion to duty. He had a passionate sense of justice and was not a
man for half-measures: both his devotion and his hatred were whole-
hearted. At the same time he was excitable, often changing his
opinions — though not the profounder principles that underlay them — and
because he became emotionally involved in ideas he could not separate
people from their opinions. One of the so-called 'socialist academics',
Mehring studied philosophy in the Universities of Berlin and Jena.
From 1883 he became celebrated as editor of the left-wing middle-class
paper, Berliner Volkszeitung, through whose pages he waged war on

the anti-socialist law, and when he ceased to be its editor he became
a regular contributor to (and later joint editor of) the socialist periodical Die Neue Zeit. At the time of the founding of the Freie Volksbühne
Mehring showed no interest. With other Social Democratic leaders he
feared such a body would divert energy from what he saw as the central
tasks of the socialist movement and was suspicious of Wille's highly
individual brand of socialism. When the split in the association became
imminent, Mehring at first declined to be put forward as Wille's
successor. It was only when Türk put it to him that the Association
must have some literary person on the executive, lest the workers
should really appear (as indeed they were later represented in some
sections of the press) as enemies of the intellectuals, that Mehring
agreed to stand for election.

Türk's argument certainly expressed part of the truth: it was
important that the Freie Volksbühne should neither in fact nor in image
lose its literary-intellectual aspect. At the same time a leader was
wanted whose loyalty to the Social Democratic Party was unquestioned,
as only such a leader could command the trust of the majority of the
working class and so ensure a maximum growth in membership. One
suspects that Mehring was also welcomed by Türk because, as a man
whose interest in the theatre was secondary to his socialism, he was
unlikely to block Türk's own growing theatrical ambitions. To Wille's
opponents in general and Türk in particular, Mehring appeared as the
ideal successor. Whether he really was so is another matter, but just
as Mehring's life was 'burdened with tensions which, naturally enough,
reflected just as much tensions of the times as the tenseness of a
receptive and sensitive mind', [29] so, within the Volksbühne movement, his presence and activity expressed the tension between political
and artistic aims inherent in the original foundation.

Why he accepted the office is more difficult to see. That he intended simply to lend literary respectability to a primarily working-class
organisation cannot be the whole explanation. Perhaps at this point in
time he anticipated a new wave of proletarian drama. When the Freie
Volksbühne was founded two years earlier with naturalistic plays in the
forefront of its programme, many socialists had supported the foundation because they 'had founded upon Naturalism the hope that it would
develop into the art of the fourth estate if it were given fruitful soil.
And', Heinz Selo goes on, 'it had not so far fulfilled this hope'. [30] In
January 1893, within a few months of taking office, Mehring was writing
that Naturalism showed the world that was passing away, and he was
asking whether it would have the courage to take the second step and
show the world that was coming into being. Mehring clearly failed to
appreciate the primarily critical function of drama and may have been
looking for something like the later 'preaching' Shaw or the products

of Russian socialist realism. Fortunately for the theatre the naturalistic writers did not take this road: Ibsen and Hauptmann were already
writing subjectively and individualistically. [31] But Mehring may well
have expected otherwise and his disappointment in the failure of such a
drama to develop may have strengthened his apparent willingness to
dissolve the Freie Volksbühne in 1895 and devote himself to other
socialist activities. He did in fact say that in the struggle of the working
class not to sink into misery and degeneration and to shape the society
of the future, <u>art is a tiny factor</u> compared with universal voting rights,
the value of strong organisation, and the influence of a flourishing
Trades Union press. [32] Whatever his motives, it was not in
Mehring's nature to do a job less than whole-heartedly and he evidently
threw all his energies into his new responsibilities.

The loss of a few hundred members did not appreciably weaken the
Freie Volksbühne; indeed, the removal of the non-working-class
'writers' and the chairmanship of Mehring led to a rapid increase in
membership. [33]

Although statistics for these earlier periods are scanty and hap-
hazard, a census of occupations of members made in the season 1893/4
shows strikingly that the association was predominantly working-class,
with a particular appeal to skilled workmen; [34] it was genuinely and
unmistakably a working-class movement. Mehring, who claimed at the
time of the split that there was no change in the policy of the Freie
Volksbühne, later called it 'a serving member in the great struggle of
the working class for emancipation'. It was to play its part in the self-
liberation and self-education of the worker; it was not revolutionary;
'to overturn the bourgeois theatre in the bourgeois world' lay wholly
outside its power. He emphasised its democratic character, contrasting
its members' freedom with Wille's 'adult-educational undertaking'.

The will of the membership made itself strongly felt in many ways,
not least in the choice of plays. From the start Mehring's own intention
was to emphasise much more strongly the political tendency of the
association. He declined an offer from Raphael Löwenfeld (1893) to
co-operate with the Schiller-Theater, stigmatising it as 'capitalistic'
and at first opposed creating a new 'section' which he feared would let
in 'bourgeois' elements, interested only in seeing plays cheaply. This
did happen. Schutzmann Gerlach, the regular police observer, made a
note on 1 June 1893 that many members did not belong to the Social
Democratic movement. Like Mehring, he assumed that these members
were only interested in cheap tickets. Similarly Mehring hoped for the
new naturalist plays that would confirm the workers' image of the new
world. When these failed to materialise he was left with a potentially
dangerous vacuum. He saw that a 'modern' form did not ensure unexceptionable content and that many 'classics' had a revolutionary
content hidden under the dust of ages.

Meanwhile the demands of the membership became more and more diverse. As a compromise it was agreed that there should be more modern plays, if very good, full of teaching and 'revolt' — and also more classics. But in fact the seasons included fewer and fewer untried new plays: Mehring's excuse was that it was easier to experiment with one or two thousand members than with seven or eight thousand, as the risk was much less.

Throughout the period 1892 to 1895 members were offered productions from the repertoire of the Lessing Theatre and productions of the Volksbühne itself at the National, as the Ostend Theater was now called. Although the association had no real control over the plays presented at the Lessing Theater, the high quality of the productions attracted a large membership, and when in the spring of 1895 a proposal was put forward to leave the Lessing Theater and rely entirely on performances at the National, membership growth was checked. [35]

Ironically enough, under Mehring's consciously 'socialist' direction the danger actually increased of the Freie Volksbühne becoming what its enemies in the Social Democratic Party called it — a 'dramatic soup-kitchen' or 'humbug education'. [36] Much of the best energy of the Social Democratic movement went into the Volksbühne and other educational bodies, though many party workers (at another time Mehring might have been of their number) regarded this as unwarrantable dissipation of resources. Mehring defended the Volksbühne's work by saying that the people needed 'recuperation', and by asking where better they could get it than in the theatre? — a sad retreat from the Volksbühne's original position, and indeed from Mehring's own.

In fact the plays actually offered to the members are not unworthy successors of Wille's repertoire from 1890 to 1892. At the Lessing Theater members saw four plays of Anzengruber, three of Sudermann, two of Lessing, and plays by Grillparzer, Kleist, Augier, Björnson and Ibsen. The standard of the productions at the National Theater was so low that apologies were made in the periodical! But the repertoire itself included Goethe, Schiller, Molière and Calderón, and many contemporaries or at least moderns. There was no shame in a programme that included Verga, Augier, Heyse and Hauptmann (Die Weber, 1893; Der Biberpelz (The Beaver Coat), 1894).

The performances of Die Weber were the high point of the work of the Freie Volksbühne in this three-year period, as indeed in their own theatres were the performances of it given by the Freie Bühne and the Neue Freie Volksbühne. This is not the place to repeat the history of the writing of this play and the struggle with the censor, nor to attempt any new or deep critical assessment. Yet all these must be touched upon if the importance of the play in the history of the Volksbühne movement, and the importance of the Volksbühne movement in the history of Naturalist drama, are to be understood. Even in its own day Die Weber was already a symbol as well as a fact; though a unique and unrepeatable work of art — strictly inimitable — it was regarded as a prototype for a new proletarian art, as well as a high achievement of the naturalist movement. The disputes with the censor and the disputes within the ranks of progressives as to the play's significance epitomise the broader disputes and disagreements of the period.

As early as autumn 1888 in Zürich, Hauptmann had conceived the idea of a play based upon the revolt on the Silesian weavers in 1844. He began working on the material early in 1890, made two journeys to the 'weaver' country, the Eulengebirge, in 1891, and by the end of that year had completed a dialect version of the play (De Waber) and about two months later, the High German version (Die Weber) — though this too is heavily weighted with Silesian dialect. Both versions were rejected by the censor — the High German version being regarded by the police as even more dangerous than the dialect version, because more intelligible. The play could, of course, have been performed by the Volksbühne, but Hauptmann was anxious for public performances and would not release the play for Volksbühne use while his appeals were proceeding. He did, however, allow a performance in February 1893 by Brahm's Freie Bühne. This association had by now little more than a nominal existence (in 1892 it had presented only one play, Strindberg's Miss Julie), but it was revived for the occasion. [37] Permission for public performance, at the Berlin Deutsches Theater only, was given, surprisingly, on 2 October 1893, though the first public performance did not take place there until nearly a year later on 25 September 1894, less than a month after Otto Brahm himself had taken over the direction of the theatre. As soon as the play had been passed for public performance, Hauptmann released it to the Freie Volksbühne and the Neue Freie Volksbühne, and within a fortnight (15 October) the latter presented the play to its members in the Viktoria Theater. The performances arranged by the Freie Volksbühne did not take place until December, at the National Theatre. During that month the play was presented to all five Freie Volksbühne sections, and in January two additional performances were also sold out.

Brahm's production at the Freie Bühne was apparently a muted one. He put the author's interests before those of his society: an explosive production might well have been good for the Freie Bühne and its reputation, but it would almost certainly have made the police even more determined to stifle the play. When Brahm produced the play — at least when Cord Hachmann produced it under his direction (at the Deutsches Theater a year later) — he departed from his normal attitude of respect for the text of a new play. Normally he would not, for the first night with the critics present, allow cuts or alterations in new plays, though to reduce length he would subsequently introduce cuts, usually of whole scenes. This time he simplified the texture of the play, cutting anything that reflected badly on the workers, and anything contributing to Dreissiger's humanity. Brahm's Weavers must have been a thinner and poorer thing than Hauptmann's.

The arguments about the play continued stormily throughout 1893. Hauptmann himself in a letter written in August declared that the play was indeed social, but not socialist [38] and Julius Hart wrote about it in these terms in the Tägliche Rundschau. Gerhart Hauptmann, he said, is one of the very few in our times 'who bear on their shoulders the wings of the true poet and raise themselves upon them high above the fog and fume of everything party-political'. [39] Mehring responded to this in a piece of characteristic polemic: 'Mr Julius Hart is just as well informed as we are how deeply Die Weber is rooted in "the fog and fume of everything party-political".' [40]

In December 1892 the enrolment fee had been lowered to 50 Pfennigs to encourage working-class recruitment. The monthly subscription of 50 Pfennigs was called a 'minimum', but 99 per cent of members paid only the minimum. In 1893 both the enrolment fee and the monthly subscription (for eleven months per year) had to be raised to 60 Pfennigs. But Die Weber was so costly a production — with large cast and five distinct settings — that a special supplementary fee of 30 Pfennigs was required for this play in December; this did not prevent its being a complete success. It was also exceptional in being twice as expensive to stage as most productions at the National Theater. The police reported that at the Freie Volksbühne performance (presumably the first) the applause and cries of 'Bravo!' at the end of the fourth act (when the weavers storm Dreissiger's house) seemed as though they would never end.

What appealed to this audience was the subject-matter, not the style of the dramatist or the skill of the direction or acting. It was not Naturalism as an art form that attracted the working-class audience, and the greatest successes of the first five years — with the exception of Die Weber — were not naturalistic plays. In this respect the working-class audience was no different from the middle-class, though the squalor of some naturalistic settings did not offend them as it did the middle classes. Mehring himself came to see that there was a cleavage between the aims of the contemporary playwrights and those of the working classes. Modern art, he thought, was deeply pessimistic; the modern proletariat deeply optimistic. In seeing only pessimism in plays of social criticism Mehring again showed the limitations of his understanding of the nature of drama. He also failed to realise that the working classes were (and usually are) conservative in art even when

revolutionary in philosophy. They were more interested in hearing
their own views and prejudices emphasised than in seeing an art work
presented in a consistent convention. Thus Alfred Loth's two socialist
speeches in Vor Sonnenaufgang were delivered straight at the audience
in a way quite out of key with Naturalism — and gained great applause.
Nor did this audience distinguish between the actor and the role: it
was the role, not the actor, that was applauded. Bruno Wille understood perfectly well this inability of the audience to appreciate the art
of the theatre.

Nevertheless, this audience, which so impressed Ibsen, had many
positive qualities as well as other often laughable faults that could not
have been predicted by middle-class theatre people. Much stemmed,
on the one hand, from their goodwill and on the other from their lack
of education as theatre-goers. The Freie Volksbühne was felt to be
their own theatre — therefore it was good. They wore their best clothes
and thought of the Volksbühne performance as a 'day out'. The performance was for them a symbol of social ideals and aspirations. Thus
they applauded heartily whether they liked and understood the show, or
not. Such an audience fascinated the critics. It was the unpredictable,
apparently unprejudiced audience that some twentieth-century dramatists have claimed to long for. Its members showed their feelings
openly, expressed their laughter and fear without inhibition. They
would shout out their anger at individuals in the play, loving, hating,
anxious and rejoicing, watching the drama breathlessly. They were,
as Brahm saw, a naïve audience in the best sense. To a factory
worker with no job-satisfaction it was of immense psychological value
to give human feelings expression. He knew once more what it was to
be a person — ein Mensch zu sein (Schiller).

The naïvety and lack of 'theatre-education' brought corresponding
shortcomings. Like the middle classes, the audience arrived late — but
perhaps for different reasons. The women did not know that they ought
to remove their hats (but in the second season the programme asked
them to do so); the men used to variety houses, with a bar in the room,
took spirits into the auditorium. Not knowing what to do with children,
parents tried to bring them to the theatre; later they realised the advantage of husband and wife belonging to different sections and taking
turns at baby-sitting.

However presented, certain aspects of life produced stock reactions. Drunks and bad language were something familiar and amusing,
even in the context, for example, of Vor Sonnenaufgang. The audience
was anti-clerical and ready to laugh at the celibacy of the parson in
Der Pfarrer von Kirchfeld (The Pastor of Kirchfeld). Erotic scenes
were enjoyed with a smirk. References to class evoked immediate
response. A working man who refused money from a wealthy one,

saying, 'I'm not no beggar' (<u>Keen Bettler bin ich nicht</u>) produced a
terrific reaction. The audience responded warmly to human love, a
sense of justice or a fine deed. They became angry at intrigue. They
wanted above all to laugh. So they liked inoffensive comedies and often
laughed where laughter was really out of place. Even Die Weber drew
some inappropriate laughter.

The worker in the theatre usually forgot his class-consciousness
unless the play itself (helped by the introductory essay in the periodical)
reminded him of it. There was always the 'danger', in the eyes of
Mehring and others, of the Volksbühne audience becoming 'simply' a
'Sunday afternoon public'. In fact, the relationship of socialism,
Naturalism, theatre-going, working-class culture and the Volksbühne
movement was far more complex than anyone involved at the time could
appreciate. The bifurcation into Freie Volksbühne and Neue Freie
Volksbühne at least enabled people who saw the relationship in different
terms and with different emphases to continue working with enthusiasm
and good conscience right up to the First World War, growing gradually
closer to each other until reunion became the natural step. Had the
split not occurred, the whole venture would probably have foundered in
its first few years, destroyed by internal divisions.

v The Neue Freie Volksbühne to 1895

If Mehring's Freie Volksbühne carried on the Social Democratic tradition of the association, Wille's Neue Freie Volksbühne preserved the
artistic and educational ideals which he had expressed in his original
appeal. And simply <u>because</u> it was educational, Wille argued, it could
not be fully democratic. The proletariat, he said, could not educate
itself; and anyway, the principle of the association was of free agreement. 'No one is obliged to belong to the association against his
inclination.' [41] It was, he said at the founding meeting (30 October
1892), to be a society for 'uplift' not for 'amusement', and in a series
of articles he tried to convince his members that the value of a work
of art does not depend upon the opinions of the artist, but on the artistic
form. Like Hart and unlike Mehring, he valued Die Weber just because
it was not one-sided or party-political, though ironically enough, the
programme of the Neue Freie Volksbühne contained more new plays,
problem plays and plays of social criticism than that of the 'social
democratic' Freie Volksbühne. [42]

Most of the productions in this period were the association's own,
and Wille was fortunate in obtaining the services of Emil Lessing as
artistic director of the productions. No leading personality, Lessing
was artistically serious, industrious and sensitive. Working within the
naturalistic framework, he was not doctrinaire. He was able to get
together some of the best Berlin players, and though they could not

work together continuously he was able to create something like an
ensemble. The keynote of high artistic ambition was struck in the first
production: Goethe's Faust, Part I; and if some of the new plays produced were not of the highest quality, their inclusion was artistically
adventurous.

Even so, Wille found experiment within the association difficult.
Two attempted 'special performances' led to misfortune. Wille wanted
to give two performances of Meister Oelze by Johannes Schlaf. To be
sure of two houses Wille offered one of them to the Academic Dramatic
Association, who guaranteed 750 Marks for it. Schlaf, however, hoped
that Brahm might produce his play at the Freie Bühne (he never did),
and when rehearsals were well advanced, he sent his friend Arno Holz
along to cancel the arrangement. When Wille refused, Holz, very
angry, went to the Academic Dramatic Association and persuaded it to
withdraw. Wille went ahead; the result was heavy loss. On another
occasion Agnes Sorma offered to play Voss's Eva for the Neue Freie
Volksbühne. This would have been an enormous attraction, and the
Zentral Theater was booked for two Sunday afternoons in February 1895.
But then her own management, the Deutsches Theater, insisted that she
play for them on those afternoons, so the whole thing came to nothing.

The experience with Schlaf, however, had already shown Wille the
difficulties of experiment in the Volksbühne, so he founded in 1894, an
experimental theatre specifically to produce plays by young literary
talent. A special periodical, Die Versuchsbühne, was also produced
under Wille's editorship. In the event there were only two productions,
before the police shut the venture down. The response to these productions was disappointing and the future of the experimental theatre might
well have been in doubt quite apart from the police.

Wille's proud comment that no one need belong to the Neue Freie
Volksbühne who didn't want to was answered by the fact that very few
did want to. About three hundred people left the meeting with him on
12 October 1892. A call for new members did no more than double this
number, and towards the end of the year membership had reached a
thousand. As only nine hundred could see a performance at the Belle-
Alliance a second section was needed. A recruiting slogan 'Every
member a booking office' resulted in several hundred new members
and in February 1893 a second section was launched, even though the
total membership was only about fifteen hundred. The next season also
opened with two half-filled sections, but the release of Die Weber to
the Volksbühne associations brought in hundreds of new members. Two
sections were filled and a third and fourth set up. But membership
quickly declined again. The fourth section dropped out; by January
1894 amalgamation of the second and third was threatened. By the end
of the season there were under two thousand members, and at the start

of the 1894-5 season the second section had only four hundred; so that there were five hundred empty seats at its performances. By the second half of the season one performance was enough for the total membership.

There are no statistics, but probably the members were largely working-class, though in a smaller proportion than in Mehring's association. They applauded during performances and were openly rebellious during Ostrovsky's The Storm, evidently having not lost the spontaneity that was one of the original Volksbühne virtues. Antoine, founder of the Paris Théâtre Libre, was present at a Neue Freie Volksbühne performance of Die Weber, and was impressed by the audience much as Ibsen had been impressed at the Freie Volksbühne two years before. 'It was worth a journey from Paris to Berlin to see that', was Antoine's comment on the audience.

In the 1893-4 season frictions developed between the technical and artistic organisers, and a group comprising some three-quarters of the technical organisers called a meeting for 30 May 1894. On 13 September 1894 a further protest meeting was held, this time to question the whole relationship of membership and management. The principal speaker, Julius Müller, thought he had produced a trump card in accusing Wille of being well paid for his post on the executive. Into this situation a brief note from Wille burst like a bombshell:

> Weary of the persistent agitation that frustrates my efficiency and that of the Executive and Committee, I am hereby resigning from my post. I wish the beloved association well in every way but I have little hope. [43]

The resignation gave many members second thoughts, and a commission was appointed to meet Wille, who refuted the charges against him and resumed his post. Only a month later, however, at the ordinary general meeting (22 October) strong feeling against Wille was again expressed, especially over the power to assign good seats. Adjourned, the meeting continued eight days later. Wille finally won the battle, insisting that the players must retain the power of giving good complimentary seats. The ringleaders, Hermann Berger and Julius Müller, however, continued to agitate and were struck off the list of organisers. They then (27 November) called a public meeting on the theme 'The corruption of the Neue Freie Volksbühne'. Only 120 people came, including some of Wille's supporters; but these eventually left and a unanimous vote of no confidence in Wille was then passed, and the meeting decided to found a Third Freie Volksbühne. Berger, Müller and a third, Stehl, were appointed to carry this into effect. They began negotiations with theatres, and misused the name of the Neue Freie Volksbühne. Wille threatened legal action and the whole thing collapsed.

vi Struggles with the authorities, 1892-96

The judgement of January 1892 that the Freie Volksbühne was a
category (ii) association made possible a degree of police control; but
this was not strongly enforced. Early in 1893 an official statement was
made that the performances could no longer be said to be really
'private', and it appeared for a time as if both bodies might have to
submit to censorship. But in spite of the judgement nothing was done.
It seemed as if troubles with the police might be over, but the truce
proved to be only temporary. Already the Volksbühne idea had aroused
interest outside Berlin, the strongest movement being in Hamburg and
the neighbouring Altona. [44] In the autumn of 1894 the Altona police
sent to the Berlin police saying that an attempt was being made in
Altona to found a Volksbühne on the Berlin model and asking whether
the Berlin Volksbühne performances were entirely private or whether,
because of the large membership and because apparently anyone could
get in by paying enrolment and entrance fees, they were not in fact to
be regarded as public. This enquiry seems to have set the ball rolling
again. At all events, on 18 April 1895 the Freie Volksbühne, the Neue
Freie Volksbühne and the Versuchsbühne all heard from the police that
they must now submit all scripts to the censor, fourteen days in advance of the performance. The message reached the chairmen on 19
April and on the 20th the directors of the National Theater (Freie
Volksbühne) and Zentral Theater (Neue Freie Volksbühne) refused
further performances of uncensored plays.

It was, however, too late to cancel the scheduled first performances of Einsam (Alone), a dramatisation by Agrell of a novel of
Anzengruber, by the Neue Freie Volksbühne at the Zentral Theater on
21 April. The players and the audience both turned up, but the police
lieutenant 'stood between them with the flaming sword of the censorship
order' [45] and there was no performance. This production may well
have been one of those other factors that led to the end of the 'provisional' freedom from censorship. The play was a passionate attack on
clerical arrogance and parsonical intolerance. Nevertheless, the
police action took the associations completely by surprise; they had
been lulled into a sense of false security, and now, overnight, their
meaningful existence was threatened. Both arranged general meetings.
That of the Freie Volksbühne was immediate (23 April). A resolution
was passed instructing the executive to fight the police decision. At
the same time the association decided to suspend its operations, rather
than continue, even temporarily, under censorship. The periodical
was to continue in order to hold the membership together.

The administration of the Neue Freie Volksbühne, although unanimous that they should fight the police in the courts, could not agree on
other aspects of policy. Some of them wanted to follow Mehring's

example and suspend operations. Wille, characteristically putting
theatre before politics, wanted to continue, replacing private performances by public ones. Eventually Wille's views prevailed and they were
endorsed by a general meeting held on 17 May. The experimental
theatre also decided both to continue its activities and to fight the
police. Thus, to begin with, there was a three-pronged legal attack on
the police action, but the two smaller bodies soon ran out of money and
only the Freie Volksbühne was left in the field; and indeed, only one
successful court action was needed for the whole movement.

There were long delays before judgement; even the first court did
not meet until the summer. The whole of 1895 passed. The Freie
Volksbühne, with a good fighting fund of 1600 Marks, arranged a 'Heine
evening' and a concert. The Neue Freie Volksbuhne tended to stagnate.
There were four 'open' productions of established plays at the Schiller-
Theater, but these ended in the autumn, and the general meeting in
November 1895 decided to suspend regular performances. Meanwhile
plans were afoot to alter the constitution so as to make it acceptable to
the police.

While the official associations thus stagnated, the restless, stage-
struck Julius Türk saw his opportunity to win his 'theatrical laurels'.
Immediately after the suspension of Freie Volksbühne productions he
established himself as a private manager and took over the Freie
Volksbühne's agreement with the Ostend Theater (National Theater) —
though the theatre director, Max Samst, had to take part of the risk.
At Whitsun 1895 he advertised in <u>Vorwärts</u>, 'Popular Performances in
the National Theater, arranged by Julius Türk'. The first production
was Hebbel's <u>Maria Magdelena</u>. Tickets were all one price, 75
Pfennigs, but for Freie Volksbühne members they were reduced to 60
Pfennigs. A long list of ticket-agencies was given: precisely that of
the Freie Volksbühne. As treasurer of the association Türk obviously
had excellent contacts here. After two productions at the National
Theater Türk moved to the Alexanderplatz-Theater, and after that took
his Volksbühnen-Ensemble on tour to Magdeburg, Halle, Leipzig and
Hannover. Although he had some quite respectable actors, he did badly,
especially on the tour, which was a complete fiasco. The Freie Volksbühne general meeting in July wanted to stop his activities, but were
unable to do so. Nor was he now to be deterred by financial difficulty.
He had tasted theatrical blood. In the autumn he offered Sunday afternoon performances at the Belle-Alliance — once more with single price
tickets, using the Freie Volksbühne agencies. He just scraped through.

The appeal was laid by the Freie Volksbühne's lawyer, Kauffmann
on 26 April 1895. Judgement was not given until January 1896. Meeting
on 3 January, the High Court could not reach agreement. It did so on
24 January. Judgement was against the Freie Volksbühne, but a rider

clearly hinted that constitutional changes might radically alter the
position. The hint went unheeded. Perhaps Mehring welcomed the
opportunity to get the Old Man of the Sea off his back. [46] The executive did not wait for the written judgement (which anyway didn't come
until months later!) but called a general meeting for 9 March 1896. It
was poorly attended, and after a short debate it was agreed to wind the
association up. Five liquidators (including Türk!) were appointed. The
assets, about a thousand Marks, were divided between the Social Democratic Party, the Workers' Education School and the weavers on strike
at Cottbus. 'A burial without pomp and touching speeches of farewell',
remarks Nestriepke. The experimental theatre was also dissolved and
only Wille's own Neue Freie Volksbühne remained in existence, though
dormant, to keep a faint line of unbroken continuity in the history of the
movement. The general meeting held on 22 August 1896 formally
resolved to seek alterations in the constitution to allow the association
to continue. The new constitution, passed on 28 November, was far
from ideal and some of the police requirements were very pernickety.
It was not an easy rebirth and for many years it must have required a
vast amount of faith to keep the association in being with fewer than
two thousand members. But the faith was there, the continuity was
maintained and the Neue Freie Volksbühne was ready when, early in
the new century, the opportunity arose for its unprecedented growth.

2 INTO THE TWENTIETH CENTURY

i The Freie Volksbühne from 1897

The success of the Neue Freie Volksbühne in reconstituting itself so as
to be able to resume active life made a great impression on many of
those former members of the Freie Volksbühne who had agreed in
March 1896 to throw in the sponge. The wounds inflicted by the split
had not even yet healed however, and the Freie Volksbühne men could
not suggest that the work be continued with one joint organisation. So
a committee set about quietly drafting a suitable constitution, though
some of the former officers, including Mehring, made it clear that
they would not be prepared to resume their posts in a re-founded Freie
Volksbühne. On 7 March 1897, a year almost to the day after the
formal dissolution of the 'old' Freie Volksbühne, an advertisement
appeared in Vorwärts for a big public meeting on the subject: 'What is
the attitude of the Berlin working classes to founding a Freie Volksbühne association?' The meeting took place on 12 March with Robert
Schmidt in the chair. Paul Dupont, the advertised speaker and former
vice-chairman, called for the re-establishment of the Freie Volksbühne,
putting aside the idea of uniting with the Neue Freie Volksbühne. Adolf
Löhr, bringing a forcefully worded message from Bruno Wille, fluently

put the case for unity on behalf of the committee of the Neue Freie
Volksbühne. After a lively debate the suggestion of a united Volksbühne
was rejected, but it was rejected politely, with expressions of regret
and the assurance that the reasons were objective, not personal. In
spite of this, Wille took the decision badly.

The question must be asked whether the 'new' Freie Volksbühne
of 1897 was in fact a direct continuation of the 'old' Freie Volksbühne.
Heinz Selo, in his closely argued but highly tendencious thesis of 1930,
maintained:

> This investigation proves that the Freie Volksbühne lived and went
> under with Social Naturalism. It should have been originally the
> 'literary organ' of the German working class, as the Social
> Democratic Party was its political organ and the Trades Unions
> its economic organ. It did not succeed in this. Instead it brought
> the working class to a taste for theatrical art. For when in 1897
> the possibility presented itself to revive the association, it was
> newly constituted at the pressing wish of many earlier members,
> now of course in completely altered inner structure. [1]

As Selo's thesis includes nothing after 1896 he brings no evidence to
support this last assertion, while his definition of what the Freie
Volksbühne should have been rests on a very one-sided view of its
roots. In whatever sense we take the phrase 'inner structure' it is
difficult to see that it was 'completely altered'. The 'aim' was
expressed less provocatively with no mention of the topicality and truth
of the plays, but most clauses closely resembled the old ones. As to
the character of the membership, a census of occupations made at the
turn of the century shows that this was still primarily proletarian. [2]
The association had the sympathy and trust of the workers. It soon
outstripped the Neue Freie Volksbühne (which at this time had only one
section, of eight to nine hundred members) and for six or seven years
its leadership was never in question. In just over a fortnight one section was full. Steady growth continued until in the season 1907-8 there
were over fourteen thousand members in twenty sections.

Although Mehring and Dupont would not stand as chairman and
vice-chairman they remained on the committee with other former
members and one new, Dr Bruno Borchardt. The members of the
executive were new to office, but not to the movement. Dr Conrad
Schmidt, the chairman, had been one of the founders in 1890, but in
1891 he had gone to Zürich as a university teacher. Now he had
returned to Berlin and was working on Vorwärts. For decades to come
he was to be a most important personality in the Volksbühne movement.
In contrast with Mehring he was meditative rather than pugnacious,
judicious rather than rash. His profound and many-sided education

enabled him to write play-introductions which were both understandable
and full of understanding. His was a lovable personality. He was a man
of absolute openness and willingness to serve. He lacked certain qualities required of an active leader, however. Nor was he businesslike or
tactically clever. The new vice-chairman, Heinrich Schulz, was a man
who had sacrificed his career as a teacher to devote himself absolutely
to the service of the Social Democratic Party. The general secretary
was Julius Cohn, already on the committee, a man of known qualities,
though with dangers hidden in his energy. His assistant Max Buschold,
a former painter, was a good subordinate. The most onerous post was
still that of treasurer. Being a paid appointment it developed in time
into that of general manager. Julius Türk had no intention of becoming
an organisation man again and in his place Gustav Winkler was elected.
His candidacy was supported by Dupont and by Robert Schmidt: he was
treasurer and later manager of the Freie Volksbühne for nearly a
generation. Winkler, a stonemason, had been a member since the
foundation in 1890 and had become an active one, though without a
specific function, after Wille's exodus. He had been a correspondent
to Vorwärts and assistant secretary in the Berlin Trades Union office.
He had led the wage-battles of his fellow stonemasons, even being secretary of an International. Consequently he had been blacklisted within
the trade and at the age of thirty-five found it hard to make a living.
He was proposed by the stonemasons.

In constitution, working-class membership and socialist leadership,
then, the re-founded Freie Volksbühne was the true child of the old one.
But Heinz Selo's principal argument for discontinuity relates to the
programme: '... the Freie Volksbühne lived and went under with Social
Naturalism.' We must examine the programme of the first decade of
the 'new' Freie Volksbühne. In the first place, no change in policy was
intended. Most members saw the Freie Volksbühne as a member of the
working-class movement, but an independent one, neither the supporter
of an agit-prop political theatre, nor having a mere average eclectic
programme. Plays should be enlightening, educational and such as to
tend to liberate the people. The leading figures, of course, realised
that every great work of art has a stimulating and educational element,
and Conrad Schmidt expressed this in the first issue of the periodical
in 1897. Nevertheless, the feelings about ideology were so strong that
in the same year the association declined an invitation from Raphael
Löwenfeld to participate in honouring Tolstoy's seventieth birthday,
because of his belief in suffering and his primitive Christian mysticism.
(But three years later, The Power of Darkness was included in the programme.)

Conrad Schmidt, more than Mehring, was committed to the
Naturalist movement in drama and would have included a high proportion of new naturalistic plays in the programme had these been

forthcoming: but they were not. The history of dramatic writing,
expressed in the development of the established playwrights and the
interests of the younger ones, was determined by many factors other
than the desires of the Freie Volksbühne. The lack of these plays was
repeatedly lamented in the periodical and in general meetings, and
Schmidt had to point out that if an unbroken series of productions was
to continue, a broader idea of what were suitable plays was essential.
Nevertheless, apart from the paucity of completely new plays and plays
still banned by the censor, the programme presented over the next six
years, or even over the next decade, does not differ radically in
character from the earlier. There were fifty-two productions of
sixty-two plays in the next six years; eleven were classics, ten were
foreign, and the rest modern German. [3] In the following period
(1902-8) seventy-two different plays were presented (a few being one-
acters) of which twenty-one were classics, twenty-two by modern
foreign authors and twenty-nine by modern German authors. Thus
there were many more classics, and the number of works that would
not have been found in any ordinary theatre repertoire was extremely
small. The repertoire was varied and lively, but not bold. By that
time, however, the Freie Volksbühne was competing with the pheno-
menal growth of the Neue Freie Volksbuhne (now collaborating with
Reinhardt) and might well be forgiven for popularising its programme.

Even so, the programme was not entirely unadventurous, and
certainly not without plays of social and political criticism. In 1902
the Freie Volksbühne presented The Good Hope by the Dutch socialist
playwright Herman Heijermans; in 1905 followed two more of his plays,
both of which had been blocked by the censor: No. 80 and Armour,
both works of trenchant social criticism, the one of law and punishment, the other of militarism. As a result the author released to the
association his unperformed Ora et labora. Tschirikow's The Jews
was an exposure of Russian pogroms. But perhaps more significant
than these was the Freie Volksbühne's introduction of Shaw to Germany.
At the beginning of the century he was virtually unknown there, but by
the time the Freie Volksbühne decided to include Arms and the Man in
its programme, Lindau had already planned to present it at the
Deutsches Theater. The Volksbühne production took place first, though
not without friction. The Börsen-Courier claimed that the Volksbühne
performance was an illegal trespass upon Lindau's theatre; it went
further and claimed that the performance was not only without Shaw's
permission, but against his will. The executive replied that they were
totally unaware of Lindau's plans and published a letter from Shaw
which said: 'Among all German theatres there is none by which I would
rather be produced than by the Freie Volksbühne.' [4] Productions of
The Devil's Disciple, Mrs Warren's Profession and Widowers' Houses

followed. Shaw's plays of keen social criticism were closely in harmony with the basic ideals of the Freie Volksbühne, and in the absence
of new naturalistic plays the association could hardly have done better
than introduce Shaw to its audiences.

If, as is true, the Freie Volksbühne became less experimental in
the early years of the new century, 'safer' in its general choice of
plays, the reason is not to be sought in a change of intention or aim,
but in the sheer size of the growing body. Franz Mehring, who had
justified similar policies as early as 1892 on the grounds that it is
harder to experiment with large numbers, brought forward the same
argument again, out of his own experience, in 1906, when opposing a
further expansionist plan within the movement. 'The greater the number of members', he wrote, 'the less can the tendency to experiment
exist'. No great human movement, political, ethical, artistic or
religious, can retain in its enlarged maturity the purity and intensity
of its infancy.

When the Freie Volksbühne was re-founded in March 1897 it was
already too late to produce any plays under its own direction in that
season. Julius Türk, however, was still presenting Sunday afternoon
performances, with the tickets sold through the Freie Volksbühne's
own agencies. They were not very good productions. Türk had a
shrewd head, but was no Director. The Freie Volksbühne, having no
choice, went to his plays, but with little satisfaction. A proposal was
put forward to offer Türk the post of play director under Freie Volksbühne management — in this way the association hoped for greater
control over him. But he refused. He valued his independence and
preferred to negotiate independently with the association. The association responded, but at the same time sounded out other theatres.
Several threatres were needed if its members were to be given a
satisfactory programme. Türk could offer only one, so the negotiations
collapsed. Türk was offended and embittered, and some of the Volksbühne officials became his advocates. The executive remained firm,
and eventually the agencies were forbidden to work for Türk. So it
came about that Türk, incurably bitten by the theatre bug, and having
himself worked for the resurrection of the Freie Volksbühne, now
found that its very existence precluded him from any future in Berlin.

In later years need drove him into several different walks of life,
those of touring lecturer, of hotelier, of publican; but he always came
back to the theatre whenever he saw an opportunity. At one time he
worked with Reinhardt, but usually independently, as director of small
or medium sized municipal theatres. His theatrical activity took him
to Silesia, Saxony, Switzerland and south-west Germany. Sometimes
he did well, at others he had to draw on his savings. Inflation after the
First World War finally ate up his reserves and he committed suicide,

a broken man. He was one who had always meant well, whose aspirations had been fundamentally good. But his actions lacked the guidance
of a fine insight, and the movement which he loved might well have been
better without his fight against Bruno Wille.

The first theatre manager with whom the Freie Volksbühne made
an agreement was its old friend Max Samst, now at the Friedrich-
Wilhelmstädtisches Theater. At the same time there was an agreement
with Oscar Blumenthal at the Lessing Theater, where the artistic
director was Carl Waldow. In the following season the same theatres
were used, and the Freie Volksbühne engaged as its own artistic
director Adolf Steinert, Hungarian by birth, an eccentric, but a crafts-
man of the theatre, with imagination and originality. He was to play an
important part in the movement for a long time. For the season 1901-2
an additional agreement was concluded with Paul Lindau at the Berliner
Theater. In this season each member saw four productions at the
Berliner Theater, four at the Lessing Theater (now managed by Fritz
Witte-Wild) and two at the Ostend — now called the Carl-Weiss-Theater.
This combination of arrangements was far from ideal and it is not
altogether surprising that at a general meeting on 25 January 1900 the
suggestion was actually voiced that the association ought to build its
own theatre. Of course, neither the membership nor the financial
reserves were anywhere near adequate and the idea was quite utopian.
Any attempt to put it into practice would have been disastrous; but it
was a pointer to the future. At the beginning of the new century the
association also temporarily lost Steinert who took a post in Barmen
(Wuppertal), but he had hardly arrived there when his theatre was
burnt down and he returned to Berlin and to his post.

More serious and important were the changes in theatre management that occurred between 1904 and 1906. In 1904 Witte-Wild left the
Lessing Theater, and Otto Brahm, ending his historic decade (1894-
1904) at the Deutsches Theater, took over from him. The Freie
Volksbühne was unable to reach agreement with him, but followed
Witte-Wild to the Metropol Theater. At the same time Paul Lindau
took over the Deutsches Theater and made a new agreement with the
Freie Volksbühne. But early in the 1905-6 season, Lindau went bank-
rupt and his successor Max Reinhardt, who had already, as we shall
see, a relationship with the Neue Freie Volksbühne which placed him
under obligations to that body, would not honour Lindau's contract. The
Freie Volksbühne was thus driven to various unsatisfactory resorts,
including arrangements with the old Ostend — now, under another new
management, known as the Bürgerliches-Schauspielhaus. About this
time, too, after a brief and unsatisfactory arrangement with Carl
Waldow as artistic director, the Freie Volksbühne engaged Steinert
(for whom an anticipated post in Cologne had not materialised) as
artistic director for the third time.

Through this whole period the Freie Volksbühne avoided performances of plays outside the series which members were committed to
see. An exception was two performances of The Lower Depths. Otherwise extra performances were all of opera. There were also two or
three 'festivals' each year, though the open-air summer event was
dropped after 1897. They often took the form of concerts, but also
included recitation and lectures. The festivals were a mixture of
culture and dancing; one might have a Mozart or Heine evening,
followed by a social dance — all for 50 Pfennigs. In the spring of 1905
the festival was a Schiller Festival, celebrating the centenary of the
poet's death. Instead of a single evening there were lectures, performances of Die Räuber and Kabale und Liebe and a performance of
Beethoven's Ninth Symphony with the 'Ode to Joy'.

In the 1903-4 season came a decision to hold Cultural Evenings in
each of which one composer, author or painter would be celebrated
with lectures on and examples of his work: the first was on Beethoven.

Another special activity was the choir. Ernst Zander, a young
dentist who had earlier successfully led the choir of the Neue Freie
Volksbühne, proposed the idea in September 1903. Soon there was a
membership of 150. Discussions arose about financial responsibility
and in February 1904 the choir declared itself to be financially and
organisationally independent. The original name Volksbühnenchor was
changed to Volkschor. Zander wanted it to have a professional conductor, but the members insisted on his continuing, and even though at
first he said he was doing it only 'provisionally', he was still its
leader in 1930, by which time it was the oldest mixed choir in the
Deutscher Arbeitersängerbund.

Throughout this time the periodical Die Freie Volksbühne was
published. Johann Sassenbach, a well-known trades unionist who ran
a press purely to help the workers' movement, published it for the first
year, the cost being covered by advertisements. At first the periodical
was not much to look at. It was improved in the season 1902-3 with a
new cover, showing the back view of a father with his son his knee
looking towards a proscenium. It was criticised on the grounds that
children were not admitted as members!

It is not easy to believe that the periodical was edited and written
on an entirely honorary basis and that, like the organisation as a whole,
it had no office. All posts, indeed, were honorary, except that of
treasurer, which was poorly paid. Winkler got 150 Marks a month to
begin with, which rose by irregular increments to 250 Marks in the
early years of the twentieth century: and there was great trouble in
1901 because the resolution that his salary be raised to 225 Marks per
month had been proposed by a person not in full membership! That

same winter it was decided to get a proper office (even a telephone was
suggested) so that Gustav Winkler need not work from his little flat in
Rixdorf. But the scheme did not materialise. Just how Winkler worked
at home, and at what inconvenience to himself and his family, he has
himself vividly described:

> For thirteen years my private flat, the sitting-room and kitchen,
> served for carrying out the association's business. There could be
> no question of regular working hours. Only the hours of night
> interrupted the hours of work. When the regular audit of the ac-
> counts took place we had first of all to put my little girl Lisa's cot
> in the kitchen, so that the auditors could be offered seats. (Lisa
> was three when I took on the job.) As a part-time job my wife
> helped me to deliver to the agencies the numerous items of printed
> matter, and packets of cards and tickets. The leaflets were stowed
> away with little Lisa in the pram, and so she went, tightly bound in
> Volksbühne ideas, zigzagging through Berlin to the thirty-six
> agencies we had established. [5]

Obviously such a body, carrying out such a large-scale operation from
so small a base, physically and financially, could not run without frictions or changes. In the spring of 1898, about a year after the new
beginning, Schulz, the vice-chairman, left for Erfurt to edit the party
paper there; he was replaced by Johannes Gaulke, stonemason and
writer. Then Franz Mehring resigned. The immediate cause was
differences with the chairman, Conrad Schmidt. Ever since 1892
Mehring had carried on a feud against what he called a 'writer's
clique' which was particularly represented by Schönhoff, editor of
Vorwärts. Schönhoff had taken Wille's side against Türk at the time of
the split. An honest man, Schönhoff had reviewed some Freie Volksbühne productions very unfavourably, and in particular he had criticised
justly, but sharply, the production and reception of Blumenthal's
one-acter, Abu Seid. Schmidt himself commented strongly on this in a
general meeting and was supported by others, some of whom wanted a
complaint to be made to the Press Commission, while Mehring wanted
a 'boycott' of the 'clique'. Schmidt, who realised that Vorwärts was
basically sympathetic to the association, did not want this and would
only agree to a retort on the tone of the critique. The committee
agreed and Mehring, wounded, resigned. Many regretted his leaving,
and with reason. Though one-sided, rough in judgement, obstinate,
unjust, lacking in understanding and balance, he had nevertheless done
much for the Freie Volksbühne, where, particularly on the political
side, he had made a contribution that probably no other man could have
made. Benno Maass was co-opted to fill his place and a year later a
seventh member was elected to the committee by a general meeting
held in April: this was Curt Baake, whose return to office was most
valuable.

This clash with the Vorwärts critic was the first of several such; another was with Kühl, when the critic actually defended himself at a general meeting in January 1899; another was with his successor Erich Schlaikjer. This time Schmidt's objection was backed by everyone except Maass, and Schlaikjer later took his revenge by giving the name 'Conrad Schmidt' to an unsympathetic character in his play Des Pastors Rieke.

The 'critic' problem came to a climax at the beginning of 1902 when Schmidt himself was appointed theatre critic of Vorwärts. His opponents said at once (perhaps with some justification) that this was incompatible with his remaining chairman of the Freie Volksbühne. The committee passed, by a bare majority, a resolution of Dupont's to this general effect, with the expected consequence that Schmidt resigned. A stormy general meeting inevitably followed (29 April 1902) in which, as his clinching argument, Cohn suggested that Schmidt had some kind of relationship with the justly hated police chief Merscheidt-Hüllessem! Nothing, of course, could have been further from the truth. But the trick back-fired on its perpetrator and the meeting rallied to the support of Schmidt. Cohn, Dupont, Fraenkel and the auditor Sahm, resigned their posts and ultimately a 'provisional leadership' was set up consisting of Conrad Schmidt himself and two members whose speeches from the floor had swung the meeting round in his favour. Winkler, of course, remained as treasurer. The triumvirate continued for only a matter of days, for at a further general meeting held on 9 May 1902, Schmidt was re-elected to the chairmanship with Baake, his ideal complement, as vice-chairman. The secretary was Dr Hans Davidson, assistant Max Buschold. This was the last major political crisis within the management of the association for many years.

In 1906 Kurt Eisner fell foul of the Social Democratic Party leadership and had to give up the editorship of Vorwärts, so that shortly afterwards he left Berlin and had to resign from the Artistic Committee of the Freie Volksbühne — a great loss. He was replaced by Dr John Schikowski. Schikowski was already a leading figure in the Freie Volksbühne Charlottenburg that had come into being in 1905. He was particularly interested in the visual arts and through his preference for abstract painting and sculpture became in later years an enthusiast for modern ballet, so that under his influence the Volksbühne became an important factor in the promotion of this branch of theatre. Schikowski was not only expert in his field, but an original character, uniting Prussian crustiness with dry humour.

ii The Neue Freie Volksbühne from 1896 to 1908

The decisive year in the history of the Neue Freie Volksbühne — and as it transpired, for the whole movement — was the season 1905-6 when Max Reinhardt went to the Deutsches Theater and the membership of

the Neue Freie Volksbühne leapt in one season from six thousand (in
seven sections) to ten thousand (in twelve sections). In the following
year (1906-7) it overtook the Freie Volksbühne, ending the season with
fifteen thousand five hundred members in eighteen sections, and in
1907-8 it had eighteen thousand members in no fewer than twenty-two
sections. That is to say, it had to lay on twenty-two actual performances and distribute eighteen thousand theatre tickets each month of
the season.

But such success must have been beyond the wildest dreams of its
officers in the autumn of 1895, when the problems of censorship had
still not been overcome and membership was two hundred at the most.
In the summer of 1896 preparations were made for the next season's
performances, but although the association had an autumn and winter
free of competition (the Freie Volksbühne being non-existent then) this
did not greatly help, even the modest goal of two sections not being
achieved. In truth the association could not reach the mass of the
workers, though its very forcible recruiting leaflet issued at the turn
of the year 1896-7 was addressed to them, and though, as censuses of
occupations taken in October 1900 and 1902-3 showed, the proportions
of various workers in membership were much as in the rival body (e.g.,
the largest single group was that of the joiners) but on a much smaller
scale. [6]

The continuation of work in the autumn of 1896 had to be in the
form of participation in public performances, as the long negotiations
with the police over the new constitution were still in progress, but an
arrangement with Brahm enabled the association to book part-houses
at the Deutsches Theater. Then, after the new constitution had been
passed on 28 November, it was able to present its own, closed performances, and for some years (until 1902) in contrast with the Freie
Volksbühne, it took very few productions from existing repertoires.
[7] Its own list of productions contained fewer classics than that of
the Freie Volksbühne, but only because so many of these were too
costly to stage, and the classics chosen were economical ones such as
La Malade Imaginaire, Nathan der Weise (Nathan the Wise), Maria
Magdalene etc. As a whole the repertoire was considerably more
adventurous than that of its larger competitor. For example it included
the first German productions of Björnson's Beyond our Power II and
Büchner's Dantons Tod, and world premières of Björnson's New
System and Paul Lange and Tora Parsberg, as well as six of less
lasting worth. The production of Paul Lange and Tora Parsberg
involved the association in a dispute with the publisher, Alfred Langen,
Björnson's son-in-law, who had already given the rights to the Munich
Hoftheater. The Neue Freie Volksbühne retorted that its private performances enabled it to play what it liked, and that anyway Langen
ought to be thankful that it was so enterprising or he might have waited

a long time for a German production of Beyond our Power II. This
more adventurous programme had to be staged very modestly, with
great economy in the settings and casting, though a few well-known
names (e. g. Emanuel Reicher) appeared from time to time.

Inevitably such a programme did not attract a large membership.
Time showed that it was not simply Wille's failure to win the trust of
the workers, but also his uncompromising artistic policy and its far
from lavish execution that kept the Neue Freie Volksbühne small during
these years, for as soon as this policy was changed, and the association began to include more plays from the programmes of existing
theatres, the membership began to increase, until it reached six
thousand in 1904-5.

Naturally this development, and the policies that led to it, must
be traced back ultimately to the men in charge of the association. Not
all were ideally suited to their posts: the first treasurer, Eduard
Möller, was no good at detailed 'niggling' work. He kept the money in
two cigarette tins; and when his brother-in-law, Siebenmark, the
proprietor of a printing works, was imprisoned for his part in the
production of the anarchist periodical Der Sozialist and Möller took
over the works for the time, he paid Neue Freie Volksbühne bills with
the firm's money! Naturally that was the end of him as treasurer.
His successor, in February 1897, was Adolf Löhr, a type-founder also
connected with Der Sozialist. In 1899 he became too ill to do the job
properly and August Müller, a compositor, undertook to help him un-
officially. Müller at once showed that he was a first-class man who
wanted no public credit. [8] He soon recognised a problem. Löhr was
a Schlafbursche, that is a man who rented only a bed, not a room, and
was virtually without an address from which to conduct the association's
business. So Müller suggested a change.

Heinrich Neft was a man of thirty-one who had been a member of
the Neue Freie Volksbühne from its foundation. He had been an Organiser. Though regarded by many people as a wild man he was only
apparently superficial. A socialist even in the days of the anti-socialist
laws, he had joined the Independent Socialists and had become an
anarchist. Having the courage to put his signature to Der Sozialist he
had been accused of treason and blasphemy, but was eventually acquitted.
Originally he had political motives for working with the Neue Freie
Volksbühne but it became for him ultimately an end in itself. No doubt
the scope it offered for individual initiative suited Neft better than the
democratic control of the Freie Volksbühne would have done. In the
late summer of 1899 Müller proposed that Neft, who was about to marry
Müller's sister, should take over the treasurership; at the same time
he assured the sceptics that he himself would be in the background to
help. The proposal was accepted. At first Neft leaned on Müller, but

he soon became master of the situation. The former wild anarchist
became a quiet observer of economic and social struggle. He lived for
the organisation which he served, and under him it made great progress. The opposition to him soon came to an end, and a proposal in
October 1900 to have Löhr as treasurer again was defeated by ninety-
eight votes to fourteen. [9]

Like other Volksbühne officers, Neft worked in his spare time at
home until 1902 when the association began to expand and the work
became too much. Then the association was able to get him a cigar
shop and his wife was able to look after this while he did Volksbühne
work. But the shop did not pay too well, and the treasurer's honorarium
was increased. Finally, in the spring of 1905, Neft was completely
freed of the need to do other work, and a house in the Bremer Strasse
was obtained which provided both an office for the association and a new
home for the Nefts. In December 1905 as expansion continued, an
assistant had to be engaged: the successful candidate was — August
Müller.

On the whole, the officers and artistic committee in 1896 constituted a strong group including such men as Gustav Landauer, Fritz
Mauthner, Emil Lessing, Max Dreyer (the dramatist) and Dr Ludwig
Jacobowski, editor of Gesellschaft. Jacobowski soon became vice-
chairman and achieved sudden importance in the summer of 1897 when
Bruno Wille, on a lecture tour in Austria, was arrested on accusations
of 'disturbing religion and spreading unbelief'. He was released on two
thousand Gulden bail but had to remain in Austria until the case was
over, which was many months, during which Jacobowski had to carry
the whole burden of the association. At the end of it all Wille was sen-
tenced to six days' house arrest. Jacobowski had not really the personality of a leader, and suffered, too, from a speech defect; but he had great
gifts. He was a fine, sensitive lyric poet and a serious, creative
thinker. He had the courage to publish meaty and substantial extracts
from the works of the greatest poets in penny numbers for working-
class readers, an enterprise which proves at once his determination
to popularise the arts, and his own daring. He had a likeable manner
and was a good worker, which compensated for his immaturity and lack
of practical sense. He stood by Wille for four years: the artistic
activities and particularly the experiments of these years were largely
due to him. His retirement was due to eye trouble and he died a few
weeks after it, in December 1900.

He was followed by Max Martersteig, who found after a few months
that the work demanded too much time and in the summer of 1901 made
way for Dr Joseph Ettlinger, whose name first appears in the records
in 1896. Ettlinger was the architect of the great expansion. In 1901 he
was just over thirty, established as a good translator, novelist and

critic. He had made the Literarisches Echo a respected periodical.
He was not 'brilliant', but was what the association needed — a man of
taste and good judgement, possessing both solidity and initiative. He
was trustworthy, always eager to help, and had good connections. No
trouble or sacrifice was too great for him. A year or so later he became chairman, Wille becoming vice-chairman, as he had done when
Jacobowski took over. (Later Wille even became deputy vice-
chairman.) Ettlinger remained chairman until 1908. He was a busy
man and it was not easy for him to find time for honorary work, but it
was characteristic of him that in the season 1906-7 he was making
himself available to members for the whole of every alternate Sunday.

Ettlinger considered that his policy was completely in the spirit
of Wille's original foundation, and his decision to go over gradually to
the use of productions from existing theatres was conceived as an expression of this. He wanted complete political independence, with no
one-sidedness in the programme. Of course, the policy had its critics,
and Ettlinger, answering them in 1906, said,

> What is the tendency which, it is claimed, should or could be
> destroyed? Our whole tendency, the aim of our association is one
> and only one: to offer elevating and liberating works of art to the
> working population. [10]

It was thanks to Ettlinger that the Neue Freie Volksbühne in 1903
established a relationship with Reinhardt, a relationship which he
cemented by co-opting Reinhardt and his dramaturge Felix Holländer
as non-voting 'advisers' to the artistic committee of the association —
though both were in fact too much occupied with their own affairs to be
of much practical help to the committee. At this time Reinhardt was
not yet universally recognised as an outstanding artist, though his
productions in the Kleines Theater, especially that of The Lower
Depths, which was performed five hundred times, had already attracted attention. Therefore Ettlinger must be given the credit for
realising that he was the rising star of the theatre to whom the Neue
Freie Volksbühne would do well to hitch its still lowly wagon.

The partnership of the Neue Freie Volksbühne and Max Reinhardt
has a symbolic quality. Both were in some sense unruly children of
Otto Brahm. If the Freie Bühne had not existed, the Freie Volksbühne
would probably not have done so, and the naturalistic movement with
which Brahm was identified was that with which the Volksbühne
originally identified itself. Brahm first saw Reinhardt, then a young,
unknown Viennese actor, playing in Salzburg and immediately engaged
him for the Deutsches Theater, of which he was then director-
designate. From 1894 for nearly nine years, during which he made a
high reputation as an actor of old men, Reinhardt worked under Brahm
at the Deutsches Theater. Sharing from the start many of Brahm's

fundamental leanings, he learned from him indelibly the great principles of unexaggerated truth, ensemble-playing and unconditional
respect for the dramatist's text. And though the great eclectic
later employed every device and every style that the theatre offered,
part of his greatness was that he never wholly lost touch with these
roots. Brahm he honoured to the end of his life. So too the association founded by Wille, while it came to express in its play policy
the fact that the plain Naturalism practised by Brahm was not the
whole of theatrical experience, nevertheless always retained his
high conceptions of art and truth.

   Not that Reinhardt had ever believed that Brahm's theatre contained all that drama needed or offered. As an impoverished young
man he had been a 'Child of the gods' (Kind der vierten Galerie) at the
Vienna Burgtheater and in the acting of Sonnenthal had experienced
something neither known to Brahm nor sympathetic to him. Except for
Kainz, Reinhardt said later, Brahm's actors 'lacked the grand manner,
necessary for the classics, which made those old artists so outstanding'. [11] Even while working under Brahm, Reinhardt, with other
like-minded actors, had played in matinées of works that held no
interest for Brahm, and founded a cabaret, Noise and Smoke. Then,
with financial help from one of his colleagues, Louise Dumont, Reinhardt found himself in a position to set up his own management in the
Kleines Theater — though Brahm inflicted a fine of 14,000 Marks on
him for breach of contract! At first he had only some successes; [12]
then came The Lower Depths in which Reinhardt played Luka (the last
of the young actor's old men) and which was nominally directed by
Richard Vallentin, who also played Satin. But it was in this production
that Reinhardt first realised his gift of tuning actors to each other and
awakening in them things they themselves had not dreamed of. This
close personal work with actors was probably Reinhardt's greatest
gift, too easily lost sight of behind the vast spectacles of his later
career. Gerda Redlich, an Austrian actress who trained under Reinhardt in Vienna and made her first stage appearance walking on at
Salzburg in Jedermann (Everyman), and whose architect father was,
with Poelzig, responsible for the Grosses Schauspielhaus, has said of
him:

> Reinhardt was a very modest, quiet, gentle person. What was
> typical of him was that when he would sit, he would always sit on
> his hands, watching what was going on. He would never raise his
> voice. He did most of his directing by taking actors aside and
> telling them privately what he wanted to get from them, not in
> front of the others. It was all gentle and civilised and no showing-
> off at all, just marvellous.

In reply to the remark that Reinhardt's actual productions were in fact showy, she continued:

> Tremendous, but you see, in England Reinhardt is only known through his World Theatre and Miracle and that sort of thing, and that — that wasn't his strength: chamber theatre, small detailed, subtle work with actors — and that was his real strength. And he was a fantastic teacher. [13]

The financial success of the Kleines Theater also enabled him to rent a larger theatre, the Neues Theater, and at this point Ettlinger brought about an agreement between him and the Neue Freie Volksbühne. His artistic successes multiplied: this was the year of his new-furbished Minna von Barnhelm. In the next season the association required only three of its own productions to complete its programme, and in 1905 the decision was made to have none. Friedrich Möest, the director, was honourably discharged from his post, and the agreements made with the theatres gave the association not only a say in the programmes, but even some influence over the casting! Then Reinhardt, without giving up the Neues Theater, took over from Lindau the one thousand-seater Deutsches Theater. Because of his existing relationship with the Neue Freie Volksbühne, he refused to honour Lindau's agreement with the Freie Volksbühne, and the Neue Freie Volksbühne immediately booked all Sunday afternoons in the Deutsches Theater. The original intention was that these should replace the performances at the Neues Theater, but the news of the Deutsches Theater agreement brought such a flood of new members that Neft, without consulting his colleagues, went ahead and booked the Neues Theater as well, although thousands of new members would be needed to fill both theatres. The other officers were shocked, but Neft's instinct had led him to act rightly, if rashly; for this was the beginning of the real development of the association. The Neue Freie Volksbühne had gained a monopoly of Reinhardt's Sunday matinees with all the drawing-power this implied. Success breeds success, and the monopoly of the two Reinhardt theatres led to further growth. In the 1905-6 season, the association still went to the Schiller-Theater, and when the limited liability company that managed it got a second theatre, this was used too. In the following season, 1906-7, the Neue Freie Volksbühne was using five theatres: Reinhardt's two, the Schiller-Theater North and Schiller-Theater East, and a new theatre in Charlottenburg, built by the city and rented to the Schiller Theater Company. In 1907-8 a sixth was added.

The change from the policy of mounting its own productions to that of using productions already in other repertoires raised the overall standard of what was presented to members in terms of quality of acting and settings, and the technical resources available. The

Schiller-Theater productions were good; but these were put in the shade
by Reinhardt's which opened up a new world to the members. They
were able to see actors like Reinhardt himself, Kayssler and Agnes
Sorma. The real quality of what the association was now offering
to its membership can be assessed when we realise that to this period
belong most of Reinhardt's great classical productions — his Minna von
Barnhelm, his Midsummer Night's Dream (at first too expensive for
the Neue Freie Volksbühne), The Winter's Tale, The Merchant of
Venice and Twelfth Night. His Lower Depths entered the Volksbühne
programme when it transferred from the Kleines Theater to the Neues.
Typically, Reinhardt offered variety of plays: Nestroy, Björnson,
Courtelines, Shaw, Ibsen, Hauptmann, Holz, Anzengruber and Tolstoy
were all included. His historic production of Wedekind's Frühlings
Erwachen (Spring Awakening) in his recently opened Kammerspiele in
1906 was put into the Volksbühne programme as an 'extra', the smallness of the theatre (three hundred seats) making it impossible to use it
in the regular series.

At the Schiller-Theater members saw some less often performed
classics such as Schiller's Braut von Messina (Bride of Messina) and
Wallensteins Lager (Wallenstein's Camp) with Piccolomini, and
Hebbel's Nibelungen, Parts I and II. At the Lortzing Theater, they
saw some operas, including The Merry Wives of Windsor, Zar und
Zimmermann (Tsar and Carpenter), Die Zauberflöte (The Magic Flute)
and Fra Diavolo. The association's own productions included The
Marriage of Figaro. Among these productions of its own, along with
Gerhart Hauptmann, Björnson, Ibsen and Anzengruber, the association
included several world premières (for example Marianne by Carl
Hauptmann, Gerhart's brother) and a remarkable resurrection, Die
Kindesmörderin (The Childmurderess) by Heinrich Leopold Wagner, a
Sturm und Drang poet. Ettlinger had re-edited and published this play,
which had previously been regarded as of literary-historical interest
only, but was now given life on the stage.

Giving up its own productions did not mean sacrificing its freedom
of choice. Between 1905 and 1908 theatres produced at least eighteen
plays at the special request of the association. These included German
and foreign classics (Grillparzer, Lessing, Calderón) and many modern plays. Some were revivals of plays that had previously impressed
Volksbühne audiences; some were chosen with little regard for the
taste of the main body of members (e.g. The Seagull). One of these
'Volksbühne' plays, Schmidtbonn's Mutter Landstrasse (Mother
Highway) made such an impression that Reinhardt took it over into his
ordinary evening repertoire where it became a 'best seller'.

In this period the Neue Freie Volksbühne was especially active in
arranging extra (non-obligatory) performances and special events. In

the earlier part of the period the smallness of the association and the
need for extra income provided a spur, while in the latter part, the
time of great growth, purely social events were left for the voluntary
workers to arrange, while the association itself provided a rich programme of concerts and artistic evenings.

The audience of the Neue Freie Volksbühne remained of much the
same character as before. Wille, although he felt it his calling to
marry art and the people, found it hard to reconcile himself to the
audience's limitations and its inability to respond to some of the plays,
and he wrote in 1898 that sometimes he felt that the Jacob of art had
wooed Rachel only to marry Leah, 'a splendid housewife, and, of
course, Rachel's sister ... but often Jacob cannot but sigh over his
Leah'. Inappropriate laughter at The Lower Depths led the association
to issue a pamphlet telling people not to laugh in the wrong place! This
rather heavy-handed rebuke led, naturally, to the situation in which
people were afraid to laugh at a comedy, and those who did were hushed
by their more timid neighbours.

iii   Progress towards unity 1908-1914

The development of the Neue Freie Volksbühne from 1907 to 1912 was
spectacular. It grew from eighteen thousand members (twenty-two
sections) in the season 1907-8 to fifty thousand (sixty-three sections)—
the population of a small town— in the season 1911-12. This meant the
sale and distribution of half a million theatre tickets a year. Ten years
before, there had been only two thousand members, one-twenty-fifth of
the present size!

By contrast, and, of course actually because of the success of the
Neue Freie Volksbühne, the Freie Volksbühne barely expanded during
the same period and reached only about eighteen thousand in the 1911-12
and 1912-13 seasons.

Nor was the growth of the Neue Freie Volksbühne merely quanti-
tative. In 1908 the constitution was revised and made a little more
democratic, and in the following year Wille became honorary chairman,
thus leaving an opening for new blood. In 1910 one of the new 'experts'
without voting power on the Artistic Committee was Julius Bab. Bab
was the son of the owner of a small woodwork factory who was himself
a theatre enthusiast. Even as a grammar school boy, Bab played
walk-on parts under Otto Brahm and watched his great Ibsen productions from the gods of the Deutsches Theater. His earliest ambition
was to be an actor; in his twenties he also had two plays produced in
Stuttgart; but he soon realised that his true calling must involve both
his practical abilities and his critical awareness. Nearly every issue
of Die Schaubühne (founded 1905) in its early years contained an article

by him, while he also distinguished himself as a dramaturge and
regisseur. He had a deep understanding of the Volksbühne idea and
of how it could lead to healthy theatre even in a capitalist society, and
the movement also appealed to the pedagogical side of his nature. In
1911 he became a regular member of the committee, and in 1927 he
was able to write that he had been active in the Berlin Volksbühne for
over half a lifetime, and later in the Federation of Volksbühne
Societies also. [14] Had the Volksbühne been a mere cheap-ticket
organisation 'he would not have devoted two hours of his life to it'.
Nor did he wish for a 'theatre of ideas' in a political sense:

> It is the 'ideas' of the artist which (like those of the pious and
> wise, in other ways) lead to the irreplaceable moments in which
> we are blessed again by a feeling of the meaning and purpose of
> life. That is really the 'idea' for the sake of which I serve the
> Volksbühne. [15]

Even in 1945, when the Volksbühne had not yet been recreated after its
destruction by the Nazis, we find the exiled Bab in New York com-
mending the pre-war Volksbühne as a possible model for certain
aspects of an American National Theatre.

In 1911 Dr Josef Ettlinger felt obliged, because of family
responsibilities, to leave Berlin and take up a post on the Frankfurter
Zeitung. To him the association owed its sound financial footing, the
relationship with Reinhardt, and the remarkable development of special
events. He left with deep regret: 'It is with a very heavy heart that I
part from the association to which my love and care have so long been
directed.' Sadly enough, Ettlinger fell ill soon after going to Frankfurt
and died in February 1912 after a painful illness of nine months. His
place was taken for one year by Hans Land, and after that by Georg
Springer, who was to prove to be the vital force of the movement for
the next few years.

As the administrative work multiplied, the treasurer was renamed
the manager, and an additional office helper was taken on (1908).
Apart from the periodical, the association published three guides, two
to museums, one to an art gallery; but the sales of these were disappointing. In autumn 1911 the association founded a Volksbühne
bookshop specialising in quality books.

The period saw many extra performances, several evenings
honouring great writers, many concerts (Arthur Schnabel, who always
gave his services, was a frequent performer), and a whole round of
festivals, including balls attended by six to seven thousand people.
These more social events, cabarets, horse-displays, Moritat singers
and so on, engendered a great sense of unity as well as raising money
for what had become the great project of the association— the building

of its own theatre. In 1912 an attempt was made to found an experimental theatre club. By the autumn there were only eight hundred
members. Four plays were staged, the most successful being
Hebbel's Julia, formerly thought to be unstageable. But at the end of
one season, partly because of a lack of suitable plays, the scheme
ended.

The practical work of the Freie Volksbühne during these years
was naturally more modest. There were few 'extra performances' or
special events. Even the loose connection between the Freie Volksbühne and the Choir was threatened. The choir had always had a
special place in the great combined 'Workers' Choir' (Arbeiter-
Sängerchor) which performed for Socialist Party events, for it refused
to rehearse propaganda songs and did not wholly avoid spiritual works.
Now the choir began to object to its connection with the Workers'
Choir. But all was smoothed over in the end and the Freie Volksbühne
then extended even more help to the choir.

During the whole of this period the two Volksbühnen were gradually
drawing closer together. Even ideologically the differences became
less and it would be a mistake from now on to see them as neatly representing the 'artistic' and 'political' approaches to the work, for
these arguments went on within as well as between the organisations.
By 1910 the leaders of the Neue Freie Volksbühne regarded the problem of the scope of drama with a message (Tendenzdrama) within the
programme as settled, but still debated the relationship between pure
art and entertainment. Ettlinger wrote 'Art strives towards the
heights and the depths, entertainment to breadth'. But there was a
place for entertainment in the programme.

In the winter of 1910-11 a journalistic debate in the pages of
Vorwärts and Neue Zeit took place between Heinz Sperber (pseudonym
of Hermann Heijermans) and Heinrich Ströbel on 'Proletarian and
bourgeois art'. This debate was continued within the Freie Volksbühne
and led to a clarification of its basic principles. The executive of the
Freie Volksbühne gave Heijermans an opportunity to express his views
at a general meeting in November 1911. He argued from the basis that
art and artists largely depend on the ruling and property-owning
classes of their times, and he saw it as a task of the Freie Volksbühne
to oppose consciously proletarian art to the dominant 'bourgeois' art.
On Baake's advice the talk was not debated, but in issue No. 9 of the
periodical that year Friedrich Stampfer replied to Heijermans. He
deplored the fact that Heijermans attacked as bourgeois all earlier art
from the standpoint of an 'adopted class-consciousness'. It was not
possible to tell workers that they must not enjoy this or that, because
it was 'bourgeois': the worker had the right to enjoy the little culture
he had won for himself. He argued that Heijermans must know that art

exists by virtue of its own laws, which are not those of national economics or politics. He continued:

> A work that is bourgeois through and through can be a work of art.
> ... As we now demand from art, that it gives us a picture of real
> life, we must be thankful to the bourgeois poet who is as bourgeois
> as he can be.... Ability, not opinion, makes the artist. If he can
> turn an opinion, a piece of life into artistic form, then he is an
> artist. Long live 'art with a message' [Tendenzkunst] if the mes-
> sage is ours and the art is great art. But the message is not art
> and can never replace art in any play.

Stampfer criticised earlier revolutionary movements for their artistic
intolerance:

> It will be the glory of the revolutionary movement of the working
> class, that they were the first of their kind not to take the road to
> destruction. With loving care they will carry the cultural wealth
> of the past over the broad stream that divides today from tomor-
> row.

But, he said, the working-class did also deserve its own art, and the
Freie Volksbühne would open its doors to proletarian art. Heijermans
replied in Vorwärts that the Freie Volksbühne was on the way to becoming a bourgeois theatre and that Stampfer's exposition was muddled:
but he excused himself from answering it on grounds of lack of space.
Stampfer replied that the task of the Freie Volksbühne was to open to
the proletariat all the treasure chambers in which mankind has locked
up its cultural heritage. He could as yet see no signs of real proletarian art able to stand comparison with the great art of the past.
Heijermans' final shot in reply was to describe the Freie Volksbühne
as 'a consumer association for retailing bourgeois art'. [16]

In June 1911 Heijermans was not re-elected to the committee.
Clearly an association which tacitly endorsed Stampfer's opinions was
ideologically not far removed from the Neue Freie Volksbühne.

At the same time that this movement towards ideological harmony
was taking place, various practical problems were demanding joint
thought and sometimes joint action. Among these were a threatened
entertainment tax, renewed police hostility and the need for the Volksbühne movement to have its own theatre.

An earlier attempt to impose an Entertainment Tax had been made
in 1905, but at that time enterprises such as the Volksbühne Associations would have been excluded. This time there were to be no
exclusions and there was a danger that all subscriptions would have to
be increased by 10 per cent. Ettlinger approached Conrad Schmidt
suggesting joint action. This was agreed but in practice differences

soon emerged and the two bodies acted independently. In the event the tax proposals came to nothing.

The police were always suspicious of the Volksbühnen, and made several minor attacks on the associations in 1908 and 1909. A major police attack began, however, on 23 July 1910, when the Police President von Jagow sent a directive to all theatres that had Volksbühne performances saying that in view of the size of these associations and the ease with which they could be joined, the performances could no longer be regarded as private and must therefore abide by the laws of public safety and censorship. Von Jagow claimed that he was not really concerned with the censorship issue, only that of safety. This sounded reassuring, but the safety matter could have been dealt with privately, so both associations decided to fight, as the censorship could well hamper their work in the future This time the Freie Volksbühne took the initiative, but the joint meeting was cool. Eventually each association acted independently. Dr Heinemann, the Freie Volksbühne lawyer, pursued the matter through legal channels, ending with a legal judgement against the association. Julius Luzynski, the Neue Freie Volksbühne lawyer, met with similar failure.

In the 1912-13 season Rosenov's <u>Die im Schatten leben</u> (<u>Dwellers in the Shadow</u>), a sincere play about miners, set in the 1880s, was forbidden by the censor although already performed in Frankfurt-am-Main and Mannheim. It was now clear that the police actually did wish to censor the productions of the Volksbühne. Further harassment occurred over choral works in the hall of the Neue Welt. Finally, in 1913, the police refused permission for a Berlin performance of Hauptmann's festival play celebrating the War of Independence of 1813, although this had already been performed at Breslau. Undoubtedly the fight against the censor would have become even sharper had not the outbreak of war intervened.

Even in the 1890s the need for its own theatre had been felt within the Volksbühne movement, but only in the new century did it become a practicable proposition. By the start of the 1905-6 season the membership of the Freie Volksbühne had reached ten thousand and was still rising. To meet the demand, evening performances (an absolute essential if the association were to run its own theatre) were started and were welcomed. In January 1906, therefore, Curt Baake announced to a general meeting the idea of having a Volksbühne theatre as something 'to which we must come sooner or later'. The first step would be to establish a fund built up primarily through small contributions. A start was made by giving the proposed building a name — The Independent Arts Centre (Freies Kunsthaus) — which implied

something probably more comprehensive than a simple theatre. But
in spite of help from other organisations, a favourable press, enthusiasm in the left-wing press, and solid support from influential
people (Alfred Kerr put down 500 Marks), the scheme failed,
primarily because of opposition within the Social Democratic Party,
led by Mehring. Although the Volksbühne was not formally linked to
the party it seemed hopeless to go ahead in face of its opposition.
The centrepiece of that opposition was an article by Mehring in Neue
Zeit published in mid-July. Mehring argued that the scheme showed
a lack of 'class instinct' and was not in keeping with the original aims
of the movement. He then made a most important point, one based on
his own experience as chairman, and one whose truth, or at least
partial truth, the whole future of the movement was to demonstrate:
'The greater the number of members, the less can the tendency to
experiment exist.' [17] His 'trump card' (the article being addressed
to party members) was that the whole scheme was a dispersal and
waste of socialist energy — which had been his original objection to the
whole movement before he had been persuaded to accept its chairmanship.

Undoubtedly some of his contentions were right; some were
arguable; but his conclusion was the result of a somewhat narrow
view. In fact, he probably did the movement a service, for had the
project been proceeded with it might well have broken an association
that lacked the strength and organisation to carry it through. After
this abortive effort the Freie Volksbühne lost heart, and it was left
to the Neue Freie Volksbühne to take the next initiative.

Before this happened, however, Adolf Steinert, the association's
artistic director, came forward with a plan for an independent firm
with a sleeping partner. The new building would contain a 1,400-seat
theatre and a 2,400-seat festival hall. In January 1907 a general
meeting gave the plan a cautious welcome. After this — as might have
been expected — the scheme began to change, and the terms became
much worse for the Freie Volksbühne. In April 1907 a modified
scheme was put to a general meeting which sceptically left a decision
to the committee. The proposal was changed more and more from its
original form, until in the end there was to be no new building at all,
merely alterations to the Zentral Theater. By spring 1908 it was
clear that the idea had come to nothing.

The Freie Volksbühne's own original plan for building a theatre
was naturally discussed also within the Neue Freie Volksbühne, and
some members would have welcomed a joint enterprise. But as the
rapid growth of the Neue Freie Volksbühne continued, its need for its
own theatre became even more acute than that of the Freie Volksbühne.
Heinrich Neft was greatly drawn to the idea, Georg Springer became

enthusiastic about it, and by the autumn of 1908 agreement had been reached to work towards a building project. The name proposed was The People's Arts Centre (Volkskunsthaus). Though the difficulties proved far greater than anyone anticipated, it was this decision, five years before even the foundation stone was laid, that led to eventual success, while to men such as Springer the difficulties were merely a challenge, stimulating greater enthusiasm.

At a general meeting on 29 October 1908 the matter was raised very late under 'any other business'! Neft gave a factual introduction, Springer made an emotional appeal and a motion was passed, accepting in principle the establishment of a theatre building fund and calling for an extraordinary meeting. This was held on 21 January 1909. Springer, the principal speaker, explained that a building fund would be set up as a separate association. It would be funded by an initial contribution of 10,000 Marks from the Neue Freie Volksbühne's own account, and afterwards (from 1 September 1909) by means of a 10 Pfennig levy on all entrance subscriptions and ticket sales. This money would not be 'lost' to the contributor: for every ten 10 Pfennig contributions a one-Mark token would be issued, and ten of these on a card would constitute a 'share' eligible for 5 per cent interest. If the project were not under way by 1 October 1912, subscribers would get their money back. It was hoped that some members would also buy additional shares. [18] Springer calculated that the 10 Pfennig levy would bring in 50,000 Marks in the first year, and hoped it would be doubled by voluntary contributions. He hoped to reach 300,000 Marks in the second year, when, with the help of a bank loan, work could start on a theatre with an auditorium holding fifteen hundred, two big halls for meetings and concerts, exhibition rooms, restaurant facilities and so on.

In the lively discussion that followed Bruno Wille showed himself to be one of the sceptics: he feared the 'building fund association' might become wholly independent, and he warned against over-optimism, saying that the collection could take twenty years!

Eventually a provisional building commission was elected consisting of Springer, Neft and five others. Public propaganda followed, slides were shown on theatre tabs, special events were arranged to raise further funds, and, of course, the periodical was used. Ettlinger published a leading article urging members to look beyond their individual interests and, of course, supported his views with a quotation from Schiller. [19] Autumn 1911 was the date proposed for the opening of the theatre, but during 1910 it was recognised that this was impossible: by April 1910 only 150,000 Marks had been raised, and by August only 200,000 Marks, while the estimated initial capital requirement had risen from 300,000 Marks to 400,000 Marks.

Meanwhile Adolf Edgar Licho, chief producer at the Hebbel-Theater, approached Neft with his own ideas about the proposed new theatre, evidently hoping for the post of director. When he understood the financial difficulties he suggested that there was no reason why the association should not in the meantime rent a theatre for its own exclusive use. Shortly after this came an opportunity to rent the Theater in der Köpenicker Strasse — which usually housed visiting companies — from its owner, Professor Ludwig Stein, at a cost of 24,000 Marks per year for three years. It was far from an ideal theatre. Externally it was not unlike an English nonconformist chapel, while the auditorium was decorated in bad 'Jugendstil'; the stage measured only 8 by 9 metres and was technically ill equipped. The news was announced to the members in March 1910 that this would be 'a theatre in which players engaged exclusively for us will act plays exclusively of our choice only for members of the Neue Freie Volksbühne'. The theatre was renamed the Neues Volkstheater (New People's Theatre). During the summer alterations were made in the seating, stair-carpeting, stage-equipment and lighting, and on 3 August 1910 it came into use. As the periodical emphasised, for the first time in the history of the German theatre a completely new thing had happened: a permanent theatre, with a permanent ensemble, was playing solely for the members of an association, with the public completely excluded; in other words, a public was creating its own theatre, whereas normally every newly founded theatre had to create its own public.

Ettlinger was formally 'director' to satisfy legal requirements, Licho the artistic director and Neft the business manager. The theatre's finances were kept entirely separate from those of the association, which paid a fixed sum to the theatre for seats and productions and then left it its complete independence. Thus, though the theatre had to toe the line financially it had a great deal of artistic freedom. The programme was arranged in consultation with the artistic committee of the Neue Freie Volksbühne and the executive, but there was no regular interference by Volksbühne administration.

Licho assembled a talented company, giving Jürgen Fehling his first Berlin engagement after his discovery by Licho, Neft and Springer in a touring company. He was a sensitive director with a sense of the dramatic, a good artist, but not easy to work with. Once in the middle of a season he disappeared for weeks after a quarrel, leaving the whole burden to Neft. This awkwardness of disposition ultimately led to his not even being considered for the post of director of the Volksbühne theatre when this was eventually built. Meanwhile he presented in his first season a repertoire of some character, though not extraordinary, seeking to reflect the work of the younger generation so long as this was 'popular' in a good sense. [20] As a deliberate gesture, the opening production was Ibsen's Pillars of Society, the first

Freie Volksbühne play of 1890. Plays by Hartleben, Björnson and others followed, but many practical factors limited the repertoire. Moreover, the majority of the now very large (forty to fifty thousand) membership had not grown up with the association, and as a body lacked the unity of the earlier days (as, indeed, Mehring had prophesied when the Freie Volksbühne had first tried to establish its own theatre), so that a more eclectic programme was necessary.

The movement into theatre management also introduced the element of responsibility towards the employees of the theatre, a further inhibition to reckless experiment. Naturally, the work of the Neues Volkstheater must be seen as complementing the programme derived from other theatres, a programme whose size was only slightly reduced and over which the association could exercise a certain limited influence by proposing plays to theatres. As the Volksbühne could guarantee to fill nearly two dozen houses, these proposals were often accepted. Unfortunately, members justly complained from time to time of unsatisfactory performances, including performances in Reinhardt's Deutsches Theater. All too often the actors did not trouble themselves to give their best, or even adequate, performances for Volksbühne audiences, and an almost farcical climax was reached in a performance of <u>Medea</u> in 1910 when huge cuts were made and the rest gabbled, so that the play was over in an hour and a quarter. After members had made complaints to the association and in the press, the Neue Freie Volksbühne sent a strong written complaint to the theatre, and actually refused to pay for the unsatisfactory performance. Reinhardt was away at the time. When he returned he agreed that the complaint had been justified and sent a circular to all members of his company insisting that Volksbühne matinées be played 'with the same artistic seriousness as all others'. Every member of the company had to sign a declaration to this effect, and sanctions for further offences were threatened; but the executive of the Neue Freie Volksbühne remained sceptical—not, it seems, without reason.

Meanwhile progress towards the new building went on. The opening date was postponed to the autumn of 1912, and although the authorities refused to allow a big public lottery in aid of the fund, 400,000 Marks had been collected by October 1911. An alternative plan for completely altering the Neues Volkstheater having been abandoned (its owner being unconvinced by it), the services of Oscar Kaufmann were obtained as architect. He had been responsible for the Hebbel-Theater in the Königgrätzer Strasse as well as other theatres outside Berlin. At the same time a building site was sought and found between the Bülowplatz (now the Luxemburgplatz) and the Linien Strasse. It was a slummy area, but its development, which would be enhanced by the new theatre, was already planned; and it was convenient for working-class areas of the city. The authorities would not sell the plot directly to the

Volksbühne, but the development company which was acquiring the
whole development area was interested in the theatre scheme and
helpful with a mortgage. From now on, Kaufmann worked closely with
the building commission. He saw that the means at his disposal would
be insufficient for the two concert and meeting halls, and for the exhibition rooms, so these were abandoned. In retrospect one cannot
help speculating whether this simple, negative decision, imposed by
economic limitations and nothing else, was not a major factor in the
whole later history of the Volksbühne, shaping it as a movement
firmly based on theatre, with other arts as peripheral interest, rather
than as a more widely conceived 'arts association'. The auditorium
was to be enlarged from 1,500 to 2,000 seats. Of course, this would
pay better, provided it were filled — another factor to influence future
policies.

On 23 June 1912 the decision was formally made to buy the land
and go ahead. Unfortunately for the Volksbühne, however, the money
market had strengthened during the previous months and the Deutsche
Bank, partners of the development company, would no longer honour
their verbal agreement to provide a mortgage and additional loans.
The risk without the bank's help was too great, so yet another year had
to be added to the delays while other sources of fluid capital were
sought.

The delays gave opportunities for further thought and in September
1912 another decision was reached which although again negative, must
have had an enormous hidden effect upon the inner character of the
movement in later years. The point at issue was the shape of the
auditorium. Many speakers wanted an amphitheatre, modelled on the
Schiller-Theater, rather than the proposed stalls and circles. Not only
would the amphitheatre ensure a better view of the stage from all
seats, but it was also felt to be more 'democratic'. The arguments for
retaining the circles were economic, and eventually these won the day.
In this way the Volksbühne committed itself, with strange inconsist-
ency, to a form of auditorium reflecting a society divided economically
into classes, rather than one, like the Greek, reflecting the unity and
equality of all citizens. Erwin Piscator, who referred rudely to 'the
pompous building on the Bülowplatz', wrote in 1929: 'It is not without
significance for a production how the audience is grouped, whether the
auditorium is divided by emphatic circles and boxes or held together
by its parts as a unity'. Ironically, economic considerations led the
broadly left-wing Volksbühne into building a conservative, 'capitalist'
style of theatre.

During 1912-13 intensive money-raising continued, until by
summer 1913 three-quarters of a million Marks had been amassed.
Then, with the keen support of the Second Bürgermeister, Dr Reicke,

himself a writer, the grant of a mortgage for two million Marks at $4\frac{1}{2}$ per cent was passed through all the necessary city bodies. It was 'something extraordinary and unprecedented' that a cultural undertaking should be helped financially on such a scale. 'The way was open.' The building plot was bought a few weeks later, and, thanks to a building society mortgage, the Neue Freie Volksbühne did not even have to take up all the city's offer. Building operations began in June 1913.

Before this, however, a dramatic change had taken place in the relationship between the two Volksbühne organisations. In spite of the considerable public acrimony that accompanied the separately conducted battles over the threatened Entertainment Tax and the censorship issue and the mistrust that still existed, these external struggles had actually brought the two bodies nearer together; the 'hotspurs' of the Freie Volksbühne had been somewhat cooled by the lack of success of the public protests they had urged, and now that both bodies faced the same continuing problems in relation to the police the stage was set for fuller reconciliation. In 1912, Neft approached Winkler about the possible amalgamation of the two, Neft admitting the advantage on his own side of having the support of the Freie Volksbühne in the theatre project. The Freie Volksbühne executive welcomed the suggestion, as it was important to end competition between the two Volksbühne bodies, which benefited no one but the theatre managements. Both associations had reservations about full amalgamation and a solution was found in a cartel in which each organisation would remain independent, while conflict and undercutting would be avoided. The cartel was to be only loosely binding and was to have a small executive; it was to undertake the actual bargaining with theatres, but terms having been arranged, the two associations were to fix their own choice of plays, insofar as these had not already been agreed in common.

The first joint meeting of the leading committees of the two organisations took place on 31 March 1913. It was an almost solemn occasion. Bruno Wille presided, Springer and Schmidt spoke, Landauer gave a talk on the nature and aims of the cartel, and delegates to the new executive were appointed. Although the ordinary members of the two bodies hardly noticed the existence of the cartel, it was actually of vast importance. The Freie Volksbühne decided during the first season of joint working to modify its constitution to be more in line with that of the Neue Freie Volksbühne though without becoming less democratic — no general meeting would have tolerated that.

Six months later (14 September 1913) the foundation stone of the new theatre was laid. Despite the existence of the cartel this was still a venture of the Neue Freie Volksbühne, who issued the invitations. Both Volksbühne organisations, other friendly bodies and the city of

Berlin were well represented. Prussia and the Reich sent neither representatives nor apologies! Apart from the invited guests, thousands watched the ceremony from beyond the boundary fence. Contemporary photographs have preserved vivid impressions both of the solemnity of the actual stone-laying and of the excitement and gaiety of the whole occasion, evidently a sunny and breezy day, with the crowded building site, the garlanded poles, the spectators beyond the fence and the rather grim surrounding buildings, heavy blocks of flats and what appears to be a textile mill. The order of events had the typical flavour, or blend of flavours, of the Volksbühne. First, the Typographical Choral Society sang the song 'O Guardian Spirit of all things beautiful, descend!' [21] Then Georg Springer, as chairman of the Neue Freie Volksbühne, himself deeply moved, gave a proud and hopeful introductory address. He was followed by Conrad Schmidt, as chairman of the Freie Volksbühne, John Lehmann, representing the Society of German dramatists, and Gustav Rickelt on behalf of German actors, who hoped 'this building may become a true temple of our art, in which God's words of the good and beautiful may resound for all who wish to hear them'.

Thus introduced came Bruno Wille to lay the stone, with appropriate rhetoric: 'The ancient world has sunk in ruins, but it has bequeathed us its beauty; the garment of Helen forms a costly inheritance, especially for the Faustian spirit of the German people'. He went on to refer to classical culture as founded upon slavery in contrast with the culture sought by the Volksbühne, founded upon freedom, equality and fraternity. The new theatre was to be a temple dedicated to humanity:

> It is not to be lifeless, a mere building of cold, rigid stone. It should become a cathedral, a forest cathedral, dedicated to Beauty. The singers of the heavens rejoice in its sunny treetops, and at the roots below, couched upon flowers, men hark to the exalted song which Beethoven's Ninth Symphony pours forth in harmony. [22]

And he quoted Schiller's words, by now almost a Volksbühne anthem, which, after Kaufmann, Neft and others had also struck the stone, were then sung by the Typographical Choral Society. An emotional social evening with speeches and poetry followed later in the Brauerei Friedrichshain.

Very soon, in the autumn of 1913, another external threat forced the two Volksbühnen into an even closer association. Reinhardt had plans to transform the Zirkus Schumann, already his 'mass theatre', the 'theatre of a thousand', into a 'theatre of five thousand'. This plan threatened serious competition with the new theatre in the Bülowplatz.

At the same time the District Education Committee of the Social Democratic Party and the Berlin Trade Unions agreed with Reinhardt to take up ninety thousand seats per annum. This was a serious threat to the Volksbühne movement and led to talk of actual re-unification. Complete fusion, however, presented too many difficulties, and on 6 February 1914 the draft of yet another new scheme was accepted by the executive of the cartel.

This was for a Verband (Federation) der Freien Volksbühnen. Its executive was to consist of the executives of the two constituent bodies meeting together. There would be full unification of administration, cash and theatre bookings. Each body was still to recruit its own members, but within agreed limits, to avoid competition, and when one was filled, applicants were to be directed to the other. Subscriptions would be the same in each. Money would be divided proportionately at the end of the financial year; there would be a joint periodical for 1914-15. The whole plan was for a three-year trial period, but renewable. This left the Neue Freie Volksbühne still sole owner of the Bülowplatz theatre. But it was now evident that complete fusion would come sooner or later.

The Federation immediately found it was in a strong position to negotiate with the Social Democratic Party and Trade Union Education Committee, which now gave up its idea of taking seats in Reinhardt's proposed theatre. The Volksbühne offered the committee blocks of seats, at a price 10 Pfennigs higher than the Volksbühne's. Ultimately Reinhardt's plan collapsed.

The Neue Freie Volksbühne was to have three times as many members as the Freie Volksbühne, and both about 20 per cent more than at present. A big propaganda campaign was undertaken, and by July enrolments for the new season had already reached thirty thousand. Then came the outbreak of war, and the question as to whether the Volksbühne could even survive. An executive meeting held the day war was declared decided to go on with the building, but within a few days fourteen out of seventeen fitters and twenty-four out of thirty bricklayers had been taken for war service. There were material delays, too, and lack of transport. The opening was fixed for Christmas Day, and then postponed from that to 30 December.

Apart from the building itself the most important task was to choose a suitable director for it. Licho was not even considered; Neft refused to work any longer with so difficult a person. The number of candidates seriously considered was soon reduced to three. Two were young men — Hermann Sinsheimer from Mannheim, an enthusiast but perhaps too theoretically minded, and Leopold Jessner — a man who had served his time in the theatre from the bottom up, but whom Neft

thought no businessman; and the third was Emil Lessing, a man in his
mid-fifties who had directed for the Neue Freie Volksbühne as early
as 1892! His abilities in the theatre and in business were known. He
had been Brahm's right-hand man at the Deutsches Theater and later
at the Lessing Theater. He was, however, wedded to Naturalism and
unlikely to take up any new ways and styles. His candidacy was supported by Bruno Wille and others who had valued his work in the
nineties. The conflict between the supporters of the two younger men
was extremely bitter, and when Neft declared himself for Lessing, the
supporters of both the other two decided that they preferred Lessing
to their opponents' candidate. Lessing was therefore chosen, though
very few people really thought him the best man.

Lessing could afford to hire no big names, so, aiming at a good
ensemble, he engaged a company of thirty men and fifteen women.
When, at the outbreak of war, the theatre-opening had to be postponed,
the Neues Operetten-Theater in the Schiffsbauerdamm was rented and
Lessing had to make his start there in unfavourable circumstances.
He produced good, homely fare, no more. In December Götz von
Berlichingen was rehearsed. Bab wrote a verse prologue to be spoken
by Götz's faithful page, Lerse. On 30 December there was a full
theatre for the festive occasion, and everyone of importance in the city
had been invited. But two days before, disaster had struck. One of the
technical features of the stage was a revolve designed by the engineer
Knina, 21 metres in diameter, of which half could also be raised and
lowered. Two days before the opening performance the lift-system
was overloaded, a screw sheared off, and half the revolve fell into the
under-stage cavity. Wire ropes used to try to lift it from the depths
only broke. As only half the stage area was now available it was impossible to present Götz as planned, so the première had to be a less
demanding play from the existing repertoire — Björnson's When the
Vineyards are in Blossom. The opening speech was given by Julius
Bab. Georg Springer modestly thought his own Saxon dialect might be
bad on such an occasion and wrote an article instead. Bab apologised
for the technical trouble and made a speech in which he called the new
building 'a memorial to that unconquerable strength of feeling, that
strength of idealism for whose sake we love in the true sense our
national song "Deutschland, Deutschland über alles"'. He described
the building as a means to lead 'the people to art, art to the people'.
The play was well received, despite disappointment, and Götz was
presented a few days later.

Whatever criticism may be made of the Volksbühne Theatre, it
was a remarkable achievement. It had cost four and a half million
Marks and the shares were in the hands of 14,500 people, mostly small
contributors, so that it was genuinely 'owned by the people'. The site,

though it covered 3,500 square metres, had not been easy to use and
was too narrow to allow an adequate side-stage to be included. There
were nearly two thousand seats. The stage, with its great revolve,
was 40 metres wide, the cyclorama 26 metres high and the stage tower
42 metres high. An orchestra pit could be sunk for operatic performances, and the lighting was by the Fortuny system. It has been
described as a fulfilment of Goethe's dictum of 1817, when he laid
down principles for theatre-building: 'The outward form [to be] the
result of the inner, practical arrangements, and thus expressing the
purpose of the building.' The curve of the cyclorama, answered by
the curve of the auditorium back, was repeated externally, and then
strengthened by the square corners. Although an amphitheatre had
been eschewed, there were no boxes. These were definitely felt to be
exclusive and undemocratic. The result, a theatre with circles but
entirely without boxes, was, at that time, unique. Although the auditorium was so large, a feeling of vastness was avoided by the use of
mahogany cladding throughout the interior, contrasting with a lighter
yellow wood and red curtains in the foyer. The design of the façade
was symbolic of the theatre's purpose, and across it was carved the
Volksbühne motto: Die Kunst dem Volke.

FIRST INTERMISSION

1914-1918 War and revolution

The opening of the Theater am Bülowplatz is the 'curtain line' of the first act of the story of the Volksbühne. The second act runs from the end of the war to 1933, when the movement was taken over by the Nazis, while the third act, which is still running, begins with the re-establishment of the Volksbühne after the Nazi defeat. What happened during the First World War may be regarded as an interval between the acts, a sustaining operation simply to keep the movement in being.

With Emil Lessing as director the Volksbühne survived the first winter remarkably well, but at the end of the season the leadership felt that the risk of continuing its own theatrical business in wartime was too great. It was Reinhardt, friend and rival of the Volksbühne, who provided the solution. He offered to take over the theatre for a period of two years — no doubt in part as a substitute, with its two thousand seats, for his own unrealised 'Theatre of 5,000', and in part through good will towards his old colleagues. The former successful co-operation with Reinhardt encouraged the Volksbühne to accept the proposal. Reinhardt took over the theatre rent free, but made half the seats available to the Volksbühne for its members The Volksbühne was responsible for all costs connected with the house, Reinhardt for all artistic costs. Though the Volksbühne was disappointed that its great aim of operating a theatre and ensemble completely of its own was once again postponed, Reinhardt saved it from hibernation and possible extinction during the hardest years. The membership began to rise again - it had fallen by half in the early months of the war — and in three years had reached fifty thousand. Reinhardt's programme was supplemented by outstanding Sunday morning concerts in the theatre under Leo Kestenberg, and by performances in the Lessing Theater and Deutsches Künstler-Theater.

In the fourth year of the war the Volksbühne decided to revive the old ideal of having its own company in its own theatre. Friedrich Kayssler, an outstanding actor, who also wrote comedies and children's plays, was appointed as director, a post which he held until 1923. In him the Volksbühne obtained the services of one of the most distinguished artists in the German theatre. The new season opened on 4 September 1918 with Immermann's Merlin. Written in 1832, this play had never before been performed and the world première gave the new venture a striking send-off. From other points of view the choice was curious. Immermann (1796-1840), director of the Düsseldorf theatre from 1834 to 1837, was a believer in the Prussian State who rejected liberalism and individualism, and though an apologist for the Volksbühne has called the play 'One of the noblest poems of the Germans', [1] it has also been described as 'a Faustian hotch-potch of medieval myth, pantheism, gnosticism and neo-Platonism'. [2] Today, with its sub-Wagnerian, sub-Faustian rhetoric, its Arthurian cast - with Lucifer, Satan, Lohengrin and Klingsor thrown in for good measure— its tedious speeches, ubiquitous cliffs, gorges, dwarfs and snakes, it is almost unreadable; but it could lend itself to spectacular and colourful staging and production, with flames and transformations. Certainly it is, if not in the best sense, 'Germanic'. That the Volksbühne should open with such a play by such an author is an oddity that can perhaps be most charitably accounted for by the distorting influence of a wartime situation.

The first year of Kayssler's directorship was shaken by even fiercer storms than accompanied the opening of the theatre four years before. Even as the season opened the final German military collapse was beginning. Two months later (9 November) came the abdication of the Kaiser, the proclamation of the Republic by Philipp Scheidemann and— two hours later— Karl Liebknecht's rival proclamation of a Russian-style Socialist Republic. The chairman of the Social Democratic Party, Friedrich Ebert, was appointed Reich Chancellor. Overnight the friends and supporters of the Volksbühne movement became the rulers of Germany, while its opponents in high places were driven into opposition or exile, and the Volksbühne itself became allied with the establishment. The following months, however, with the great strikes and street battles, the Spartacist revolt and the short-lived Bavarian Republic, were hard ones for a theatrical enterprise. For days together the theatre had to remain closed. Once it was rumoured that the building itself had been shelled and lay in ruins. Fortunately this was not true, but glancing shots had done a little superficial damage. With the coming into political power of the Social Democrats several leading members of the Volksbühne had to take up important posts in the new government. Gustav Landauer was killed in the revolutionary fighting in Munich. All in all the stage was set for the Volksbühne movement to develop its changed and important role in the new Germany.

ACT II

1918-1933   The Berlin Volksbühne in the Weimar Republic

1   TO 1923

The dominant figure of the Volksbühne movement during this period, and indeed until his death in 1963, was Siegfried Nestriepke, the 'Grand Old Man of the Volksbühne' as he has been called, without whom the Berlin — and indeed the whole German — Volksbühne move-ment is unthinkable [1] and to whom Oscar Fritz Schuh referred as 'the expert master-builder of the greatest theatre-audience organisa-tion in the world, to whom not only the German, but the European theatre owes so much gratitude'. [2]

Siegfried Nestriepke was born on 17 December 1885 in Bartenstein, East Prussia. His mother came of an old East Prussian family, but his father, an official surveyor, was Silesian. He went to school from 1891 in Bartenstein Bürgerschule until 1895 when the family moved to Bremen, where Siegfried attended first the Vorschule and then the Gymnasium. He was a clever boy, drawn to literature and poetry, and at the same time, even as a fifteen-year-old, he showed a keen inter-est in public affairs and contemporary problems, supplementing the study of Horace and Homer with that of modern stories, commentaries and articles which he found in the newspapers and from which he en-deavoured to form his own opinions. The struggle of the Boers for national independence kindled his imagination and one of his first published poems was dedicated to General de Wet.

From 1905 to 1910 he studied literature, history and national economy in the Universities of Berlin and Marburg, coming under the influence of such noteworthy teachers as Gustav Schmoller and Adolf Wagner, the so-called 'academic Socialists' who sought to give econo-mics an ethical basis and whose preoccupation with ameliorating the

effects of class differences anticipated the idea of the Welfare State.
But the intensive study of Marx and his analysis of the power of modern
capitalism made Nestriepke recognise the inadequacy of the study of
merely national economics in the face of the serious problems of the
time. At Marburg he was able to become acquainted with the teaching
of the great philosopher, Hermann Cohen, without, however, adopting
his transcendentalist neo-Kantian philosophy. Under the economist
Walter Troeltsch, Nestriepke wrote his first important work on Trades
Union Methods of Agitation, while the writings and teaching of his
literature Professor, Ernst Elster, inspired his choice of doctoral
thesis, the Swabian Sturm und Drang poet Christian Friedrich Daniel
Schubart, who appealed especially to Nestriepke because of his revolt
against the tyranny of the absolutist Herzog Carl Eugen von Wurttem-
berg, which earned him ten years' imprisonment.

At least as important in his personal development as the academic
study was Nestriepke's involvement in student politics. He soon
attached himself to an independent student movement, the Deutsche
Freie Studentenschaft, which strove for the reform of the whole of
academic life. Inspired by the 'black-red-gold' ideals of the Wartburg
Festival of October 1817, when revolutionary students met to celebrate
the death of Luther and the Battle of Leipzig, the movement also
wanted to make a breach with the mindless, 'dashing', but actually
reactionary Korpsstudententum—members of expensive and exclusive
student clubs with great emphasis on the initiation of freshmen,
duelling and heavy drinking. This independent student organisation
came into conflict during the winter of 1907-8 both with the conservative clubs, who had an overwhelming majority on the allegedly
representative student committee, and the university authorities.
Nestriepke and others were brought before an academic court and
reprimanded: the activities of the independent society were suspended.
The twenty-three-year-old Nestriepke, filled with 'righteous indignation' wrote a pamphlet, The Fight for Freedom in Marburg University,
which the Deutsche Freie Studentenshaft published in 1908.

Even as a student he also became involved in German politics. In
the 1907 elections he spoke on behalf of Helmuth von Gerlach, the
'enfant terrible' of the Prussian Junkers, and when von Gerlach and
others founded the Democratic Union (Demokratische Vereinigung) in
1908 this became Nestriepke's first political home. Two years later
he was its party secretary for Rhineland-Westphalia, while pursuing
at the same time his chosen profession of political journalist. Within
the political field Nestriepke developed a special enthusiasm for Trades
Unionism and in 1912-13 he was economic policy secretary to the
Federation of Technical-industrial Public Servants and editor of The
Commercial Salaried Employee. His progress as a left-wing journalist
reached its climax when he was appointed political editor of Vorwärts,

the central organ of the Social Democratic Party, a post which Philipp
Scheidemann himself urged him to accept. From 1915, however, he
was able to continue this work only when on leave from war service,
until 1917 when he was wounded and returned to civilian life and other
journalistic positions. In 1917 he attached himself to the Independent
Social Democratic Party, but left it in 1919 as he felt the need for unity
in the struggle to build a democratic order, and from 1922 was vice-
chairman of the Central Office for the Union of the (two) Socialist
Parties, founded by Eduard Bernstein in 1922. Meanwhile he had
written a three-volume study of The Trade Union Movement, which
became a standard work, and, as a development of the theoretical part
of volume I, a further book, The Theory of Trades Unionism.

Such was the man who immediately after the end of the war came
into close association with the Berlin Volksbühne and the movement
that was to be his life's work. In temperament and interests he seems
to have been ideally suited to the Volksbühne. On the one hand an
aggressive social democrat and trades unionist, with both journalistic
and organisational experience in politics and trades unions, he was also
a genuine scholar and lover of literature with something in him of the
schoolmaster, the academic and the author. With astonishing speed he
familiarised himself with the nature, history, organisation and problems of the Volksbühne and in 1919 he was elected to the executive
committee of the Freie Volksbühne. He made his first important
appearance in a general meeting on 8 May 1919, when he delivered an
address on the communalisation of the Berlin theatre, coming down
heavily on the side of non-commercial but autonomous bodies, rather
than nationalisation (the two possible developments of socialism which
were being hotly debated in Berlin at this time).

When Nestriepke entered the Volksbühne movement it was, of
course, still divided into the two organisations, though the establishment of a good external relationship between them had already led to a
steep rise in membership (eighty-two thousand altogether), and they
were taking up ten thousand seats in theatres other than their own. Just
as he had felt the need for socialist unity, so too Nestriepke became the
driving force for the amalgamation of the two Volksbühnen. In an
imaginative and disinterested move — which one imagines must have
been inspired by Nestriepke — the Neue Freie Volksbühne, on 8 April
1920, revised its constitution so as to bring it completely in line with
that of the Freie Volksbühne. A few days later the Freie Volksbühne
dissolved itself and a new association, the Volksbühne e. V., [3] subtitled Vereinigte Freie und Neue Freie Volksbühne (United Independent
and New Independent Volksbühne) came into being. Thus the Theater
am Bülowplatz became the property of the united body. At the first
annual general meeting under the new statutes (21 October 1920) Georg

Springer, Anton Wagner and Curt Baake (by now an ex-undersecretary of State) were elected as chairmen, and as general secretary Dr Sieg-fried Nestriepke. At this meeting a decision was taken to publish, in addition to a free newsheet, a periodical for the encouragement of the arts, called Die Volksbühne, devoted to serious articles and free from necessary but space-consuming information. Nestriepke became editor and the first number appeared in autumn 1920. A year later this peri-odical was taken over by the Verband.

Alongside the Theater am Bülowplatz the Volksbühne also managed the Neues Volkstheater in the Köpenicker Strasse where a representa-tive of the society worked alongside the director as adviser and colleague and a programme closely in line with the demands and needs of the Volksbühne was possible. In the winter of 1923-4 the Neues Volkstheater became a subdivision of the Theater am Bülowplatz under Nestriepke's direction. In 1926 this theatre was given up and for one year the Theater am Schiffbauerdamm rented instead. Meanwhile the Volksbühne wanted an opera house where it had some control of the programme and in the spring of 1920 agreement was reached with the State Administration over the Krollschen Oper am Platz der Republik (the Krolloper as it was more simply referred to). The interior of this building, the former Neues Operntheater, was more or less a ruin. The authorities were willing to make over the Krolloper to the Volksbühne for twenty-five years, and to service it with operatic and straight productions, using the Ensemble of the State Theatres, provided the Volksbühne took responsibility for restoring the interior. Mere renovation was inade-quate, and Oscar Kaufmann was asked to design a new auditorium. After some hesitation the work was begun in the early summer of 1921 and should have been completed by spring 1922, but there were delays caused by the weather and shortage of materials and soon inflation began to catch up with the money-raising. Despite heroic and sacrificial efforts on the part of the members, the Volksbühne had to give up in the end; all rights in the Krolloper were returned to the State, which com-pleted the work and assumed financial responsibility for the undertaking, nevertheless guaranteeing to the Volksbühne over seven thousand seats per week for twenty-five years at prices within the means of the Volks-bühne members. The theatre came into use purely for opera at Christmas 1923, with almost 2,200 seats and what had become one of the largest and most modern of stages.

The period of Kayssler's direction of the Volksbühne theatre from 1918 to 1923 was a highlight in the history of the movement. Kayssler gave the Volksbühne a distinct character, and the theatre exercised great drawing power. The seasons included many world premières and other noteworthy productions. Outstanding in the first season was Georg Kaiser's Gas, which opened on 25 February 1919, just a fort-night after Ebert's election as President of the Republic, and only four

days after Kurt Eisner's assassination in Munich. This play, in which
the workers in a socialised industry are so seized with greed for profit
that eventually their fanatical labours lead to a gas explosion that lays
the whole plant in ruins, was both topical and prophetic. The world
première had been at the Neues Theater, Frankfurt and the Düsseldorfer
Schauspielhaus on 28 November 1918, but it was the Volksbühne production that brought Kaiser the public recognition in Berlin which he had
long sought for.

Among the actors in Kayssler's ensemble was Jürgen Fehling, who
had been given his first Berlin engagement in the Neues Volkstheater in
1911 and had been playing since 1913 at the Volksbühne in Vienna.
Fehling soon had ambitions to direct plays himself, ambitions which
were for some time frustrated by Kayssler. Kayssler, as director, was
also his own principal actor, and eventually Fehling was given an opportunity to direct Gogol's comedy Marriage (March 1919). The production
was praised by Herbert Ihering, who as dramaturge in the Vienna
Volksbühne already knew Fehling well and saw him as a coming director
of comedy rather than of tragedy. Fehling followed Marriage with
Shakespeare's Comedy of Errors (1920), Shaw's Captain Brassbound's
Conversion (February 1921) and Der Bauer als Millionär (The Peasant
a Millionaire) by the early-nineteenth-century Austrian dramatist,
Ferdinand Raimund (May 1921). Between these last two, in April, he
produced his first tragedy, Sophocles' Antigone. Critics were struck
by the production's independence of the example of Reinhardt and the
use of music in the choral sections. Herbert Ihering coolly dissected
its virtues and shortcomings, but less analytical critics were carried
away with enthusiasm.

During the following months Fehling firmly established himself as
one of the leading Berlin directors. At the end of September came the
first public production of Toller's Masse-Mensch (Masses and Man),
(first performed, privately in Nuremburg, 15 November 1920). One of
the greatest and most poetical of all Expressionistic plays, Masse-
Mensch was written in the prison-fortress of Niederschönenfeld, where
Toller was imprisoned for his part in the short-lived Bavarian Republic
of 1919:

> It literally broke out of me and was put on paper in two days and a
> half. The two nights, which, owing to my imprisonment, I was
> forced to spend in 'bed' in a dark cell, were abysses of torment....
> In the mornings shivering with fever, I sat down to write and did
> not stop until my fingers, clammy and trembling, refused to serve
> me.... The laborious and blissful work of pruning and remoulding
> lasted a year. [4]

At the time of the first night, Toller was on hunger strike in the same
prison. The play itself deals poetically and expressionistically with the

problems of ends and means, the central conflict being between the
Nameless One who advocates violence in the cause of the masses, and
the Woman (Sonia) who, though deeply involved in the revolution,
believes in a non-violent solution:

> If I took but one human life,
> I should betray the Masses.
> Who acts may only sacrifice himself.
> Hear me: no man may kill men for a cause.
> Unholy every cause that needs to kill. [5]

The critics objected that Fehling made no distinction in the production
between the three 'dream pictures' and the other scenes, but Toller
wrote from prison to Fehling (October 1921), saying:

> I want to tell you myself that you have carried out my meaning.
> These pictures of 'reality' are not realism, are not local colour;
> the protagonists (except for Sonia) are not individual characters.
> Such a play can only have a spiritual, never a concrete, reality.

He added later: 'I am surprised at the critics' lack of understanding.
Possibly the play is insufficiently worked out.' [6] Fehling himself has
written an enthusiastic note on the play and its production. He has
emphasised that though Toller is 'a social writer',

> this does not mean that his play is political propaganda, for he is
> a poet. But his poem, his play, was conceived in the midst of a
> social upheaval and inspired by the wrath of a war against social
> injustice. Though his battle-cries may at times sound grotesquely,
> the living breath of anger and sorrow informs his work and gives
> his politics their universal dramatic values.

He concludes:

> The whole cast was young, for only the young can adequately trans-
> mit the fiery outpouring of Toller's own enthusiasm. If this
> statement seems to hold a latent criticism, I would say that the
> author himself desires and need desire no better valuation of his
> play. It is a prelude to the poetry of world-revolution, a stormy
> morning which may, in happier hours of daylight, be surpassed in
> lasting poetic value, but never in the passionate humanity from
> which it springs [7]

And Toller himself ended the letter to Fehling:

> I need not dwell on the fact that proletarian art must ultimately
> rest on universal human interests, must, at its deepest, like life
> or death, embrace all human themes. It can only exist where the
> creative artist reveals that which is eternally human in the spiritual
> characteristics of the working people. [8]

These comments have been quoted at length as exemplifying the Volksbühne attitude to the relationship of art and politics, and the nature of
its continuing commitment to the socialist cause, and they will be
recalled when later the left-wing criticisms of the Volksbühne are
described. They are of immediate importance in the way they reveal
the aims and sympathies of Fehling himself.

Later in the same autumn he produced (less successfully) King
Lear, and ended the extraordinary year's achievement with a remark-
able production of the eighteenth-century satirical comedy of Tieck,
Der gestiefelte Kater (Puss in Boots). Later in the same season (March
1922) he set the seal on his rise to eminence with his production of
Hauptmann's Die Ratten (The Rats). This play, having failed when first
produced in 1911, had been revived at the Volksbühne in 1916 by Felix
Holländer, working under Reinhardt: the success of that production
made the critic Siegfried Jacobsohn withdraw his earlier condemnation.
But Fehling's production, with Kayssler himself and Helene Fehdmer
in the leading parts, lifted the play into another dimension. That production and one of Raimund's Verschwender (The Spendthrift) were his
farewell productions for the Volksbühne. In the autumn of 1922 he went
to work as regisseur under Jessner in the Staatstheater.

The Volksbühne's second theatre, the Neues Volkstheater, also
made its mark during this same period.

The leadership of the association took over this theatre again in
1921, and after its directors Berisch and Heinz Goldberg had left,
Nestriepke took over the direction in addition to his other tasks. He
attempted a programme that even Piscator described as 'politically
coloured', including plays by Ibsen, Hauptmann and Shaw as well as
minor writers. One of his most important acts was the production by
Paul Günther, in May 1923, of Ernst Barlach's first play Der tote Tag
(The Dead Day). Apparently the theatre lost money, and for the
following season, 1923-4, it was taken over formally as a subsidiary
of the Bülowplatz theatre. [9]

Kayssler's years of office included the terrible period of inflation,
during which the membership of the Volksbühne actually rose to the —
largely illusory — figure of 167,000, falling to about 140,000 in 1924
and slowly settling to a steady hundred thousand in the later twenties.
Also during the Kayssler period the Volksbühne was hit by the two-week
strike of actors in 1922, even though the Volksbühne publicly declared
that it had no part in the dispute.

Kayssler remained the director of the Volksbühne theatre until the
end of the 1922-3 season, when his contract was prematurely ended.
Some difficulties had arisen because of his playing leads as well as
directing, and when various business and organisational problems were

traced back to the arbitrariness of the artistic director, it became
more and more difficult for the officers and committees of the association to work with him. With his going the first post-war phase of the
Volksbühne's work ended.

2 THE PISCATOR AFFAIR

Friedrich Kayssler's successor as director of the Bülowplatz theatre
was Fritz Holl, up till now principal regisseur of the Württemberg
Landestheater in Stuttgart. His term of office was the stormiest in the
whole history of the Volksbühne in Berlin, and, primarily because of
Piscator, the best known. But, partly because of Piscator's enormous
international reputation, partly because he himself published the story
from his own point of view as early as 1929 in his book Das Politische
Theater, and partly because of the hostility of the press to the Volksbühne at that time, Piscator is usually represented, even in books
written in recent years, as the 'hero' and Nestriepke as the 'villain' of
the piece — and this in spite of the fact that in 1963 the two men worked
together again with mutual respect in the new Freie Volksbühne of West
Berlin. In this book the events will, of course, be seen from the point
of view of the Volksbühne, and Piscator's debt to the Volksbühne, as
well as the Volksbühne's debt to Piscator, will be examined in addition
to the conflicts between them.

When Piscator was invited by Holl to direct a play for the Volksbühne he felt himself ripe for the opportunity to use for the first time
the resources of a large, well-equipped modern theatre. His experience
in the war, including amateur theatre at the front, had turned him away
from 'pure' art ('Art is shit') to politics, and from Social Democracy to
Communism. Piscator (sometimes 'Piskator' — really Herr Fischer)
made his first serious steps at Königsberg in 1919-20 where his company Das Tribunal played Strindberg, Wedekind and Sternheim, using
the lesser hall of the town hall as a chamber theatre. Meanwhile in
Berlin, Karl-Heinz Martin had founded Die Tribüne — where he produced
Toller's Die Wandlung (The Transformation) — and then the first Proletarian Theatre. [1] Now came the twenty-six-year-old Piscator to
Berlin and founded the second Proletarian Theatre which, he said, was
distinguished from the Volksbühne — on whose model it wished to create
an audience organisation — and also from Martin's Proletarian Theatre,
in that the word 'art' was banned, and that the 'plays' were proclama-
tions 'with which we wanted to sieze on contemporary events and act
politically'. They acted in halls smelling of stale beer and men's
urinals. Once John Heartfield (Helmut Herzfelde) arrived at a performance half an hour late with the backcloth he had designed and painted,
and insisted on stopping the show to put it up! Except for a few

sympathetic professionals, the actors themselves were working people.
Six plays were presented in the first year; no bourgeois critics were
admitted; the audience was organised exactly on the lines of the Volksbühne and consisted of five to six thousand members recruited largely
from the Allgemeine Arbeiter-Union, the Kommunistische Arbeiter-
Partei (KAP) and Syndicalists. There was no support from the
Kommunistische Partei Deutschlands (KPD) whose organ Rote Fahne
accepted the traditional distinction between art and propaganda and
refused to accept Piscator's theatre as art.

The Proletarian Theatre posed great financial problems and wound
up in April 1921. Piscator's next venture was to join with José
Rehfisch in acquiring the Zentral Theater. Inflation being rife, they
paid three million Marks for it and sold some scrap iron in order to
pay! Zickel, the former director, had some Volksbühne bookings and
at first these were handed over, but when the Volksbühne realised
Piscator's political intentions, it withdrew them: it was his first
conflict with the Volksbühne. Indeed the Zentral Theater project was
conceived, he says, as an opposition to the Volksbühne, but, in common
with the Volksbühne, Piscator could not avoid admitting middle-class
members — the number of working-class ones was not enough. [2]

Piscator here directed three highly naturalistic productions —
Gorky, Suburbans, Rolland, Le Temps viendra and Tolstoy, The Power
of Darkness. Eventually Piscator had to give up the theatre; the year's
work there, he says, had enabled him to make great progress into the
theatrical life of Berlin, but at great financial loss.

It was at this point that Piscator was invited to direct Alfons
Paquet's Fahnen (Flags) for the Volksbühne. He himself says it was by
chance: 'My invitation came purely by chance, for by chance there was
no Director who would have been willing to produce a piece by Alfons
Paquet, chosen equally by chance'. [3] It is difficult to accept this
view. Piscator had already modelled his audience organisation on the
Volksbühne and thought of his Zentral Theater venture as its rival.
Further, to him the Volksbühne itself was the historical root of what
he called 'political theatre':

> The political theatre, as it has worked out in all my undertakings,
> is neither a personal 'invention' nor a result of the social re-
> grouping of 1918. Its roots reach back to the end of the last century.
> At that time forces broke into the intellectual situation of bourgeois
> society which, consciously, or through their mere existence,
> altered that situation decisively and to some extent raised it up.
> These forces came from two directions: from literature and from
> the proletariat. Where the two intersected a new conception came
> into being in art — Naturalism — and a new form in the theatre — the
> Volksbühne. [4]

It is usually said that the invitation came from Holl, but Piscator's widow, Maria Ley-Piscator, writing admittedly long after the events, says: 'Siegfried Nestriepke made the daring step of asking Piscator to direct the forthcoming play at the Volksbühne.' [5] Though the invitation would undoubtedly be extended to Piscator by the artistic director of the theatre, it is interesting that Maria Ley thinks of it as actually originating, like so many bold and imaginative Volksbühne developments, from Nestriepke himself. She may well be right.

Piscator clearly regarded himself as the potential saviour of the Volksbühne. That very movement which he saw as the root of his own political theatre, seemed to him to have been betrayed by the exaltation of art over class struggle. It was, he said, a mere artistic 'Co-op' (Konsumverein), whose only business was to engage the best experts. 'Everything here cooked in butter', he remarked sarcastically and quoted at length a pamphlet by Herbert Ihering, The Betrayal of the Volksbühne, which formulated three stages of degeneration — Reinhardt, 'a prodigal genius'; Kayssler, 'a priest of the art of acting; a temple-ward of the theatre; art as a religious service, the stage as a cathedral'; and Holl, 'now formlessness succeeds to formlessness'. Piscator was far too penetrating to charge individual directors with responsibility for the development of the Volksbühne: he blamed the circumstances of the time, particularly the non-emergence of authors and plays:

> Where was the drama? Where were the authors? All forces, all the forces of the drama, production, direction, political leadership, administration and, finally, of the public, united to guarantee the Volksbühne long and undisturbed sleep. [6]

Piscator saw Paquet's play as one of those for which the theatre, and especially the Volksbühne, was waiting, and himself as the appropriate director — because for him, technical and political developments were inextricably bound together. Maria Ley tells us that the surprise invitation produced a crisis of conscience in Piscator, who asked himself how he could work in the theatre which he had condemned for not living up to its own ideals. In spite of his losses at the Zentral Theater, he had not yet come to terms (if he ever did) with the economics of theatrical production. Later, having had his own theatre at the Nollendorfplatz, 'he realised the pressure of the economic battle which was the true reason for Siegfried Nestriepke's sometimes crafty administrative measures'. [7] He decided, however, to accept, hoping to 'turn the tide' at the Volksbühne.

The action of Alfons Paquet's play takes place in Chicago at the time of the unrest among the workers in 1886. [8] Written for a German audience, it concentrates upon the community of German immigrant

workers in Chicago, and at one point relates the events to Germany
itself by references to Bismarck and the anti-socialist law. The central
events of the play are that Cyrus McClure, the capitalist, bribes the
Police Captain Shaak to provoke a disturbance at an open-air workers'
meeting: he does so. A bomb is thrown and shots are fired. Workers
are arrested and accused. One commits suicide in prison and four
others are executed. In the final tableau the flags which give the play
its name are dipped over the coffins of the martyred workers.

The play is in eighteen scenes, divided into three acts, and is
written in a completely factual and naturalistic style without any poetic
language or non-naturalistic stage directions. The numerous characters
[9] are clearly and simply seen — Fielden, the Englishman, who speaks
of the Lancashire Luddites; Parsons, with his Old Testament rhetoric
and Indian wife; Governor Ogleby; Lingg in his cell reading his mother's
letter and so on. The scenes are similarly plain — the editorial office of
the workers' newspaper; Seliger's house with its home-made bombs;
McClure's office; a cellar; a court; a citizens' club where a buffalo is
being roasted; a prison cell. There is a documentary plainness, too, in
the presentation of the sequence of events. No attempt is made to knit a
plot, lead up to climaxes or construct shapely acts, and although all the
incidents are relevant to the central story, the method is discursive
rather than concentrated, narrative rather than dramatic. When the
play was printed in 1923, the author subtitled it A Dramatic Novel (Ein
dramatischer Roman), but when Piscator directed it he changed this to
An Epic Drama (Ein episches Drama). [10] It is the first appearance
of the phrase which Brecht made famous and upon which he constructed
a whole theory of theatre. Alfred Döblin described the play as belonging
to a fruitful 'middle ground' (Zwischengebiet) between narrative and
drama, saying that it was none the worse for that: 'One can not re-
proach a mule for being neither an ass nor a horse: it is only bad, when
it is a bad mule.' [11] Leo Lania, writing in the Wiener Arbeiterzeitung
(2 June 1924) distinguished it from plays like Dantons Tod and Die
Weber in that the author had renounced all artistic form and limited
himself to allowing the bare facts to speak for themselves.

Piscator was delighted at the response of the Volksbühne Ensemble
to his ideas, and began to put into operation his distinctive kind of production, later known, as he remarks, as 'epic theatre'. This, he says,
briefly consists of a broadening of the treatment, illumination of the
background, and the development of the piece beyond the compass of the
merely dramatic. 'Out of the play to be seen, grew the teaching material' ('Aus dem Schau-Spiel [sic] enstand das Lehrstück'). He placed
projection-screens on both sides of the stage, and, consistently with
his aim of presenting the play as clearly and objectively as possible he
used these for what he calls 'display texts linking the individual scenes'.
Piscator said that as far as he knew this was the first time that slide-

projections had been used in this way in the theatre. In fact they had
been similarly used four years earlier by the Dadaist, Ywan Goll.
Piscator was associated with Dada in 1919, but minimised its artistic
influence upon him in his book. [12] The play had a Prologue in verse
in which the characters were introduced and the play declared to be a
'puppet show'. Piscator projected photographs of the characters as
they were named. [13] At first all went well, but two days before the
first night everything began to disintegrate and at the dress rehearsal
the invited guests gradually slipped away. At the end Piscator wrote
'Shit' in his notebook and walked slowly upstairs, accidentally over-
hearing one sentence from a conversation between Holl, Neft and the
actor Paul Henckels: 'That's the worst we've had! How could we
engage this man! Simply frightful!' To Piscator's honour, he walked
straight into the room and declared, 'Gentlemen, I entirely agree with
you!' He offered to give up the production; he suggested putting off the
opening for a week. The others would not agree. So Piscator went to
the actors and proposed that they rehearse, with all properties and
effects, from after that evening's performance until the following
evening. They agreed! The rehearsal began at 1.0 a.m. and continued
until the performance, which had to begin half an hour late. During the
performance the applause became more and more stormy, and 'when in
the final tableau three great black flags had descended from the flies, a
round of applause broke out which almost had something revolutionary
in it'. [14]

'A storm of applause answered the storm on the stage. And with
justice', were the opening words of Max Osborn's enthusiastic critique
in the Berliner Morgenpost two days later. Projections, scenery, the
use of the revolve, the enthusiasm with which the actors were fired, all
were seen as contributing to the whole and silencing any carping criticism of imperfect particulars.

The anonymous critic (Fh ...) of Vorwärts welcomed the fact that
a writer of note had treated 'the most important problem of the present',
and was prepared to forgive the 'dramatic shortcomings' of the play,
which he felt were, at least tentatively, compensated for by the light
and sound effects and the dramatically moved scenery.

Monty Jacobs, in the Vossische Zeitung, was more scathing about
the play itself which, he said, owed its place in the Volksbühne to its
propaganda value only. 'Paquet's hand trembles uncertainly, but
Piscator's fingers work energetically and firmly.' But Piscator is not
left blameless. If Paquet shows himself to be his own critic in calling
the piece 'a dramatic novel' (and what can that be, asks Jacobs, but an
undramatic play?), Piscator reveals a lack of confidence in the play, in
his use of projected texts. He uses them like sub-titles in the (silent)
cinema, so that, when the prisoners are condemned, the words appear

CONDEMNED TO DEATH, or when the police commit the outrage —
THE POLICE THEMSELVES THROW THE BOMBS (though the author
has been objective enough also to show the anarchist domestic bomb
factory). 'A director', says Jacobs, 'who thinks such crutches necessary, does not even discreetly hide the lameness of the play ... These
superfluous bits of cinema rubbish show that Piscator must make
himself strong enough, if he is to help his author's weakness — which
the actors, under his direction, already can'.

Soon after this success the Volksbühne and Piscator entered into a
contract under which for some years he would direct plays of his own
choice in the Volksbühne theatre. He himself admits that, largely
because he could not find the kind of plays he wanted, several of the
productions were mere journeyman work. His next production in the
theatre, in December 1924, was Under the Caribbean Moon — Berlin
was just 'discovering' O'Neill. It does not seem to have been very
successful, though Ihering rather grudgingly admitted it to be the best
O'Neill play so far, while at the same time asking when the Volksbühne
was going to realise its true vocation. Piscator makes no comment at
all in Das Politische Theater. The O'Neill was followed at the end of
January by Wer weint um Juckenack? (Who Weeps for Juckenack?), a
comedy by Hans José Rehfisch, jurist turned dramatist, who had
worked alongside Piscator in the Zentral Theater in 1923. Although
this play marks the beginning of Rehfisch's success as a dramatist it
was of no more than secondary importance to Piscator — though Ihering,
whose hopes for Piscator had been sustained since Fahnen, in spite of
O'Neill, said that the production was a great credit to the Volksbühne,
the greatest since the production of Fahnen.

Piscator was much more interested in his next Volksbühne production, Rudolf Leonhard's Segel am Horizont (Sails on the Skyline).
This title was suggested by Georg Kaiser, whose friend and disciple
Leonhard was, the original having been Towarischtsch (Comrade). The
germ of the play lay in a report in a Berlin newspaper (7 November
1924) of a Russian ship, Towarischtsch, under the command of a
woman. In the play itself Angela Alexandrovna Dialtschenskaya, the
dead Captain's wife, is elected captain by the crew of sixty. A sexually
explosive situation develops, as the men are unable to regard Angela
simply as a comrade — she is for them a woman, the one woman among
sixty men. They insist that, in order to ease the tension, she must
choose one man from among them. She chooses the telegraphist, an
intelligent and articulate man, who says, 'No'. She then chooses
Kaleb, the illiterate. The tension, so far from easing, becomes worse,
and Kaleb is thrown overboard to drown. Angela eventually gains full
command of the situation and explains to the crew that her husband had
in fact committed suicide because he was jealous of the two sailors

Oleg and Morten. The sense of comradeship and duty to the collective gains an uneasy victory.

Piscator liked the play for the way in which an intellectual thesis was developed out of starkly realistic material — sex, murder and violence — though he said that Leonhard had created only a mosaic out of the disparate elements, not, like Kaiser, an entirely new form. Traugott Müller designed a three-dimensional, practicable ship on the revolving stage which 'attained an independent function through which the weakness of the conclusion became dramatically one of the strongest moments of the piece.' [15] Unfortunately Piscator does not explain exactly how this was achieved.

After Fahnen the next of his Volksbühne productions which Piscator seems to have regarded as important was another play by Paquet, Sturmflut (Storm Flood), though he says he selected it through lack of time while fully aware of its weaknesses. He calls it 'a paraphrase of the Russian Revolution', and summarises it thus:

> The revolution is winning; but money is lacking to carry it through. Granka Umnitsch, its leader, therefore sells Petersburg to an old Jew, who re-sells it to England. Granka and his band withdraw into the forests. There, a battle of love between him and a Swedish woman who goes over to the other side (embodied in the White Guard Sawin). Granka returns secretly to Petersburg, rouses the proletariat and reconquers the city for the revolution. [16]

The weakness of the play lay in the unreality of the symbolism. As one critic wrote: 'Because I am, as I have said, lazy and superficial, frivolous and childish, I require first of figures in drama that they are something, before they signify something.' [17] Piscator writes similarly:

> Symbol is condensed reality.... But it is not a trade-mark. It may not become a cliché for reality.... High points of history are themselves symbols in their complete, concrete extent. It is a mistake to drain what is material from such material, [von solchen Stoffen das Stoffliche abzuziehen], for through that not a heightening but a disembodiment is achieved. [18]

Thus Piscator, filled, as he says, with the events of the Russian Revolution, with which he was familiar in all their political and social relationships and interrelationships, had to produce a play in which everything 'ran together in confusion, entangled, unclear, pale and half-baked'. [19] Small wonder if, feeling like this about it, Piscator virtually remade the play during the three and a half weeks of rehearsal, 'splitting the piece to its foundations, rebuilding its structure, adding new material, and right up to the opening night demanding further new text from that harassed creature, the author'. [20]

The 'harassed creature' later defended himself in the Preface to
the printed edition of the play:

> It is not the history of a revolution; not a description of the life of
> Lenin; not a representation of Soviet Russia.... It was not a
> question of a transcript of reality, but of epitomising the driving
> forces of our time in a few figures, which would rouse the
> emotions vividly, as reality arouses them. [21]

Meanwhile, what the audiences and critics saw had, as Piscator said,
come into being on the stage. It had done so with the author's full
co-operation, and to his satisfaction, as Paquet makes clear in a
passage omitted from his Preface, which he prints as a Postscript to
the play:

> Piscator gave me the opportunity of working directly with him and
> the actors at rehearsal.... The revolutionising effect of this close
> contact of the dramatist with the essential laws of the theatre
> working themselves out in a thousand particulars and possibilities,
> cannot be overvalued. [22]

Apart from the type-characters that Arthur Eloesser found so
unconvincing, but which Ihering found to be an exciting, individualised
and extended political typology, the most discussed aspect of the production was its use of film sequences. It was this, too, that interested
Piscator himself most.

> With this production a great step forward was made in working out
> and refining the film scenes. For the first time it was possible to
> have whole sections of film specially photographed for the play. [23]

Ihering, who wrote about the production in two successive issues of the
Berliner Börsen-Courier, devoted much of his second article to the
film, giving more details about its use:

> Radio news: Revolution in China — on the screen in the background
> a Chinese mass meeting; speech by Lloyd George — Lloyd George
> speaks in the film.... Or at the beginning: the stage is the shore,
> the harbour, the square at Petersburg. The film: ships, sea,
> inundation. Or at the end: fighting. Or between: motionless back-
> ground that suddenly becomes alive; contrasts or parallels from
> other revolutions, or aeroplanes, the stone canyons of the city,
> forest. [24]

Ihering, who was pleased with the experiment ('The film is no longer ...
a trick.... The film is dramatic function') [25] also pointed out that
it did not always come off. It was best, he thought, when documentary.
Eloesser reached a more negative conclusion. Having remarked that
we should murder Piscator if he provided visual aids to poetic passages
in Goethe's plays, he continues:

The stage abdicates when it renounces the magic of language,
which makes our ear a spiritual eye.

How sweet the moonlight sleeps upon this bank.

If Herr Piscator ... but perhaps we have murdered him already. [26].

Four more productions must be mentioned before that over which
the storm broke — appropriately enough Gewitter über Gottland (Storm
over Gothland). Two of these are Piscator's intervening Volkbühne
productions, one is his Die Räuber at the Staatliches Schauspielhaus,
and one Jessner's Piscator-influenced Hamlet at the same theatre.
    The next Piscator Volksbühne production was Paul Zech's 'scenic
ballade', Das Trunkene Schiff (The Drunken Ship). As the title suggests,
this is a play about the poet Rimbeau, and is in fact simply Rimbeau's
life from his running away from home as a teenager, to his death.
Rimbeau is thought of as his own 'bateau ivre' and the scenes of the
Ballade are named as if the play were a voyage: 'Setting sail', 'First
port of call', 'Second port of call', 'Harbour'. Best are the closing
scenes and those which show Rimbeau's relationship with Verlaine.
Piscator was clearly disappointed that though the play covered an
important period in French history it limited itself to the study of
individual psychology (though it contains some side-swipes at imperial-
ism), and to compensate, as it were, for this, Piscator substituted
for the elaborately naturalistic scenes described in the author's stage
directions, projections on three great screens of designs by George
Grosz which introduced the social and political environment. He also
projected film, not only as illustration, but also, when Rimbeau on his
last homeward voyage lies dying of fever, as interpretations of his
delirious fantasies.

    The other Piscator Volksbühne production in 1926 was Gorky's
The Lower Depths. Although the play attracted Piscator, he was not
satisfied with it as it stood. 'In 1925 [actually 1926] I could no longer
think on the scale of one small room with ten unfortunate people, but
only on the more extended scale of the slums of a great modern city.'
[27] Piscator asked Gorky himself to adapt the play along these lines,
but to his disappointment Gorky declined to do so. Piscator therefore
fell back upon scenic devices and stage effects. In two places he moved
the play in the direction he wished:

The beginning — the snores and heavy, rattling breath of a mass of
people, which filled the whole stage space; the awakening of a
great city, the clang of tram-bells, until the ceiling descended and
contracted the whole social milieu into the room; and the riot — not
just a minor rough-house of private characters in the yard, but the
rebellion of a whole quarter against the police, the uprising of the
masses. [28]

Meanwhile, in September, Piscator had produced Schiller's Die Räuber at the Staatliches Schauspielhaus. Following the example of Brecht's adaption of Marlowe's Edward II [29] and Erich Engel's production of Shakespeare's Coriolanus, [30] Piscator set out deliberately to give Schiller's play a modern political significance. It is not relevant here to describe or discuss this famous production in detail. [31] Schiller's play was, as Bab expressed it, stood upon its head, and Spiegelberg — in cutaway coat, dirty brown bowler and Trotsky make-up, became the hero, the true proletarian revolutionary, and Karl Moor reduced to 'a romantic fool'. The production brought into debate the whole question of whether the classics should be thus adapted and in part rewritten in order to give them new life in the twentieth century (the view supported by, for example, Herbert Ihering) or whether the classics must remain themselves and new plays be written to express new ideas: 'A Spiegelberg drama cannot be derived from Schiller, but must be newly written — let us say by Brecht. Or let us turn directly to Piscator's poetic ability and demand something home-made from him.' [32]

The debate was intensified by Jessner's own production in December of Hamlet. This, said Bab, did not actually falsify the play as Piscator's production had falsified Die Räuber but developed as its main theme the background of court cabal, aristocratic brutality, and stupid convention, that Shakespeare needed for presenting his main themes through Hamlet himself. The play was so directed that it was easy to see actual parallels implied with modern German history: Claudius as Kaiser Wilhelm II; Polonius as Bethmann-Hollweg.

These two productions, coming after Piscator's other work at the Volksbühne and elsewhere, set alight a controversy in literary periodicals and serious newspapers on the politicisation of the theatre — though it also took the form of debates on freedom of thought and the protection of pure art. 'The signs are multiplying. The flags of literary questions are being unfurled.' [33] Left and right began to take to the intellectual barricades. 'Why are we not as active as Piscator?' demanded a speaker at a public meeting of the right-wing National Women's Circle, when the Greater German Theatre Society (Grossdeutsche Theatergemeinschaft) was founded (it achieved only one production); while Herbert Ihering joined Balázs on the left, and called for 'Clear relationships! Decisions, not mixtures.' Piscator admits that on the right this demand was taken up not only as decisively as on the left but with stronger political insight. Could Piscator, writing in 1929, have by then become aware that he was among those who, through his dipping flags and modern techniques for playing upon mass emotion while claiming only to present sober fact, [34] helped to let out of the bottle the genie who stage-managed the Nuremburg Rallies of the 1930s?

Nowhere was the conflict felt so keenly as within the Volksbühne itself. While on the one hand the Volksbühne had its contract with Piscator, on the other hand, during the same period it had made 'many concessions to the customs of the Berlin Private Theatres in the "star" system and the shaping of the repertoire'. [35] As Georg Springer's left-wing adversary Arthur Holitscher pointed out:

> After every first night of works of the political opinion that we demand, works which demonstrate a proletarian feeling in contemporary events, hundreds of letters fly from the membership into the office of the Volksbühne, all to the same effect: 'Leave us in peace from all these problems — hunger, revolution, class-war, misery, corruption, prostitution. We have enough of these at party-meetings, in our jobs, at home, in our neighbourhood.' [36]

The magnificent theatre ('catastrophically magnificent' according to Holitscher) demanded a large membership that could not be drawn from one class or one political persuasion, and even had the executive of the Volksbühne wanted its theatre to become a speaking-trumpet for the Communist Party, it would have been economically impossible for it to have done so. But within the Volksbühne the Youth Section strongly supported Piscator and continuously demanded that the Volksbühne 'accept the consequences of taking the road to political drama, so far followed only hesitatingly and unhappily'. [37]

The conflict came to a head in February and March 1927. In the article by Arthur Holitscher already quoted the Volksbühne is accused, along with the whole Social Democratic Party, of betraying the ideals of its founders, and of entering into a 'coalition' with the 'reactionary' Volksbühnenbund. [38] On 14 March the Youth Section unanimously passed a resolution which stated:

> The Volksbühne, whose support is the working class, must express a clear conviction in a lively and consciously purposeful repertoire. The proletarian youth in the Volkbühne refuses to accept the bourgeois interpretation of the neutrality of art. As the theatre is an important instrument in the working class struggle for freedom, the stage must reflect the purpose and life of the proletariat fighting for a new order in the world. [39]

While denying that there was a 'crisis' in the Volksbühne, Georg Springer answered Holitscher in _Weltbühne_ on 22 March (the day before the opening of Piscator's next production!):

> The Volksbühne has not the tradition, intention or possibility of equating the word _Volk_ in its name with 'radical-socialist working-class'. Of course it grew out of the aim of opening up the arts,

in the first instance the theatre, to the workers, and today it still
regards it as its principle task to free the way for the proletariat
to the good things of art. But the membership of the Volksbühne
in Berlin does not consist exclusively of proletarians, and still
less in the country as a whole, and if we wanted to narrow the
conception of the Volk entitled to an opinion and worthy of help, to
radical-socialist convictions, that would be equivalent to blowing
up the Volksbühne. [40]

It was into this explosive situation that Piscator deliberately
injected his production of Elm Welk's play Gewitter über Gottland.
He represents the play as a 'concession' by the executive to the left,
a compromise. Herbert Ihering saw it in similar terms, but Piscator
must have known better. He himself suggested the play, and says that
the executive accepted it because the action took place in the year 1400,
'and so even in my production must still be safe from too dangerous a
contemporary significance. The executive had only overlooked one
trifle, one sentence. It was on the title-page and said: 'The drama
does not only take place in 1400'. [41] From that one sentence
Piscator developed the contemporaneity of the theme in a way which
could not have been foreseen and was in fact nakedly party-political.

The actual story of the play concerns the struggle between the
great trading Hansestadt Hamburg and the Vitalian Federation, a com-
munistic group established on the Island of Gottland. Störtebeker, a
'kind of maritime officer of the Baltic provinces' (Ihering) is taken into
the service of the leaders of the Vitalians, Michelsen and Asmus
Ahlrichs; but his outstanding success in the war at sea makes him
independent of them. His revolutionary ideas are primitive and he is
personally ambitious. Piscator himself calls him an emotional revolutionary and says that today (1929) he would be a Nazi. He wants to
be king, but is eventually handed over to the Hamburgers by Asmus,
fanatic of the communist idea. Welk certainly intended his audience
to infer the more general, and particularly the contemporary political
implications of the play, but Piscator was not content with this. His
sympathetic critic Ihering has given an account of the production:

It begins by illustrating on film the political and religious power
relationships and the social structure of the Middle Ages. An
historical sketch.... The characters of the play, Störtebeker and
Asmus among them, make their impact on the audience in the film,
and by stages change their clothing until Asmus has become
Lenin.... Finally, the play begins.... [42]

The result as described in Der Tag was:

There was really absolutely no more question of Art this evening.
Politics had devoured it, skin, hair and all. We had unsuspectingly

> come into a communist election and propaganda meeting, we stood
> in the midst of the jubilation of a Lenin Celebration. At the end
> the Soviet star rose shining over the stage. [43]

Small wonder that the leaders of the Volksbühne, themselves social
democrats, could not let the matter rest there, specially as Der Tag
wrote challengingly:

> The leaders of the Volksbühne emphasise again and again that their
> exertions are purely artistic, beyond and above all politics. So
> how can they permit this performance? [44]

In reply the executive issued this statement:

> The Executive Committee of the Volksbühne e. V. sees in the nature
> of the production a misuse of the freedom which the Committee
> extend to the persons entrusted with the artistic leadership of the
> house of the Volksbühne. Elm Welk's play, whose acceptance was
> the result not of a certain political aim in it, but of its poetic
> merits — of course with a full appreciation of the inner relationship
> of its material to problems of the present day — received in Erwin
> Piscator's production (whose artistic significance is recognised)
> a tendencious, political reshaping and extension, for which no sort
> of inner necessity existed. The Executive Committee of the Volks-
> bühne E. V. confirms expressly that the use of the play as one-sided
> political propaganda took place without its knowledge and consent,
> and that this kind of production is in contradiction with the funda-
> mental political neutrality of the Volksbühne, which it is in duty
> bound to protect. It has already taken steps to guarantee the
> essential validity of its interpretation of the task of the Volksbühne.
> [45]

The steps taken were to cut out parts of the films.

In the 'Storm over the Volksbühne' (Piscator's phrase) which now
broke out in full force, the issues involved are tangled and confused.
On the artistic merits of the production (to which the Volksbühne
executive paid tactful tribute in its statement) the critics were at odds,
but even Herbert Ihering thought the play monotonous and wished that
Piscator had devoted his talents to one more worthy — even another by
the same author. So the executive stood on weak ground in asserting
that the play had been chosen for its poetic merits. So too, was it on
weak ground in maintaining that 'no sort of inner necessity existed'
for the political reshaping of the play, and Elm Welk himself eventually
found it necessary to issue his own open letter to the Volksbühne
executive, saying that as far as the author's intention was concerned,
Piscator was not abusing or distorting his original. But even Ihering

wrote with reservations about Piscator's actual success in carrying out his experiments. Paul Fechter, a critic less sympathetic to Piscator's political aims, says that it was shocking. The boredom made him sorry for everyone — the author, director, audience — and himself. The production was mere repetition of earlier Piscator. The Volksbühne was 'gambling with its own existence, with this foolish trickery'. There were a couple of good visual scenes from Traugott Müller, but that wasn't enough for four hours, 'especially when the rest of the scenic machinery continually creaks and gets stuck, and won't work properly....' [46] He accuses the actors of shouting.

> The applause, which likewise seemed to be well produced, was loud. It was, so to speak a failure got up as a success. Piscator and his colleagues were recalled again and again. But I must confess: wild horses wouldn't drag me to another production of that sort. [47]

And Welk, though he accepted the political interpretation and general adaptation, objected strongly to the 'ruin and bungling of the text'. He said that George as Störtebeker, for whole scenes didn't speak a single word of the manuscript, but 'twaddle, trash and nonsense'. It was the artistic success of the undertaking, not Piscator's political slant, that Welk criticised.

It is surely clear that the artistic success and validity of Piscator's production of Gewitter über Gottland is, at the least, open to great doubt. [48] It is the political intention that his supporters welcome and praise. It seems extraordinary that commentators still blame the executive of the Volksbühne for resisting the attempt to make the association merely a communist platform. Naturally Piscator was supported by his principals and small part actors — any theatrical director of even mediocre ability generates in his company a personal loyalty that will always support him against 'the management'; how much more a director of Piscator's originality and personality! Naturally he was supported an impressive list of writers, and artists, not only of the left, but of liberal persuasion: the sense that 'faceless men' are interfering with artistic freedom always, and healthily, arouses such a reaction.

The supporters on the left called a great public meeting in the Festival Hall of the former Prussian House of Lords (Herrenhaus) (30 March 1927). Arthur Holitscher took the chair, Erwin Kalser spoke for the actors, Victor Blum for the 'supers'; Toller spoke, Jessner, Karl-Heinz Martin, and Piscator himself. It was the end of Piscator's work as a Volksbühne director for over thirty years, but the beginning of a new and fruitful relationship, for in spite of Ihering's rather shrill cries for no compromise the final solution was a compromise, and a valuable one: through the Youth Sections.

The pioneer of the Youth Volksbühne in Berlin was Wilhelm Spohr. Spohr saw performances for children and young people as an influence against 'dirt and trash'. He supported the movement away from 'intellectualism' in education, welcoming such teaching methods as play-readings in class. Writing in 1923 he said that he had first seen <u>Wilhelm Tell</u> before an audience of schoolchildren, twenty-five years earlier: 'Poet and performers could wish for no more ideal audience.' His proposals for a Youth Volksbühne were taken up by the Berlin Volksbühne in 1920. For the first year children were reached only through Volksbühne members, but this provided a basis. In the second year the attempt was made to get children committed to a <u>series</u> of performances. In the third year some schools and organisations were invited to participate. The performances were all on Saturday afternoons, and personal tickets were exchanged for theatre tickets by the traditional method of lottery. The scheme of linking the Youth Volksbühne to the parent body was not wholly successful and the number of school children grew more and more in proportion to those in youth organisations. In 1927 the Berlin Volksbühne gave up these school-children's performances to the City of Berlin, and Wilhelm Spohr became Manager of Municipal Children's Plays.

Meanwhile, in 1923, new sections were created <u>inside</u> the Berlin Volksbühne for young people not at school — through youth organisations. The sections attended evening performances, and their costs and rights were identical with those of other sections. The core of these sections consisted of young working-class people, recruited through leaflets circulated in youth organisations. The appeal made in the leaflets was a serious one:

> The theatre is of the greatest significance for the continued development of human society. It receives its stimulus — as does art in general — from the tensions and life forces of the time, and if its organism is healthy and its audience ready, it must give the essence of the time artistic form.... The Volksbühne, founded from the working class, wishes to keep the theatre open to the great mass of working people who suffer most profoundly under the needs of the time.... [49]

These sections began with a membership of about a thousand, which more than doubled in a year and by the time of the Piscator 'case' had some four thousand members. They were, as might naturally be expected, the principal supporters of Piscator.

Well before <u>Gewitter</u> Piscator had felt the need for his own theatre, where he could pursue his own ideas unfettered, and in the summer of 1926, the scheme was theoretically worked out. The money needed to found the theatre and to give him at least one season in which he could feel independent of the critics he obtained from the actress Tilla Durieux

who had approached him after Die Räuber with the idea of a close
business relationship. She put up 400,000 Marks. [50] Piscator
really wanted a 'purpose-built' theatre to express his conceptions, and
it was at this time that he and Bauhaus architect Walter Gropius worked
out the famous, but 'never realised, designs for the total theatre' —
forerunner of many modern flexible theatres. Instead of this he had to
be content with the Theater am Nollendorfplatz, with only 1,100 seats,
in which Piscator, for his costly productions, required 3,000 to 3,500
Marks per performance. He therefore had to charge what he himself
admitted were the 'Kurfürstendamm prices of the Communist theatre'.
Many social democrats were sceptical and feared the influence of the
KPD (Communist Party). Piscator himself said that the Piscator-
Bühne, as the new venture was called, was not party-political but stood
nearest in outlook and politics to the KPD. Pravda thought the Piscator-
Bühne petit-bourgeois rather than proletarian, but said it saw Piscator's
problems and supported him.

The Youth Sections of the Volksbühne with the support of other
members who favoured Piscator now formed themselves into the Special
Sections whose aim was to support the new Piscator-Bühne without
breaking with the Volksbühne. A leaflet was issued: 'What do the
Special Sections want of the Volksbühne e.V.?' This leaflet reaffirmed
loyalty to the Volksbühne and said that these sections wished to go to the
Volksbühne productions but also to ones that did not avoid taking sides
or serving as political propaganda. The Special Sections put the
Piscator-Bühne in the foreground of their programme. Members were
to see three or four productions at the Volksbühne itself, up to two in
the Theater am Schiffbauerdamm or Thalia, and five at the Piscator-
Bühne. The subscription was to be identical with that of the other
sections, 1.50 Marks per performance.

> The largely autonomous leadership of these Special Sections ...
> came more and more under the dictatorship of extremist forces
> which drew their ideological weapons from the armoury of the
> Communist Party and their directives from some very revolution-
> arily disposed men of letters. The activity of these circles was
> clearly directed at winning the Volksbühne for the Communist
> Party. Representatives of left-wing youth organisations of demo-
> cratic origin ... were forced out of the working committee. [51]

The Volksbühne recognised the Special Sections, which grew very
rapidly. By the time the Piscator-Bühne opened they had sixteen
thousand members, mostly young. They took up two to three hundred
seats a performance at the new theatre, a great help, but not enough to
enable Piscator to avoid the easy sneers in left-wing periodicals at the
'bejewelled and frock-coated' audience in his theatre. The compromise
(pace Ihering) solved the problem on both sides. No doubt the Special

Sections were 'the safety-valve for the bolshevik tendencies in the
Volksbühne', [52] but the valve worked.

The productions of the Piscator-Bühne, Toller's Hoppla, wir leben!
(Hurrah, We Live!), Rasputin (with the 'globe stage'), [53], Schweik
(with the conveyor-belt stage), have been fully described by Piscator
and others. They were as artistically adventurous as financially disastrous. Some reminiscences of Gerda Redlich, who played a small
part in Hoppla, wir leben! as a girl of eighteen, may help, however,
to make the image of Piscator more vivid and personal: [54]

> I remember a terrible row between Toller and Piscator. Piscator
> being extremely quiet and cold — and Toller was a man suffering
> from consumption, a terribly excitable man — these two men
> absolutely standing there glaring at each other. We thought they
> would be fighting any moment, but it didn't come to that! But I
> cannot tell you what it was about. Toller didn't want all that
> technical to-do; he wanted everything very much simpler; that's
> what it was all about fundamentally. Piscator wouldn't give an
> inch to anyone.
> He had no time for any human touch or any human weakness,
> or anything like that. It was a bit like a parade ground, like drill,
> for the small-time actors. Quite different I am sure for Alexander
> Granach, etc. They would not have taken that. A very hard man
> on the surface ... oh ... he was obsessed. There was no human
> feeling at all. I don't every remember him saying a human word
> or cracking a joke. I suppose he was tense.

The Piscator affair was, of course, not the whole story of the
Berlin Volksbühne during these years. Various changes naturally
occurred in the theatres used by the association. A particular enthusiasm of Nestriepke's was the promotion of the 'new' dancing. Matinées
in the Bülowplatz theatre brought in as guest artists such dancers as
Mary Wigman, Gret Palucca and Harald Kreutzberg. There was also
much musical activity, and right through the twenties until 1933 a performance of Beethoven's Ninth Symphony was always given on New
Year's Eve in the Bülowplatz theatre. Until 1924 the Volksbühne also
worked in conjunction with A. Florath's Sprechchor (Choral speaking
group). Then, through Holl's enthusiasm, the Volksbühne established
its own, which was very active for the next five years.

The Volksbühne, already weakened by the internal dissensions and
external criticisms (even from the right-wing press) arising from the
Piscator affair, suffered a further set-back and more adverse publicity when Holl resigned his post at the end of the 1927-28 season.
Above all, the economic position of the whole enterprise was pre-
carious, and the first aim had to be to liquidate a deficit and set things

on a firm financial basis. Instead, therefore, of a new artistic director being appointed the whole leadership was placed in the hands of Heinrich Neft, who had now been for many years the administrative director. Neft directed in the 1928-29 season an unexceptionable programme, including three notable plays by younger writers: Weisenborn's U-Boot S.4, Horvath's Bergbahn (Mountain Railway) and Elm Welk's Kreuz-abnahme (Descent from the Cross) — the very play which Herbert Ihering had suggested as more worthy of Piscator's attentions than Gewitter über Gottland. Nevertheless the murderous attacks in the press continued.

As a further attempt to silence the criticisms, the committee appointed at the beginning of the 1929-30 season the brilliant young director Karl-Heinz Martin. He was known as an already experienced theatre director, sound on economics, strong in technicalities and organisation, and one of the most able of the great regisseurs. His leadership had distinction and character and the first season included an impressive opening production of Büchner's Dantons Tod, Frank Wedekind's Frühlings Erwachen and a memorable world première of Rehfisch and Herzog's Dreyfus Affair. But the attacks from the press, especially on the extreme left, continued. Karl-Heinz Martin held the post until 1932; his successor until 1934 was Heinz Hilpert.

On 21 September 1930 Gerhart Hauptmann delivered a speech in honour of the Volksbühne's fortieth year of existence. It was a weighty and moving speech — 'The Volksbühne was young, when I too was young. Many close friends of mine were among its founders' — which concluded by calling upon the Volksbühne to keep its true spirit alive in opposition to all 'fanatical, dogmatic, phenomena of our time'. [55] It is sad to remember that the speaker would later fly the swastika at his home. That swastika was already a strong force in Germany, and when the Nazis came to power in 1933 one of their victims was the Volksbühne. In Berlin, and throughout Germany, party members were forced upon the committees. Many prominent leaders of the movement, including Nestriepke, resigned. For six years the Volksbühne, 'a complete caricature of the former democratic Volksbühne organisation', [56] continued a nominal existence. In 1939 it was dissolved and the Theater am Bülowplatz declared State property.

SECOND INTERMISSION

The Nazis 'Night over Germany'

By 1930 the Volksbühne was a nationwide movement with a membership of half a million in over three hundred local societies: it was 'the greatest cultural organisation in Germany'. Like the inflation of 1923, the economic crisis of 1931-32 gave it, at least in some cities, a temporary illusion of even greater strength. Theatres which had closed their doors to Volksbühne bookings now welcomed them to fill their emptying seats. But the economic crisis also provided the last push needed to bring the National Socialists into power. Rudolf Ross, since 1928 Bürgermeister of Hamburg, warned the members of Hamburg Volksbühne in October 1932 that the forces of reaction were on the march:

> Just as the nation's impulses of feeling and will were stifled before the development of the Storm and Stress period at the time of Goethe and Schiller, a growing reaction might also now subjugate everything of potential greatness in dramatic art to an intellectual and spiritual autarky. That could mean a reverse from which we might not recover again for generations. [1]

That was October 1932. At noon on 30 January 1933, President Hindenburg entrusted the chancellorship to Adolf Hitler, and on 5 March the Nazis won the elections with 288 seats. Almost at once the policy of political co-ordination (Gleichschaltung) was applied to the arts as well as to all other aspects of German life. A single theatre audience organisation, The German Stage (Deutsche Bühne) was created, of which all existing organisations must become part.

Volksbühne leaders saw all too clearly what was coming and attempted to rouse the membership to some degree of resistance. For example the executive of the Hamburg Volksbühne issued an appeal to its members in April 1933:

While the Volksbühne has existed, its business has been to open
the German Theatre to <u>all</u> our fellow-countrymen — especially the
less well-off working population — who desire the arts, <u>without</u>
<u>regard for the party or beliefs</u> of the individual member ... We
work ... in the spirit of the <u>key sentences of the Jena Volksbühne</u>
<u>Policy Statement</u>: 'The Volksbühne ... <u>rejects every subordination</u>
<u>to political or sectarian points of view, of its struggle towards</u>
<u>expression in artistic form.</u>'
We have never been subject to a party, and we wish also in
future to serve only art, especially <u>German</u> art, <u>free from all</u>
<u>party ties</u>. [2]

Within a few weeks of this brave declaration the Hamburg Volksbühne
(like all others) was absorbed by the Deutsche Bühne, which took over
the administration and assets. Members attempted some resistance,
as this passage from a report from the delegates of the Deutsche Bühne
on a members' meeting on 18 May 1933 shows:

... To the question asked from the floor of the meeting, on what
grounds the political co-ordination had taken place, Herr Pohlmann
answered by referring to the fact that the only theatre audience
organisation recognised on the government side was the Deutsche
Bühne. Therefore the transfer of the Volksbühne to the Deutsche
Bühne was necessary. The meeting took an extraordinarily rowdy
course, stirred up by provocateurs, so that objective agreement
was impossible. The chairman repeatedly threatened to close the
the meeting if order was not restored. When, in spite of this,
objective discussion became impossible, Herr Pohlmann closed
the meeting. [3]

What happened in Hamburg typifies what happened all over Germany
and, of course, not only to the Volksbühne but to its Christian counter-
part, the Bühnenvolksbund. Nor were the Nazis content with destroying
the present, and, as they believed, the future existence of the Volksbühne movement; they sought also to annihilate its past by consigning
its records, in the manner of the men of <u>1984</u>, to the Memory Hole —
they destroyed, in fact, the archives of the Federation and of most of
the Volksbühne societies. [4]

In Berlin the effect of the economic crisis had been more serious
in its effects on the movement, because here the Volksbühne itself was
involved in the management of a great theatre. Even from 1924 houses
had suffered badly because of unemployment, and when after the crash
of 1929 the number of unemployed rose to six million the theatre's
deficit became really serious. Measures were taken to rationalise the
business and reduce the deficit, and Nestriepke believed that eventually
the theatre on the Bülowplatz would have overcome its own economic
crisis.

When the Nazis came to power the Volksbühne leadership in Berlin was evidently divided between those who would admit compromise with them and those who would not, and when the association expressed its position on 11 May 1933 in terms of compromise, Nestriepke resigned, leaving Curt Baake, as chairman, in control. Under pressure from the legal adviser Rudolf Pahl, Baake called a general meeting on 19 December 1933, without preliminary members' meetings or the election of delegates. Opening the meeting, he said,

> We believed we must dispense with convening members' meetings and with new elections of delegates. The principle of strict, responsible leadership has everywhere taken the place of the electoral system. That must apply to us too. [5]

Although the Federation of Volksbühne Societies had been subsumed under the Deutsche Bühne, the Berlin Volksbühne, because it owned a theatre, was allowed to retain a nominal independence. Low membership and financial difficulties, however, compelled the Volksbühne leadership to play even further into the Nazis' hands if the association was to avoid dissolution — a course that many would have thought more honourable. In the season 1933-34 the membership was down to nineteen thousand, while forty thousand was the minimum needed for economic viability, and of the required income of 700,000 RM there was a shortfall of at least 400,000 RM.

The Volksbühne leadership went to the Ministry of Popular Enlightenment and Propaganda, negotiated with Laubinger, leader of the new National Chamber of Theatre, [6] and Schlösser, National Dramaturge, and got a subvention of 440,000 RM. As the association was now in effect directly financed by the Nazi government, Goebbels' ministry could hope soon to replace its leadership with ministry nominees. During 1934 and 1935 the constitution was changed so that the chairman now nominated the executive and other important officers. In August 1935 the executive dissolved itself and invited a Nazi cultural official (Reichskulturamtsleiter), Moraller, from the National Chamber of Culture, to be leader of the association (Vereinsführer). He took up his post in September 1935 and formed a Nazi executive. Curt Baake received a letter of thanks from Moraller for his past contribution to the Volksbühne, and a pension of 300 RM. [7]

In the season 1935-36 the Volksbühne theatres (on the Bülowplatz and Nollendorfplatz) had a deficit of over 1,400,000 RM. This was covered by government subsidy, and theatre seats were filled with Sturm Abteilung men, soldiers, police, schools and military police. Graf Solms, the theatre director, was replaced by Eugen Klöpfer, and the constitution was again revised so that he became in practice head of the whole Volksbühne organisation in Berlin. Only two more steps were needed to complete the Nazi victory. In 1937 the old executive, who were still legal owners of the Theatre on the Bülowplatz, were induced or compelled to make over to the State the theatre and the land on which it stood. A year later (May 1938) the theatre firm was wound up. The Volksbühne as an audience organisation still existed. In October, Moraller's hand-picked executive again chose him as leader, and on 1 March 1939 the Berlin Volksbühne was wound up.

After his resignation in 1933, Nestriepke became a freelance writer until his exclusion from the National Chamber of Literature. After a long period of unemployment he became, in 1935, Secretary to the Board of Directors of Fritz Staar's cinema business in Berlin and Potsdam. Later he became deputy manager of the business. 'And it is only natural,' he wrote in 1956, 'that with my hope for a speedy collapse of the Nazi regime I also always united the other — that a new Volksbühne would carry on the work of the organisation which had been destroyed.' [8]

The Volksbühne theatre on the Bülowplatz was severely damaged in an air-raid in 1943. Its ruins remained as a symbol both of past achievement and of future hopes.

ACT III

The Volksbühne
since 1945
and outside Berlin

1 IN BERLIN

i New beginnings. The Volksbühne re-founded

At the end of the war the German theatrical scene was one empty waste;
nearly all theatre buildings had been destroyed, the companies were
scattered and many leading figures had emigrated. The ruined theatres
stood amid ruined cities, Berlin among them. Yet in cities without
traffic, window-panes or domestic services the Germans gave theatre,
music and the arts priority over many other pressing claims on scarce
resources. Carl Ebert, who toured Germany on behalf of the Allied
Control Commission, found there a burning thirst for culture—
hundreds of people standing for two and a half hours on a cold winter
Sunday afternoon in the shell-damaged auditorium of Frankfurt University to listen to Bach's Art of Fugue; others trembling with cold in
the ruined stock-exchange to hear a piano recital, when the only available electric heater was needed to save the pianist's fingers from
stiffening. Friedrich Luft has written an unforgettable account of
crossing Berlin for the opening of the Deutsches Theater. He crossed
a canal hand-over-hand on the remains of two pipes, was nearly
beaten up by looters, was rowed across the Spree in a leaking boat,
and on the way home was waylaid by thieves, robbed and knocked
unconscious.

> I didn't get home that night. I slept in the Zoo. It was next day
> before my family saw me again and they had already almost written
> me off and imagined me perhaps on the way to Siberia. Theatre-
> going was dangerous. [1]

In the context of such national enthusiasm for theatre and the arts the veterans of the pre-1933 Volksbühne associations all over Germany found fruitful ground for re-establishing the movement, and even before the end of 1945 the Volksbühne was being reborn throughout the country. Once more we shall centre the story in Berlin, for although this city's situation was unique, the special problems there serve to highlight those of an occupied and politically sundered country.

On 2 May 1945 the Russians entered Berlin. Less than three weeks later (20 May) Siegfried Nestriepke sent a memorandum to the Municipal Council, 'The reorganisation of the Berlin system of theatres', in which, among other things, he proposed a Volksbühne type of organisation. Bruno Henschel, an old Volksbühne colleague of Nestriepke's and later head of the East Berlin publishing house of Henschel, showed the memorandum to the Soviet Central Command. [2] Two days later a car with two Russian officers called at Nestriepke's flat to take him and Henschel to meet the City Commandant, Colonel-General Bersarin, to discuss the memorandum. Unfortunately Nestriepke was not at home and could not be found: the Russian officers had to return without carrying out their mission. So the next day Henschel and Nestriepke walked (they had no car and of course there was no public transport) from Wilmersdorf to Friedrichsfelde, but no one at the Soviet headquarters had even heard of the memorandum, and the two men had to return wearily home. On 2 June Nestriepke sent a letter to Bersarin: there was no reply. 'I mention this <u>Intermezzo</u>', comments Nestriepke, 'only as an indication of the way the Soviet Central Command functioned at that time.'

After four weeks' delay Nestriepke was invited to exchange views with Otto Winzer, Communist <u>Stadtrat</u> (city councillor — but in effect Minister) for education. Winzer wanted to see a revival of the Volksbühne, and a small commission was formed to which Nestriepke presented a detailed memorandum; but it all came to nothing, in spite of Winzer's support, because the occupation authorities were opposed to the formation of another mass organisation. Resigning himself to indefinite delay, Nestriepke took on responsibility for theatre within the Central Administration for Education and worked with Boleslaw Barlog for the reopening of the Schlosspark Theater. He also aroused the interest of the leadership of the Kulturbund (Kulturbund für die demokratische Erneuerung Deutschlands) through whom he was to give two broadcasts on Berlin Radio advocating his ideas, but at the last minute (in January 1946) these were forbidden by the Soviet censor.

This was the beginning of Nestriepke's protracted struggle with the Soviet authorities and with German Communists. His next opponent was the Independent German Trades Union Federation (FDGB) which thought a Volksbühne unnecessary, as tickets could be distributed through trade unions. Another important rival was Karl-Heinz Martin, one-time director of the Bülowplatz theatre. Karl-Heinz Martin was not a party Communist, and he enjoyed the support both of the Russians and of the Americans. He opened the former Prater Theater in north Berlin under the name Volksbühne, 'as a contribution to the Volksbühne idea', as he expressed it. Nestriepke wrote that the Volksbühne was essentially based on an audience organisation, though a theatre might follow. His comment was probably never published.

Meanwhile Volksbühne developments were taking place both in East and West Germany, though those in the West, notably at Hamburg and Hannover, were not reported in the Berlin press. In the Soviet Zone, in spite of the official opinion of Tribüne, the organ of the Communist-dominated FDGB, a number of Volksbühne associations were founded in the second half of 1946. In most of these individual membership (as advocated by Nestriepke) was possible, but corporate membership (of trade unions, etc.) was the norm. The associations were usually founded jointly by the trade unions and the Kulturbund. They did actually get people into the theatres and even reached the stage of forming Land Federations: a Land Federation for Sachsen-Anhalt was founded on 1 August 1946. These Soviet Zone Volksbühne associations were not politically independent, however, and acted as organs for the SED (Sozialistische Einheitspartei Deutschlands), effectively the Communist Party.

Frustrated in direct achievement of their aims, Nestriepke and his friends now diverted all their energies into politics. New elections for the City Parliament were imminent, and in fact in October 1946 the Social Democratic Party (SPD) defeated the SED. This appeared to open the way for founding a Volksbühne on traditional lines. At the same time Nestriepke's Volksbühne colleagues proposed him as Stadt-rat für Volksbildung (Berlin Minister of Education) and he was appointed to this important and influential post. Within a few weeks he had worked out the sketch for a new organisation, shown it to a circle of friends and written invitations to appropriate bodies to form a very broadly based founding committee, which was to include trade unions and the SED as well as other organisations and parties. The invitations were ready for posting when the Communists took action. Evidently they had wind of Nestriepke's plans and wished to forestall them. Nestriepke himself, knowing that his predecessor, Otto Winzer, had ensured that most employees in the education department were reliable party members, believed that his desk drawers had been rifled in his absence. The newspaper Tägliche Rundschau, the official organ of Russian policy, published a 'Call for the founding of a Volksbühne' in Berlin over thirty influential signatures including those of Barlog and Karl-Heinz Martin. Many of the signatories were non-Communists who probably did not appreciate the implications of their action. The 'Call'

in itself was one to which any former supporter of the Volksbühne
might have subscribed, and ended with the hope of making real the
slogan carved over the doors of the old Volksbühne theatre: Art for the
People. Nestriepke has pointed out the irony of the fact that when the
Communist Administration actually undertook the restoration of the
Bülowplatz theatre, this inscription was deliberately chiselled off!

Nestriepke promptly posted off his own invitations and wrote to the
papers himself, as if the call of the thirty signatories were support
for his own plans. His founding committee met on 20 December 1946.
The rival scheme led to no more than a meeting of trade union officials
who put forward the idea of a People's Cultural Circle. This scheme
was published on the same day as the second meeting of Nestriepke's
committee, but the FDGB representatives, Fugger and Baum (Communists) and Pickert (SPD) made no reference to it. This was on 8
January 1947. On the founding committee compromises between the
various views seemed possible; but Fugger and his supporters
apparently went straight to the Soviet authority who then cut the ground
from under Nestriepke's feet by publishing in all Berlin newspapers
(15 January 1947) the fact that a licence to re-form the Volksbühne
and rebuild its theatre had been issued to Karl-Heinz Martin, Heinz W.
Litten and Alfred Lindemann. Of these only Martin had played any
important part in the pre-Nazi Volksbühne. Nestriepke, who was
informed of the licence by word of mouth <u>after</u> the press release,
strongly attacked the Soviet move in an anonymous article in the <u>Sozial-
demokrat</u> and in an 'Interview' (he wrote it himself!) in the <u>Telegraf</u>.

A period of complex negotiations and in-fighting followed which
involved the three licensees (themselves often not in agreement), the
FDGB, represented by Fugger, and the Soviet authorities, represented
by Major Dymschitz, the influential and devious head of the Cultural
Department. In the midst of this the situation was again modified, and
the attitude of Lindemann, spokesman of the Licensees, considerably
softened, by the formation of a Committee of Allied Theatre Officers:
the officials of the western powers had been kept informed of events
by Nestriepke and warned of the danger of Communist domination. By
the end of February a draft constitution for the new association had
been agreed. The committee was to consist of two representatives of
the city administration, two of the Youth Department, four of the FDGB,
two of Trade Union 17 (which included theatre workers), the three
licensees, and representatives of the four political parties in proportion
to their strength in the city assembly. A letter, over the signatures of
the licensees was sent to the Committee of Allied Theatre Officers;
Paul Eggers (chairman of Breslau Volksbühne before 1933) was proposed as general manager, and the names of the proposed appointees
were collected. An attempt by the Soviet authorities to exclude Nestriepke and Fritz Barthelmann was unsuccessful.

The reply from the cultural committee of the Allies came at the very end of March: the whole proposed committee structure was rejected, as it was claimed that the political parties would have too much power. Instead, the Allied Theatre Officers were to nominate all the committee, which was to consist of four representatives of each section of Berlin, plus the three licensees. Nestriepke, who thought it 'grotesque' that the committee for so utterly German an organisation should be nominated by the occupying powers, was nevertheless relieved that the Communists would be in a permanent minority.

A long delay followed, with no list of nominations from the Allies. Lindemann and his two colleagues were already impatient, and even at the beginning of March had announced that a production by Karl-Heinz Martin of Hauptmann's Die Weber in the Kastanienallee theatre would be the opening Volksbühne production. The première was on 24 April. There was still no Volksbühne. Lindemann made a speech regretting the delay and threatening to go ahead without the committee. This so provoked Nestriepke that he decided to use a very dirty weapon against Lindemann. He had uncovered a black spot in Lindemann's past, and he wrote an article in the Telegraf in early May asking whether, as Siegfried Nestriepke and Fritz Barthelmann were apparently not good enough for the Soviet military administration they realised that one of their own representatives (he didn't give the name, but knew it would be easy to guess!) had a criminal record. Even though the Allied Command then opened an investigation, Nestriepke's trick partly misfired, and Lindemann was retained when the constitution of the committee was announced. He later held various offices in the Eastern-sector Volksbühne. On 22 May the list of names for the committee was received from the allies. There were twenty names, four from each sector, the three licensees and Nestriepke ex officio. While it included on the Russian nomination Fugger and Herbert Ihering, the Western nominations included such figures as Professor Dr Joachim Tiburtius, Erich Otto and Hilde Körber. Tiburtius and Hilde Körbe, with Dr Karl Forster, were Christian Democrats, and six of the others, including Nestriepke, Social Democrats. Understandably the list did not please the Communists. Fugger told the press the committee was abortive and lacked popular and youth support. 'But', says Nestriepke, 'the Allied Command had spoken.' It had taken a full two years to achieve, but the Berlin Volksbühne could at last be re-established. The new committee met first on 18 June 1947 (Nestriepke not being present) and before it met again Nestriepke's own position was changed.

Since the SPD had gained control in the October 1946 elections the Russians had made great use of the device of 'investigating' elected officials, apparently in order to disrupt the administrative machinery.

Active in this was Major-General Kotikov, former adviser to Colonel
General Kuznetsov, and very clever at conference techniques. As we
have seen, the Education Department had been thoroughly filled with
Communists, and now they held every key position in education except
that of Head of Education, Nestriepke's post. Kotikov therefore wanted
to get rid of Nestriepke and replace him with Wildangel, the deputy
head, a reliable Communist. At this time Nestriepke was only one of
about a dozen elected officials whom Kotikov had under attack, and at
this stage he would probably have been content if the responsible
American officer, Brigadier General Frank Howley (United States
Army) had been prepared to reprimand him for alleged violation of
Kommandatura orders. This Howley was not prepared to do, as it
was simply not true, though Howley himself evidently underestimated
Nestriepke's calibre, for he says of him: 'he was not a particularly
smart politician and was in fact a good example of the absent-minded
professor....' [3] Into this situation— indeed, when Kotikov was about
ready to drop the Nestriepke issue— came a new and brash American
general who thought he knew better than his colleagues. At his first
Kommandatura meeting, ignoring the briefing his colleagues had given
him, he played into Kotikov's hands.

> 'I'm used to the Germans,' he blustered, 'I know them from the
> last war. They'll twist us and take advantage of us whenever they
> can. I propose we remove this man from office!'
>   If a thunderbolt had landed on the conference table, the effect
> could not have been more devastating. That an American official
> should recommend removal of an elected official, without trial,
> stunned me [i.e. Frank Howley].
>   When I was able to speak, I leaned over and whispered to the
> Commandant,
>   'My God, General, now we're really in hot water ... the whole
> educational system of Berlin now goes into the hands of the Com-
> munists.' [4]

News of the blunder spread, American journalists demanded a press
conference and the new commandant was 'sacrificed to the press'. [5]
But Howley's fear that Wildangel would be appointed to replace Nestriepke was not fulfilled, and in fact his elected successor, Walter
May, proved himself a friend and ally of Nestriepke and his aims.
As for Nestriepke himself, he was not sorry to be relieved of his public office, as he now had more time and energy to devote to the Volksbühne.

For two months the new four-sector committee struggled for
progress, while Lindemann pursued plans of his own, and on 19 August
the press announced that Lindemann and Litten were to found a Volksbühne for the Soviet Sector only. (Karl-Heinz Martin was not involved:

he was asked by the Americans to become Intendant of the Hebbel-
Theater, where he remained until his death in December 1947.) No
legal action against Lindemann was possible, and there was relief that
the work in the three Western sectors could now proceed unhindered.
Berlin was at that time undivided, and Nestriepke has described the
split in the Volksbühne committee as a symbol of what was to come.
A new committee was formed by co-opting new members to the rump of
the old, but because there was no precedent for treating with the three
western Occupying Powers as a group, three separate, but virtually
identical, Volksbühne associations had to be formed, one for each
sector, with arrangements for some kind of co-ordinating committee
for practical purposes. Moreover, the name Volksbühne having been
pre-empted by Lindemann, the Western groups reverted to the original
title of 1890, Freie Volksbühne (now commonly known by its initials,
FVB). For financial aid sympathetic newspapers were approached and
25,000 Marks raised.

Paul Eggers, the proposed manager, had gone to work for Lindemann, perhaps not so much from conviction as through his daughter's
influence and because he was anxious to work without further delay.
He did valuable work for a year and a half in the Eastern-sector Volksbühne but was always suspect to the party, and was later given the job
of 'overseeing' the rebuilding of the Volksbühne theatre, but with no
power. In his place the FVB appointed Bruno Braunsdorf, a learned
printer who had left his business and had been in the English military
administration. His assistant, Hubert Geilgens, had ten years' experience in the Berlin Volksbühne. An office (which was used till 1953)
was found in Wilmersdorf, and by mid-October over a hundred ticket-
agencies were established. State subsidy was essential and Walter May
put through the necessary recommendations. At first only seats in
municipal theatres were to be subsidised, but shortly afterwards
private theatres were included. Although theoretically the city was still
undivided, the Western groups of Volksbühne associations were refused
the use of municipal theatres in the Soviet Sector. Membership, of
course, would be drawn from the whole city. Because the Western
municipal theatres were in a strong economic position it was not easy
to negotiate for seats in them, while on the other hand not all the private
theatres were thought to be artistically adequate. The search for a
Volksbühne's own theatre continued — even a transportable aluminium
theatre was investigated at Hannover, but found unsuitable.

The opening public meeting was held on 12 October 1947 in the
Titania-Palast, Steglitz, with Carl Zuckmayer as principal speaker.
Julius Bab sent a message and the press response was good — though
ironical in the East. Five days later Walter May made an unsuccessful
attempt to bring East and West together, but Lindemann would not

accept Nestriepke's presence and the meeting failed. Meanwhile,
Ordner were found — many of them veterans of pre-1933 days — a
periodical began to appear, several special events took place, and on
15 December 1947 the first 'regular' performance: Aida at the Municipal Opera. During that month the Soviet Theatre Officer made an
attempt to heal the split in the movement, but once more Nestriepke
himself was the stumbling block — the Russians would not accept a joint
committee while he remained. The Western group entered 1948 with
twenty-two thousand members which grew to thirty-five thousand soon
after the first annual general meeting on 23 February — at which members sat and voted in three sectoral groups, to satisfy the forms.

Although membership rose to fifty thousand by June, the first
season of the new association was a hard one. The monetary reform
of June meant that two currencies were circulating in Berlin and all
financial questions, especially those of subsidy, had to be discussed
in relation to these. On 24 July the USSR stopped road and rail traffic
between Berlin and the West and all the hardships of the blockade
began. Although tempered by the Berlin airlift this continued until
September 1949. The demand for seats rose in the early part of the
year and performances were seen in no fewer than ten different
theatres, while throughout the summer the Volksbühne was granted
the Rehberge open-air theatre rent-free on condition of putting on
worthwhile shows. Having failed to create a company of its own the
Volksbühne drew upon the theatres with which it already had contacts.
Twenty performances of opera and forty of plays were seen by some
seventy thousand people — though not always heard, as the theatre lies
near the Tegel airfield and the constant aircraft noise from the airlift
often made the dialogue inaudible. These open-air performances were
seen only as a makeshift and a whole series of ideas was mooted for a
Volksbühne theatre. Among these was the rebuilding of the Schiller-
Theater, which would have needed two and a half million Marks, as
well as virtually unobtainable building materials. At one point a 'somewhat shadowy personality' was given 80,000 Marks to bring timber from
East Berlin. He thereupon disappeared 'into the forests of the east'.
He never brought the wood, though some months later he repaid the
money. The Schiller-Theater remained in ruins.

The problems of the second working year (1948-49) were no less.
The blockade and airlift continued, with unemployment running at some
350,000. East-West tensions increased with demonstrations outside
the City Hall (which was in the East Sector) culminating in a mob attack
upon it on 6 September 1948. On 30 November a separate administration for East Berlin was set up, the city was divided and the Iron
Curtain came down. The two-currency problem persisted into the
spring of 1949. On the other hand the elections in the West, immediately after the city was split, gave the Social Democrats an absolute

majority. Walter May continued in charge of education and Ernst Reuter
became Chief Bürgermeister. The loss of its East Berlin income was
a serious blow to the organisation and had to be compensated for by
increased subsidy from the West. The railway strike in the early summer of 1949 also prevented people from going to the theatre and the
Freie Volksbühne had to pay for empty, unpaid-for seats. But for the
Freie Volksbühne, theatres would often have played to empty houses
at this time. Also, despite the Iron Curtain, the Freie Volksbühne
was an important link between East and West, for East Berliners came
West to its performances (there was no Berlin wall until 1961) and thus
Western culture went East. The authorities, thanks to Walter May's
sympathy, made several concessions to the Freie Volksbühne. All
seats, including those occupied by East Berliners, were to be subsidised
in West Marks and the 'closed' performances were to be ended, thus
relieving the Freie Volksbühne of the necessity of filling every seat.

During this season the continued search for a theatre of the Freie
Volksbühne's own met at last with success, and in January 1949 an
agreement was signed to take over the Theater am Kurfürstendamn
on 1 September in the same year.

ii The Volksbühne in the Soviet Zone

The original Volksbühne theatre lay in East Berlin on the Bülowplatz,
re-christened the Karl-Liebknecht-Platz, now the Luxemburgplatz.
Early in 1947 the licensees attempted to rebuild it with voluntary
Sunday labour, helped by a lottery — but neither the labour nor the
lottery materialised. Nor was there much help from the Russians.
But the clearing of the site began in April and May. The architect
Friedrich Demmer undertook plans: the third circle was to be done
away with, there was to be a new style of forestage, and two side
stages. But the scheme would have cost millions and months went by
without anything being done. In 1948 the Russian command cut through
the problem: the city was to provide the money and labour, and report
progress monthly. Ironically, in 1949, the Berlin Commission for
Claims on Property declared the Freie Volksbühne to be the legal
inheritor of the building, though this was only theoretical. Legally
this view was confirmed in 1954, the year in which the theatre reopened.

The restored building still had shortcomings in its sightlines and
acoustics, and was too large. In 1972 it was closed for half a year for
major alterations. These included the removal of the first cicle. The
stalls were then given a much steeper rake, thus bringing the theatre
rather nearer to the amphitheatre style that some had favoured even
when it was being designed before 1914. Although the 'cold magnifi-
cence' of the decor was not entirely done away with, the auditorium now

gave an impression of being smaller and sight lines and acoustics were improved. Externally, the Volksbühne on the Luxemburgplatz now looks simpler and plainer than it did when built. Apart from the erasure of the motto, Die Kunst dem Volke, the statuary over the entrances has gone, while the flat roofs of the wings of the facade give the building a feeling of great width at the expense of height.

In mid-May 1947 a congress of East Zone Volksbühne associations led to the founding of a Federation of German Volksbühnen. Invitations were in fact sent to the re-founded Western associations, but no delegates went. Several 'Western' people were co-opted to the Praesidium, but all the speeches were given by Communists. Karl-Heinz Martin was elected chairman.

Within a day or two of Lindemann and Litten's announcement (19 August 1947) that they were founding a Volksbühne in the Soviet Sector only, they issued a hastily written appeal for members, with over 140 signatures. A week later the FDGB decided to encourage membership of this Soviet Sector Volksbühne, while the SPD specifically warned its members not to join, but to wait for the Western Volksbühne. A plan already conceived by Lindemann for taking over the Colosseum theatre fell through and seats had to be taken in the municipal theatres. An opening meeting was held in the Deutsches Theater on 21 September with Wolfgang Langhoff (theatre Intendant), Herbert Ihering and Paul Eggers as speakers. Walter May represented the city. By November preparations could be made for performances. In March the Volksbühne presented the first of its own productions (Der Zimmerherr (The Gentleman Lodger) by Hermann Mostar) in the Oberschöneweide Accumulator Works, but by July it was settled for the season in the Prater Theater in the Kastanienallee where Karl-Heinz Martin had run his so-called Volksbühne from May 1946 to August 1947. In September 1950 the company moved to the Theater am Schiffbauerdamm where it remained until 1954, when the old Volksbühne theatre was reopened and Brecht's Berliner Ensemble took over the Schiffbauerdamm theatre – though by this time the Volksbühne as an audience organisation had ceased to exist in the Soviet Zone.

In the two years following the founding of the East German Federation of Volksbühnen in 1947 the growth in membership in East Germany as a whole was enormous, and in August 1949 the executive of the Federation, supported by the SED, reorganised itself as a central, combined German Volksbühne. The East Berlin Volksbühne, by far the strongest in East Germany, still retained some independence until the following year. In November 1949 the SED issued guide-lines which were endorsed by the Federation in January 1950. These made the Volksbühne in future especially responsible for 'the political, cultural and intellectual care of the working-class theatre public'. But it

was not— in East German opinion— in a position to fulfil these new
demands, because in effect it was too independent. So in 1953, apparently at the instigation of the cultural conference of the FDGB, a
delegate conference of the German Volksbühne decided to bring the
whole movement to an end in East Germany. This was done, and at
the end of the 1952/53 season the East German Volksbühne ceased to
exist. Its work was in some sense continued by factory groups and
collectives, and its name persisted as the name of the Theatre on the
Bülowplatz — Volksbühne.

iii The 'Theater am Kurfürstendamm'

Meanwhile in West Berlin in 1949 a special limited liability company was
formed to run the Theater am Kurfürstendamm, so that the Berlin
Freie Volksbühne's finances as a whole should not be put at risk. This
theatre had been constructed in 1923 by adapting the Exhibition Hall of
the Berlin Independent Secession, the architect responsible being Oskar
Kaufmann. This rather overdecorated theatre was burnt out towards
the end of the Second World War and rebuilt in the autumn of 1947 with
a very insignificant exterior, but an interior at once dignified and com-
fortable, though with only 736 seats. Nestriepke became Intendant and,
after a number of more distinguished men had declined the post, the
artistic direction was entrusted to Rudolf Hammacher, who had made
a name for himself under Hilpert at the Deutsches Theater.

Aiming at ensemble rather than star acting, Hammacher engaged
his whole company of twenty for a year. But he overestimated their
abilities and it became necessary, as far as the limited finances permitted, to engage guest artists to play leads. It was obviously rash to
open with Hamlet. The company was not equal to it and Vasa Hochmann's Slavonic accent did not help the title-role. The critics did not
like the production, though the public did. The season that followed
was mixed, the most disastrous failure being a play favoured by
Nestriepke because of its side-swipes at East European dictatorships.
[6] Two of the most successful were directed by Ernst Karchow, who
was appointed artistic director for the following season.

Karchow, described as 'noble, distinguished, modest and extremely
cultivated', had been for years an actor of high repute in the Bülowplatz
theatre before 1933. Since then he had worked as deputy to Reinhardt
in Vienna, and after that at the Bremen Kammerspiel. He was a man
who knew his own mind, and disagreements over the choice of the very
first play provided an opportunity for the independence of the artistic
director and the status of the advisory committee to be settled. From
September 1950 until the end of the 1952-53 season Karchow not only
made some noteworthy productions himself (especially Hauptmann's

<u>Fuhrmann Henschel</u> (<u>Drayman Henschel</u>) with Walter Bechmann and
Maria Becker) and acted in others very successfully, but also brought
in some very distinguished guest directors, above all, Oscar Fritz
Schuh, who, although he already had an international reputation, had
not before directed in Berlin. Karchow changed Hammacher's 'ensemble' policy. He engaged about six actors on long contracts and the rest
for single shows. This enabled him to get better leading actors more
economically, though the Freie Volksbühne executive had doubts, and
the actors' trade union protested. His one-year contract was extended,
but in February 1952 he had a stroke while directing Zuckmayer's version of Hauptmann's <u>Herbert Engelmann</u>. Otto Kurth of Hamburg took
over the production which earned forty-two curtain calls on its first
night. Another unfortunate incident during this season was the letting
of the theatre to the city for a visit of Werner Krauss with Ibsen's
<u>John Gabriel Borkman</u>. Krauss had played <u>Jew Süss</u> and though he had
publicly repented of his Nazi associations the visit gave rise to demonstrations and even to fighting in the auditorium, which ended when the
stage-hands came in front of the curtain, took the law into their own
hands and ejected the trouble-makers.

Karchow continued as director in the next season, but by November
(1952) it was plain that ill health would force him to retire soon and that
a successor must be sought. Nestriepke approached Oscar Fritz Schuh
and before long had contracted him for two years from October 1953.
Karchow retired at the end of the 1952-53 season and was dead by
October.

Schuh's five seasons at the Kurfürstendamm were brilliant. Born
in Munich in 1904, Schuh gained a reputation in the 1930s as director of
the Hamburg State Opera. In 1940 he moved to the Vienna Opera whose
tours gave him a foreign reputation. After 1945 he recreated the
Salzburg Festival. His guest production of Pirandello's <u>Six Characters</u>
for the Freie Volksbühne in October 1951 was a major theatrical event.
He had plenty of opportunity in Berlin to express his ideas — about
which he was very articulate. He did not wish the Kurfürstendamm
theatre to be merely an 'all-round' theatre, but to have a special
artistic character of its own, serving quality and intellectual progress.
Not fearing experiment, he did not wish to be 'avant-garde at any price':
nor did he take progress for granted. While regarding a good ensemble
as a necessary basis, he did not want contracts to go on for ever. In
direction he called for clearsightedness, cutting through emotional
factors and showing the reality of the dramatic creation and making its
intellectual background clear. 'The work of art should not pester and
importune the listener, but persuade and convince.' He was able to put
many of his ideas into practice, and though he could not have a complete
ensemble he drew on a regular pool of actors, eliminating those who did

not fit in and inviting over again those who did. He was wholly devoted
to his work. What he continued to do in Vienna and Salzburg took second
place, but cast reflected glory on the Freie Volksbühne. Unlike many
great directors, he kept economic realities in mind and though he might
explode when asked to retrench, he invariably did so. After two years
his status was raised so that he and Nestriepke were equal directors.
Among the productions he directed, Chekhov's The Seagull, Strindberg's
A Dream Play and O'Neill's A Touch of the Poet were outstanding. The
company visited Wiesbaden twice, Recklinghausen and London once,
and undertook two tours of West Germany.

When his contract was renewed for the 1955-56 season Schuh stip-
ulated that a second theatre should be made available to him in the
foreseeable future, as he was not fully extending his talents in the one
small theatre. The Freie Volksbühne itself, with a waiting list of many
thousands for membership, could also have welcomed a second theatre —
if subsidy were available. Nestriepke tried in vain to rent a second
theatre; he then got plans for a new theatre of seven hundred seats,
and finally in 1958 drew up a scheme for a large new theatre which
would entirely replace that on the Kurfürstendamm and be economic to
run. Such a scheme was likely to obtain credit and to materialise, but
Schuh felt unable to wait longer — he was in his mid-fifties — and accepted
the post of Intendant for the municipal theatres at Cologne. He departed
on good terms with the Freie Volksbühne, but his going was a terrible
loss.

At this time too, Nestriepke, now well over seventy, decided he
must give up his post as director. His place was taken by Hermann
Ludwig. Originally an actor, he had ten years' experience with the
Volksbühne and experience as an Intendant. In Schuh's place came
Leonard Steckel, an actor and director of great experience who had had
his first job under Nestriepke at the Neues Volkstheater. He had,
however, never had charge of a theatre. Nor was his temperament
compatible with that of Ludwig, and he remained only a year.

His successor, Rudolf Noelte, also failed to co-operate with
Ludwig, who resigned for the sake of the theatre, to be succeeded by
Walter Papproth, for many years deputy Intendant and administrative
director of the Municipal Opera. But Noelte could not work with him
either, resigned, then withdrew his resignation. But the leadership
of the Volksbühne decided that they could not sacrifice yet another
experienced administrator to this less experienced man, and sacked
him. Very unpleasant conflict followed, culminating in legal action,
which brought a great deal of unwelcome public interest in its train.

Learning from this bitter experience, the Volksbühne abandoned
the 'two-headed' leadership of the theatre and appointed one man as
director, Günter Skopnik, who had held a high position in the Frankfurt

theatres. He remained for two years, when he left for a better-paid
post in Kassel. By then the opening of a new Freie Volksbühne theatre
was less than a year away.

iv Opposition and difficulties

Throughout this period the greater part of the West Berlin press was
extraordinarily hostile to the Freie Volksbühne, and especially to its
theatre. The company was referred to as 'democratically licensed
barnstormers'. Friedrich Luft, implacable enemy of the Volksbühne,
said that the Kurfürstendamm theatre 'had done the reputation of
Berlin gross injury with improper assistance from the taxpayer'. Of
course the East Berlin press was consistently hostile.

Any excuse seemed to serve to attack the Volksbühne. In February
1952 Frank Lothar directed at the Tribüne the world première of a
play by Tettenborn, Perspektiven (Perspectives), whose subject was the
persecution of the Church in an unidentified Communist State. The
production clearly identified the State as East Germany. The Freie
Volksbühne executive thought it misrepresented East Germany and
feared for its East Berlin members if they were seen by spies at the
play. It was therefore not included in the 'obligatory' list, but optional
tickets were made available, and the play offered as an alternative.
This action was seen by the press as prejudice against young writers
and against Christianity.

In 1950 there came an extraordinary attack on the Volksbühne in
the form of a footnote to the city's subsidy recommendation for the
next season. This footnote derived from a document which the Allied
Kommandatura had sent to the city authorities on 4 April 1950. It (i)
expressed the concern of the Allies for the development of the cultural
life of Berlin; (ii) proposed a special committee of all interested
circles, on the cultural situation; and (iii) made a series of specific
proposals, one of which was: 'to close down the uneconomic Theater
am Kurfürstendamm as one of the undertakings controlled by the Freie
Volksbühne' and to limit the activity of the Freie Volksbühne to supporting other theatres by providing them with audience (that is, to become
a mere ticket-agency). The Theater am Kurfürstendamm would then
be turned into a concert hall. Apart from its lack of factual knowledge,
the impertinence of this brought angry responses even from newspapers
normally opposed to the Freie Volksbühne:

> The Allied Command informed the city authorities by letter that
> they were very concerned for the development of culture in Berlin.
> That is charming of the Berlin Allied Command. We don't know
> whether the letter began, 'Hello, Boys, make a bit more Culture!'
> It's possible we're a clumsy people politically and are open to good
> teaching in this area. But they had better leave concern over our
> cultural development to us! [7]

The Freie Volksbühne executive also reacted strongly, pointing out that its theatre was more soundly based financially than any other in Berlin.

A public meeting with a thousand present was held at the end of April at which support for the FVB and its theatre was evident, and the cultural committees of both main parties (SPD and Christian Democratic Union) favoured the FVB Theatre. Consequently the city parliament unanimously threw out the footnote (20 June 1950). Even so it was not until after October 1950 that the threat of subsidy-withdrawal was finally removed — and all this happened at the time when Schuh had already firmly established the theatre's artistic standard and reputation!

The FVB was not without internal difficulties. During the 1952-53 season the association had to leave its rented offices, and after using an unsatisfactory alternative decided to build its own. The new building was completed by December 1954 at a cost of 230,000 DM, without grant aid or mortgage.

During the seasons 1952-53, 1953-54 constitutional disputes led to a general meeting on 26 May 1954 at which the executive committee resigned in a body — only to be asked to continue in charge until another general meeting could be held. The crisis concerned the relationship between the executive and the administrative council. A solution was worked out and a new arrangement was accepted in November 1954.

The last serious blow to the FVB during the period of the Theater am Kurfürstendamm was the closing of the Brandenburg Gate and the sealing off of the border between East and West Berlin on 13 August 1961, followed by the building of the Berlin wall a few days later. The last cultural links between East and West were broken. The twenty-five thousand East Berlin members of the FVB were immediately cut off, as were the equal number who came from East Berlin as ordinary box-office theatre audience. At the time no one could believe that the closure could last long, and on 15 August (that is, before the Wall was built) the FVB executive broadcast a message on the West Berlin radio to the East Berlin members urging them to be faithful to the FVB and not to be shaken in their relationship with the cultural life of the West. The East Berlin members were promised that their membership rights could be taken up again as soon as the 'infamous closure' was ended.

v The new theatre and the return of Piscator

When Oscar Fritz Schuh pressed for a second theatre, Nestriepke not only approached the architect Fritz Bornemann to draw up plans for a new seven hundred-seat theatre, but also opened a building fund. It soon became clear that this second small theatre would be uneconomic both to build and to run, so the aim was changed to that of building a

single new theatre with 1,000 to 1,200 seats — the Theater am Kurfürstendamm to be given up. Bornemann estimated the cost of this at nine
million DM. The scheme was approved by the city planning authorities,
a credit of four and a half million DM was obtained from Bonn, the
Berlin Senate and House of Representatives agreed to a bank credit of
three million DM, help was given by friendly organisations, especially
trade unions and the West German Volksbühnen, money was made available from the Berlin lottery, and, of course, the members themselves
helped by contributing to the loan fund. Despite the inevitable delays,
the scheme moved forward. A fine open site in the city centre was
bought for 788,000 DM and the foundation stone laid on 6 October 1960.
From this moment progress was steady and rapid. The topping-out
ceremony took place on 15 December 1962 and the theatre was opened
according to schedule on 1 May 1963. Bornemann had almost kept
within his estimate of nine million DM, and even with the cost of the
site and of financing the project the total cost was little over ten million
DM.

The theatre, as conceived by Bornemann, is an integral part of the
park-like open space on which it stands. The foyers and box-office hall
are fully glazed so that except in the actual auditorium one is conscious
of being in close relationship with external nature — for the surroundings
of the theatre are fully planted and rich in trees. The spacious
uncluttered auditorium seats 1047 and the stage is wide, deep and fully
equipped — though the architect was also fully aware of the danger
that modern technology can as easily come between the play and its
audience as help to project it. The theatre, which houses excellent
workshops and wardrobes, occupies only a small fraction of its tri-
angular site, the rest of which is taken up partly by car parks — some
on two levels — and partly by parkland. Though he gave careful con-
sideration to the claims of an open-space theatre, Bornemann eventually
designed a traditional, but flexible theatre, with proscenium stage 21
metres broad and 20 metres deep, with a 15 metre revolve, and side-
and rear-stages with wagons.

Such a theatre called for an artistic director worthy of it. In
October 1961 Erwin Piscator directed Arthur Miller's Death of a
Salesman at the Theater am Kurfürstendamm, and when Günter Skopnik
moved to Kassel in 1962, Piscator succeeded him. In 1932 Piscator
had gone to the USSR to make films, in 1936 he was in Paris and from
1938 to 1951 in New York where he founded the Dramatic Workshop.
Since 1952 he had directed many productions in Germany, including
some in West Berlin. His return to the Volksbühne, especially at this
time, ready to direct the still unfinished new theatre, was an event of
special significance.

... for Siegfried Nestriepke's friends it was an unforgettable
experience, how these two self-assertive men, who in the twenties
had disagreed vehemently over ends and means in the Volksbühne,
met again for new work in common. [8]

Some say that when he returned to the FVB, Piscator was still trying to
fight battles of the twenties over again. Indeed, he had little sympathy
with much that was typical of European theatre in the late fifties and
early sixties: 'What is called avant-gardism today is bourgeois deca-
dence. It is Waiting for Godot, it is the so-called Nothing, Emptiness,
Angst.' [9] But in what was lasting in his outlook, his belief in 'understanding, humanism, humanity, greatness of thought', [10] he still
had much to offer.

> This man, who is committed to the eternal rights of man, was
> always a moralist, a zealot, as Savonarola was, for the theatre
> to him is not aesthetic self-indulgence, but a tribunal of the times.
> [11]

What is perhaps the fairest assessment of his post-war contribution to
the Volksbühne was made by Dr Günter Schulz on 24 June 1966, less
than three months after Piscator's death. Piscator should have been
the principal speaker at the twenty-second Volksbühnen conference at
Dortmund with the subject 'Zeittheater — Theater unserer Zeit' (a neat
title that may be less neatly translated as 'Theatre of contemporary
problems — the theatre of our time'). In his place Dr Schulz (assistant
general secretary of the Federation of Volksbühne Associations) spoke
on the same subject. After describing Piscator's idea of Zeittheater
about 1930, when he called for a 'teaching theatre' and 'the education
of the audience even against its will', Schulz added,

> We know, that Piscator too gave up this standpoint later. [12]
>   When Piscator came home from exile he had experienced, if
> only from a distance, the second world war, the even more exten-
> sive extermination of people, the effect of atomic horror. He
> came back not as an altered man but rather as a man transformed,
> whom things as they had been no longer satisfied and could no
> longer satisfy. He had outgrown the ideological propaganda-
> theatre, the theatre of party-political outlook. He himself defined
> the position he had reached, thus:
>   'For me the Political is nothing other than it was for Aristotle,
> who defined man as a political animal, that is to say, a creature
> that is capable of community, in need of community and able to
> create community, and that lives in a Polis, that is, in a place in
> which communal functions and interests are ordered on a communal
> basis. Political art, political theatre, is in this sense an art, a
> theatre art that chooses as its subject what pertains to the com-
> munity, or to use a modern word, to society, that demands social
> attitudes and calls forth social reactions.'

In the face of humanity threatened in its existence by the
means of mass destruction, an ideology for changing this situation
no longer sufficed for Piscator. So, from the theatre of political
Weltanschauung he arrived at a theatre which he still called
'political', but which I, to avoid error, with a distinction that is
perhaps rather pretentious but justified by the broadening of the
material, may call 'human-political' [Menschheitspolitisches]
theatre. This theatre, too, is with him consistently not an exclusively teaching theatre, even though, now as before, it naturally aims
at teaching and changing ... 'Perhaps we don't want a teaching-
theatre, but we certainly want a seeking-theatre ...' [13]

The first three productions of the 1962-63 season were the last
in the Theater am Kurfürstendamm: all were directed by Piscator,
who, by a happy coincidence was immediately called upon to present
a representative work of Gerhart Hauptmann for the celebration of the
centenary of his birth. He chose the Atrides Tetralogy. The name of
the author of Die Weber evoked memories of the Blütezeit of the Volksbühne in the 1890s, while Piscator's production reaffirmed both his
independence as a director and his concerned preoccupation with contemporary problems. Regarding Hauptmann's work as a fundamental
criticism of the situation in the Third Reich, but with contemporary
allusions disguised as mythical material, Piscator accentuated what
had relevance to Nazi Germany and added statistics, recorded speeches
and film to underscore what he claimed to be the author's original
intention. The production was better received internationally than by
the Berlin press.

His second production was of a recent play, Anouilh's La Grotte
(1961); but it was his third — the last to open in the rented theatre —
which made theatrical history: Der Stellvertreter (The Representative)
of Rolf Hochhuth. Luft characteristically remarks that Piscator

had the good fortune to get into his hands, in Rolf Hochhuth's
provocative play about the Papacy, Der Stellvertreter, a politically
explosive drama with which to demonstrate anew his conception of
primarily political theatre. [14]

The suggestion of mere good fortune is unfair. When first appointed
to the FVB Piscator had noted in his diary: 'I must find plays — the
like of which have never existed before — hard, difficult plays, saturated
with reality. Back to the style of the twenties.' [15] The right play
rarely meets the right director by mere good fortune. It is not surprising that Hochhuth should have chosen Piscator, newly appointed to
his important post, as the director to whom to submit his script. It
was what Piscator was looking for:

an epic play, epic-scientific, epic-documentary, a play for the
epic, 'political' theatre for which I have fought for thirty years;
a 'total' play for a 'total' theatre ... the fate of an individual
(treated) comprehensively enough to be symbolic, exemplary in
the original meaning of the word, 'representative' for the general-
ity. [16]

It was, however, as Dr Schulz has pointed out, a play 'that was by no
means ready for the stage'. Schulz went on: 'As is well known, Piscator
gave the play its stage-worthiness, which he distilled out of a written
mass of dramatic discussion.' [17] Having done this, he was able to
present the text without injecting extraneous material or using very
unconventional forms of staging. Reporting on the production to the
twenty-first Volksbühne conference in Augsburg in 1964, Günther Abendroth of Berlin said, 'The Representative testified how even today art
can arouse and change humanity.' [18] The play, of course, moved
into the new theatre, and Abendroth goes on: 'The inauguration of the
Freie Volksbühne Theatre discovered its true importance in a world-
wide rebirth of the "moral institution"' [19] (referring of course to
Schiller's concept of the theatre as moral institution). 'The Representative', said Schulz,'showed completely how for Piscator the problem
and not the form stood fundamentally at the centre.' [20] While on the
one hand that problem, the substance of the play, aroused fierce controversy throughout Germany and even beyond, its style fathered a
whole generation of 'documentary' drama. Piscator's own contribution
to the genre as a director consisted of the FVB productions of Heinar
Kipphardt's In der Sache J. Robert Oppenheimer (The Case of J. Robert
Oppenheimer) (first Berlin production: it was not produced at the
Berliner Ensemble until the following year), Peter Weiss's Die Ermittlung (The Investigation) (world première) and Hans Hellmut Kirst's
Aufstand der Offiziere (Officers' Uprising). It would do Piscator an
injustice to equate his conception of political theatre with the documentary drama to which it contributed. As Schulz says in his lecture:

> Piscator's political theatre has really nothing to do with document-
> ary theatre in itself, that is talked of so much and which is often
> taken for the world theatre movement which I may call 'human-
> political'.... Piscator never thought that merely quoting docu-
> ments and no more was art, or could replace the artistic effect of
> the theatre upon the audience.... Nevertheless he held firmly to
> the documentary as a starting-point. [21]

The Investigation, that almost unbearable 'Oratorio', carried the
documentary method to its extremest limits. Piscator appreciated the
utterly stark simplicity of it, and though he had assembled photographs
and films to illustrate the words, he did not finally use any of them.

Piscator explained that for him this 'Oratorio' was, so to speak,
the 'Third Testament'. In his own words: Here the theatre re-
enters the realm of religious ritual, which it had left. It turns
back from the regions of the purely aesthetic and of beautiful
appearance, and becomes the ritual exorcism of an incomprehen-
sible fate, the most moving and meaningless Passion in world
history. What is here aimed at as a cultural experience is no longer
fear of the gods, but man's fear of himself. [22]

The Aufstand was Piscator's last production. He was already mortally
ill when it opened at the FVB Theatre on 2 March 1966, less than a
month before his death on 30 March. The subject of the play was the
attempt by senior officers including Klaus von Stauffenberg on 20 July
1944 to assassinate Hitler. Schulz said of this production:

He [Piscator] had pressed the theme of 20 July — the Officers'
Uprising — almost violently upon an author [Kirst] who was a
brilliant novelist but, as this play shows, quite obviously not a
dramatist ...
     In this play, where the material or the shaping of the material
would not carry the theatrical work, Piscator once more used the
Global Stage, projection, film and simultaneous setting, as a
retreat from a development which we, who knew him, thought after
The Investigation to be almost settled ... [23]

Such a development however, depended on dramatists emerging capable
of writing plays of the quality of The Investigation, and, Schulz commented, less was done to develop young writers in Germany than in
some other countries.

The new theatre on the Schaperstrasse opened on 1 May 1963 with
a new production, the last to enter the season's repertoire, an adaptation
of Romain Rolland's Robespierre — one of Piscator's many experiments
in drawing on non-theatrical material for the stage. The narrative
form held much that Piscator wanted for his 'epic' drama, and he had
already produced stage versions of War and Peace, Sartre's Iron in the
Soul and two American novels. [24]

Surveying Piscator's work from 1962 to 1966 — a period which
included, in 1965, the seventy-fifth anniversary of the founding of the
Volksbühne — Günter Schulz inevitably recalled Bruno Wille's original
manifesto and his aim for a theatre concerned with 'great contemporary
questions': 'It' (the Volksbühne) 'committed itself at the start to a
theatre of great contemporary questions ... Erwin Piscator ... has
opened again to the Volksbühne the way to its first sources ...' [25]
To take that way the Volksbühne must heed the admonition of Alfred
Kerr: 'Occupied with the Arts? Yes, even to my heart's blood, but
art was always only an excuse for a better, juster human order.' [26]

After Piscator's death his deputy, Dr Peter Stoltzenburg, became provisional Intendant until a successor was appointed. This was Hansjörg Utzerath, director of the Düsseldorf Kammerspiele, who took up his post, after a transitional period, at the beginning of the 1967-68 season. Forward plans that still bore Piscator's stamp—for example, Hochhuth's new play Soldaten (Soldiers)—had gradually to be adapted to new personalities and situations. During the following years it is surprising how frequently it is reported that the reaction of the public and the critics sharply from each other.

Two of Piscator's aims had been to establish a permanent ensemble and with this to present plays in 'true' repertoire. But for financial reasons he had not achieved either. The idea was revived during the 1968-69 season, and the 1969-70 season opened with a small permanent ensemble playing in true repertoire—not en suite repertoire. The further problem of balancing avant garde experiments against more popular plays was in part solved during the 1967-68 season by introducing a contrasting and more adventurous programme of late-night shows. The first of these was Peter Zadek's production of Edward Bond's Saved.

The greatest loss suffered by the Berlin FVB, and indeed by the whole movement during this period was the death of Siegfried Nestriepke. Barely had he brought his life's work to a fitting climax with the opening of the new FVB Theatre than he himself died on 5 December 1963, shortly before his seventy-eighth birthday. A month later, on 12 January 1964 a memorial meeting to the 'Grand Old Man' of the Volksbühne was held in the theatre. Richard Voigt, former Minister for Cultural Affairs and Chairman of the Federation of Volksbühne Societies presided, and Walther G. Oschilewski made a memorial speech, later printed and published. 'His printed speech ought always to be for us a little book whose leaves we turn over to remind ourselves of our friend Siegfried Nestriepke.' [27]

After the blow of losing twenty-five thousand East Berlin members at a stroke in 1961 the FVB rapidly recovered and by 1964 and 1965 had reached its highest post-war membership—about a hundred and twenty thousand. It was realised that this could not be maintained. Many of the newer members did not become permanent, and the turnover of membership each year was numbered in many thousands. By 1967-68 membership had fallen to a hundred thousand and by 1969-70 to 83,000. [28] This drop was in part parallel with the so-called 'theatre crisis' that was developing in Germany by 1970, but it may also have reflected public taste. Other less seriously intentioned theatre clubs were springing up and some people moved to these because they found the FVB programme too heavy [29].

Not until the 1969-70 season was a serious attempt made to meet the more varying demands of the modern public by offering a choice of

programmes. In that season however, prospective members were able
to choose between five programmes: (i) 'The established selection',
(ii) 'Thoughtfulness', (iii) 'Topical questions', (iv) 'Relaxation' and
(v) 'Own choice'. [30]

During the season 1952-53 the FVB Berlin had investigated the
occupations and status of its members. Seventy-five thousand copies
of a questionnaire were issued of which thirty-two thousand two hundred
were completed. Of these 67.1 per cent were from West Berlin addresses and 32.9 per cent from East Berlin — about the same proportion as
the membership as a whole. Out of thirty-two thousand respondents,
nineteen thousand were in professions but of these only two thousand
in positions of financial comfort and security. A high figure for pen-
sioners corresponded with the situation in Berlin. The figure for
manual workers was very low (2,757:8.6 per cent of the respondents;
14.3 per cent of respondents with jobs). [31] The obvious contrast with
the Volksbühne of the 1890s is at least in part a reflection of the contrast between society in the 1890s and the 1950s.

The Volksbühne has nevertheless remained true to its principles
in so far as it still always regards as its urgent task to make
theatre-going possible for the worst placed class of the population.
But before 1933 this was the working class, after 1945 — along with
certain groups of the working class — it was especially the middle
and lower salaried classes. [32]

A decade after its opening the new Volksbühne theatre began to
present serious problems. With the membership of the FVB falling
towards fifty thousand it was too large, and the circle was no longer
used. The general public turned against it. Its traditional design
inhibited experiment, and its back-stage facilities proved inadequate.
With scarcity of good new German plays, young writers could get their
work produced in State theatres, and the FVB lost an important function.
It even abandoned repertoire for en suite playing.

The democracy of the FVB became a liability in an age that values
efficiency more highly, and the traditional lottery for tickets was not
liked, when other organisations sent tickets through the post.

2 DEVELOPMENTS OUTSIDE BERLIN

i To 1933

During the 1890s Volksbühne associations existed in Hamburg (1892-99), Kiel (1894-98) and Munich (1898-99), but none survived into the new century. The only others to be founded before 1914 were Charlottenburg (1904-11) and Bielefeld, founded in 1905, with a continuous history to 1933, and Vienna (1906-14). In 1892 in Frankfurt, a Committee for Popular Lectures (founded 1890) successfully demanded cheap performances at the municipal theatre and from 1908 arranged closed performances on Volksbühne lines. Otherwise for three decades the Volksbühne remained virtually a Berlin phenomenon; but after the military collapse of 1918, the political emancipation of the German people, especially coming as it did at a time of great hardship, released pent-up forces which gave rise to the Volksbühne's rebirth as a nation-wide movement. At the Founding Conference of the Federation of Volksbühne Societies held in Berlin in October 1920, only two days after the first general meeting of the new united Berlin Volksbühne, fifteen Volksbühne societies and one or two similar bodies were represented; several others were in existence, and ten years later there were no fewer than 305 Volksbühne societies, with a total membership of half a million.

The Federation held conferences annually until 1929. The 1925 conference at Jena issued an important policy statement declaring that the Volksbühne recognised in the manifestation of human greatness in art — especially in drama — a value of the highest kind, and therefore rejected every subordination of this to political or sectarian points of view — and the 1927 conference at Magdeburg, led by Julius Bab's eloquence and wisdom, really ended all danger of a new split in the movement arising from the Piscator affair.

The structure of the Federation was, after 1924, twofold. Basically the conference, representing all the individual societies, elected an executive to which each society had direct access. Also there was an administrative council, a less formal 'watchdog' body, consisting of the executive together with representatives of the sixteen districts into which the societies were grouped (see Appendix C).

The strongest development was in the industrialised, poor and culturally deprived south-east — Saxony, Thuringia, Silesia — where the need for the movement was equalled by the difficulties it encountered. The weakest was in Bavaria: the area was not industrialised, theatre tradition was lacking, winter travel was not easy, and a strong amateur movement had created a poor public taste. In the north-west, Hamburg Volksbühne quickly recovered after the war, and Altona,

Lübeck and Hannover became important. Cultural backwardness in
areas like Pomerania, the French occupation of the Ruhr, the opposition of the Church and the rival Christian Bühnenvolksbund in some
predominantly Catholic areas all served to hinder and diversify the
history of the movement, while the liberal cultural traditions of Baden-
Pfalz and Württemburg assisted the growth of the Volksbühne in such
centres as Karlsruhe, Mannheim and Stuttgart.

The nationwide growth of the Volksbühne movement would have
been impossible, especially in smaller towns, without the non-profit-
making touring companies. In 1930 there were about twenty-five of
these, all subsidised out of public funds. Five were run by the Volksbühne Federation, which also had interests in four others. In the
1929-30 season more than half the total activity of Volksbühne societies
depended upon these companies. In that season the Federation's own
companies visited about 130 towns (in 90 per cent of which there were
Volksbühne societies) and gave more than a thousand performances.
Over forty other Volksbühne societies were served by other touring
companies.

The oldest was the Rhine-Main Federation Theatre, created in the
spring of 1907 by the Rhine-Main Federation for Popular Education.
This survived the war and came under the wing of the Volksbühne
Federation and two other bodies. By 1929-30, now known as the
Frankfurt Artists' Theatre for Rhine and Main, it was giving some
five hundred performances a year in about a hundred different towns.
Almost as old was the Touring Theatre of the March of Brandenburg,
founded in the autumn of 1907, which also survived the war. Extremely
important for the development of the touring companies was the Prussian
Provincial Theatre Ltd. This was in fact not a theatre but an advisory
and subsidising body (with State funds) for non-profit-making companies.
By 1030 it was helping nineteen touring companies.

In 1924 the Volksbühne Federation established two companies of
its own; three more were added in the following seasons. Between
1924 and 1930 these five companies gave altogether 4577 performances
of 349 productions. Life in them was hard, the travelling very exacting
and the practical problems difficult. They were represented corpor-
ately by the Union of Non-commercial Touring Companies, which also
looked after the well-being of their employees. As members of this
union the companies paid only half fare on the railways. A grant or
guarantee was sought in each place visited (the existence of a Volksbühne Society normally ensured this), but gaps had to be filled with
unguaranteed dates. Without the Prussian subsidy most of the venture
would not have been practicable.

Apart from the periodical <u>Die Volksbühne</u>, the Federation issued

free factual press handouts and published <u>Dramaturgische Blätter</u>
(pamphlets on plays) at regular intervals to help societies choose their
programmes. There was also a supplement to <u>Die Volksbühne</u> for the
use of societies unable to produce their own periodical. From 1924
the Volksbühne's own publishing house brought out of series of brochures
and published thirty volumes of Volksbühne Classics, representing nine
authors. Seventy thousand volumes were sold in less than a year.

<u>ii Since 1945</u>

The rebirth of the Volksbühne societies in West Germany from 1945
was generally easier than in Berlin and the East, as there was no conflict with Communist Party ideas. The refounded societies kept in touch
and the Federation was re-established in May 1948 in Hamburg with
Nestriepke as chairman. In 1951 it moved its headquarters to Berlin,
being the first major national organisation to do so. A policy statement
in 1954 re-expressed in contemporary terms the principles enunciated
in 1890 and 1925. By 1955 there were seventy-five affiliated societies
with three hundred and fifty thousand members, 26 per cent of whom
were in Berlin. But after reaching the maximum growth in 1963 the
movement steadily declined both in membership and in the number of
affiliated societies, though the Volksbühne and other audience organisations are still an integral part of the German theatre scene; in the
season 1974-75 the number of Volksbühne Societies and the number of
tickets sold through them — though not the actual membership — showed
increases in line with the small but significant increase in theatre-
going reported in that season. 'The German Theatre is unthinkable
without its <u>Spielplan</u> ... this <u>Spielplan</u> would be unthinkable without the
great audience organisations.' [1] Some theatre directors regard this
vast 'block-booking' system as a tyranny and believe that they would
have greater artistic freedom if it were abolished. But the so-called
tyranny is simply that of the economic realities of the theatre, and the
repeated assertions that the Volksbühne lowers public taste and no
longer brings the economically deprived into the theatre do not bear
strict examination.

A doctoral thesis of the mid-sixties on the taste of smaller Volksbühne societies [2] showed that within the context of the general
levelling of class differences after the Second World War, the Volksbühne had remained true to its original principles in serving the most
financially under-privileged sections of the public — now low-salaried
white-collar workers; that members tended to be better educated than
the average citizen; that the percentage of working-class people in the
Volksbühne was higher than among theatre-goers as a whole; and that
the Volksbühne helped those in the socially weakest positions to go to
the theatre. The thesis also proved that the Volksbühne flourishes best

in predominantly Evangelical, rather than in predominantly Catholic towns; that in some centres (for example, some university towns) over half the members were under thirty, though in others the figure was only 10 per cent; that the taste of a group of theatre-goers was open to be influenced, though the process was slow; that societies with a 'lighter' programme gained most membership, and that class did affect taste. Though not startling, the findings answer both the hostile critics outside the movement and the starry-eyed within it.

Hamburg Volksbühne, the largest outside Berlin, celebrated its fiftieth birthday in 1969 and in the early 1970s computerised its records and introduced a Volksbühnen-Pass, which offered a free choice of plays and dates at reduced prices in ten theatres. The idea of such a pass had originated in Frankfurt and was the brainchild of Conny Reinhold, a distinguished political cabarettist who, until his untimely death in 1974 at the age of forty-three, was manager of the Frankfurt Volksbühne. This is part of a unique organisation, the Frankfurt Federation for Popular Education, whose post-war development was the work of Carl Tesch (1902-1970). For almost twenty years he was director of the organisation, which comprises a Folk High School, the Volksbühne, and the famous Theater-am-Turm (TAT), all housed in the massive Volksbildungsheim, a few yards from the ancient Eschenheimer tower. [3]

The Frankfurt Volksbühne is the fourth largest society. The third largest is Hannover, but this has latterly lost much of its individuality through a very close relationship with the municipal season-ticket system. Fifth is Stuttgart, exceptionally active and, because it is in effect the cultural organ of the city's trade unions, having the advantage of excellent premises and facilities. The cultural climate of Stuttgart and its region, the attitude of the theatre, and the alertness and liveliness of the audiences all help the movement and its ideals to flourish.

The story of the Volksbühne is not ended. It continues now and into the future, always inextricably linked with the changing fortunes of the German theatre, the German economy and German society. It is emulated within Germany and in other countries and leads an international movement (IATO, see Appendix E) under the guidance of Gerard Schmid, who since Nestriepke's death has been the movement's leading figure and combines the duties of general secretary of IATO with those of general manager of the Volksbühne Federation.

Despite the increasing individualism of members, audience organisations are likely to remain a characteristic feature of the German theatre. They are communities of playgoers within the larger community, in a country where the civic theatre is as essential a feature of the communal scene as the town hall or the fire station. This sense of community is the basis of the emblem adopted by the Volksbühne

Federation in 1972.   To the eye the new symbol expresses unity in
diversity, movement with stability, organisation without stagnation.
Its interlinked rings of concentric circles are a fitting symbol for the
Volksbühne today, a community standing between past and future.

PRINCIPAL SOURCES

The abbreviations by which works are referred to in the Notes and
Appendices are given in parentheses.

Books and dissertations

BAB, Julius: Über den Tag hinaus: kritische Betrachtungen, ed. H.
Bergholz. Veröffentlichungen der deutschen Akademie für Sprache
und Dichtung, Darmstadt. Verlag Lambert Schneider, Heidelberg/
Darmstadt, 1960. (Bab/Bergholz)
BOCHOW, Peter: 'Der Geschmack des Volksbühnen-publikums'.
Inaugural-Dissertation, Freie Universität Berlin. Berlin, 1965.
(Bochow)
BRAHM, Otto: Kritiken und Essays. Klassiker der Kritik. Artemis
Verlag. Zürich and Stuttgart, 1964. (Brahm)
BRODBECK, Albert: Handbuch der deutschen Volksbühnenbewegung.
Berlin, 1930. (H)
Chronik der Hamburger Volksbühne. Hamburger Volksbühne e.V.,
1969. (Chronik)
DURIEUX, Tilla: Meine ersten neunzig Jahre. Herbig. Munich-
Berlin, 1971. (Durieux)
EBERT, Carl: 'Theatre as necessity of Life', in Unsere Theaterneu-
bauten nach 1945. German Section, International Theatre Institute,
Berlin, n.d. (unpaginated). (Ebert)
FELDENS, Franz: 75 Jahre Städtische Bühnen Essen. Rheinisch-West-
fälische Verlagsgeselleschaft, Essen, 1967. (Feldens)
Handbuch des Bühnenvolksbundes, Wille und Werk. Berlin, 1928.
HANSER, Reihe: Brecht-Chronik. Carl Hanser Verlag, Munich, 1971.
(Hanser)
HENZE, Herbert: 'Otto Brahm und das Deutsche Theater in Berlin'.
Inaugural-Dissertation, Erlangen, 1930. (Henze)
HIRSCH, Helmut: Viel Kultur für wenig Geld? Entwicklungen und Ver-
wicklungen der Volksbühne. ECON Verlag, Düsseldorf-Wien.

HOWLEY, Frank: Berlin Command. G. P. Putnam & Sons, New York,
    1950. (Howley)
IHERING, Herbert: Von Reinhardt bis Brecht. Eine Auswahl der
    Theaterkritiken 1909–32. Edited with an introduction by R. Baden-
    hausen. Rowohlt, 1967.
In Brief. Berlin. Presse- und Informationsamt des Landes Berlin,
    1972. (In Brief)
INNES, C. D.: Erwin Piscator's Political Theatre. Cambridge Univ-
    ersity Press, 1962. (I)
JOHANN, Ernst and JUNKER, Jörg: German cultural history of the
    last hundred years. Nymphenburger Verlagshandlung, Munich,
    1970. (Johann/Junker)
KNILLI, Friedrich and MÜNCHOW, Ursula: Frühes Deutsches Arbeiter-
    theater 1847–1918 (a Documentation). Carl Hauser Verlag, Munich,
    1970. (F)
LEONHARD, Rudolf: Ausgewählte Werke: Segel am Horizont, Dramen
    und Hörspiele. Verlag der Nation, Berlin, 1963.
LEY-PISCATOR, Maria: The Piscator Experiment. J. H. Heinemann
    Inc., New York, 1967. (Maria Ley-Piscator)
LUCAS, Robert: Frieda Lawrence. Translat. by G. Skelton. Secker
    & Warburg, London, 1973. (Lucas)
LUFT, Friedrich: 25 Jahre Theater in Berlin. Vorwort by Luft.
    Heinz Spitzing Verlag, Berlin, 1972. (Luft)
MEHRING, Franz: Beitrage zur Literaturgeschichte. Berlin, 1948.
    (Mehring)
MELCHINGER: Max Reinhardt. Friedrich Verlag, Hannover, 1968.
    (Melchinger)
MENDEL, Vera (translator): Ernst Toller: Masses and Man. None-
    such Press, 1923.
MITTENZWEI, Werner: Theater in der Zeitenwende. Henschel Ver-
    lag, Berlin, 1972.
NESTRIEPKE, Siegfried: Geschichte der Volksbühne Berlin. 1. Teil:
    1890 bis 1914. Volksbühnen-Verlags- und Vertriebs-G.m.b.H.,
    Berlin, 1930. (G)
NESTRIEPKE, Siegfried: Neues Beginnen. Die Geschichte der Freien
    Volksbühne Berlin 1946 bis 1955. arani Verlags-G.m.b.H., Berlin-
    Grunewald, 1956. (NB)
OSBORNE, John: The Naturalistic Drama in Germany. Manchester
    University Press, 1971. (Osborne)
OSCHILEWSKI, W. G.: Freie Volksbühne Berlin. Stapp Verlag,
    Berlin, 1965. (Oschilewski)
— Zehn Jahre Theater am Kurfürstendamm. arani Verlags-G.m.b.H.,
    Berlin-Grunewald, 1960.
PAQUET, Alfons: Fahnen. In: Deutsche Revolutionsdramen. Heraus-
    gegeben und eingeleitet von Reinhold Grimm und Jost Hermand.
    Suhrkamp Verlag., n.d.

— Sturmflut. Volksbühnen-Verlags- und Vertriebs-G.m.b.H., 1926.
PFÜTZNER, Klaus: Schriften zur Theaterwissenschaft, vols. 1 and 4.
Herausgegeben von der Theaterhochschule, 'Hans Otto', Leipzig.
Henschel-verlag, Berlin.
PISCATOR, Erwin: Das Politische Theater. Rowohlt Verlag, 1963.
(PT)
REUTER, Rudolf: Christen vor der Bühne. Theater-Rundschau-
Verlag, Bonn, 1968.
RÜHLE, Günther: Theater für die Republik 1917-1933 im Spiegel der
Kritik. Fischer, 1967. (Rühle)
SCHLEY, Gernot: Die Freie Bühne in Berlin. Berlin, 1967. (Schley)
SCHLIEPER, Inge: Wurzeln der Democratie in der deutschen Ges-
chichte. Siegler & Co., Bonn, 1967. (Schlieper)
SCHWAB-FELISCH, H.: Gerhart Hauptmann: Die Weber. Dichtung
und Wirklichkeit. Ullstein. Frankfurt am Main-Berlin, 1969.
(Schwab-Felisch)
SELO, Heinz: 'Die "Freie Volksbühne in Berlin". Geschichte ihrer
Entstehung und ihrer Entwicklung bis zur Auflösung im Jahre 1896'.
Doctoral Dissertation, Erlangen. Berlin, 1930. (S)
SHIRER, W. L.: The Rise and Fall of the Third Reich. Secker and
Warburg, London, 1973. (Shirer)
TAYLOR, A. J. P.: The Course of German History. Hamish Ham-
ilton, London, 1945. (Taylor)
TOLLER, Ernst: Hoppla, wir leben! Reprinted in Günther Rühle:
Zeit und Theater. Von der Republik zur Diktatur, 1925-33, Band
II. Propyläen Verlag, Berlin.
ZECH, Paul: Das trunkene Schiff, eine szenische Ballade. Schau-
spiel-Verlag, Leipzig., n.d. (1924).

Some important articles, brochures and proceedings

BRANDT, Willy: 'Theater als Politicum', Theater Rundschau, 18.
Jahrgang (November 1972).
BRAULICH, Heinrich: 'Der Verrat an der Volksbühnenbewegung —
Von den Anfängen bis zur Übergabe der Berliner Volksbühne an den
Hitlerfaschismus (1890-1939)', Wissenschaftliche Zeitschrift der
Humboldt-Universität zu Berlin, Gesellschafts- und Sprachwissen-
schaftliche Reihe, Jahrgang XVIII (1969), Heft 1, pp. 37-52.
DAVIES, Cecil W.: 'Educating a theatre audience: the German Volks-
bühne', Studies in Adult Education, vol. 3. David & Charles, 1971.
— 'The Volksbühne — a descriptive chronology', Theatre Quarterly,
vol. II, No. 5. (1972), pp. 57-64.
— 'Theatre seat prices in the Federal Republic of Germany', Appendix
V of the Report of the Committee of Enquiry into Seat Prices. Arts
Council of Great Britain, 1973.
NESTRIEPKE, Siegfried: 'Volksbühnen und Theater-Austellung', Die
Viertewand, vol. 7 (1927), pp. 2-4.

— Der Weg zur Volksbühne, Berlin, 1948.

— 'Vom Bülowplatz zur Bundesalle', Freie Volksbühne zur Eröffnung, Berlin, 30 April 1963. FVB, Berlin, 1963.

OSCHILEWSKI, W. G.: 'Mehring, ein Pionier der VB', VB Spiegel (March 1971).

— 'Ein grosser Moralist unserer Zeit [on Mehring]', VB Spiegel, (June 1971).

— Siegfried Nestriepke zum Gedenken. arani Verlag, Berlin-Grune-wald, 1964.

PAUL, Anton A.: 'Die Meinungen des Volksbühnen-Publikums', Bühne und Parkett, (September/October 1973), p. 26.

PISCATOR, Erwin: 'Volksbühne heute', Freie Volksbuhne zur Eröff-nung, Berlin, 30 April 1963. FVB, Berlin, 1963.

Schriften des Verbandes der deutschen Volksbühnen-Vereine e. V.:
Heft 11, Der 21. Volksbühnentag (Augsburg, 1964); Heft 12, Der 22. Volksbühnentag (Dortmund, 1966); Heft 13, Der 23. Volksbühnentag (Saarbrücken, 1968); Heft 14, Der 24. Volksbühnentag (Düsseldorf, 1970).

Schriftenreihe des Bundes der Theatergemeinden e. V.: Heft 6, Düssel-dorfer Theatergespräche '71: 'Theater wozu— Theater wohin?'; Heft 7, Mainzer Theatergespräche '73: 'Politik und Theater. Theater und Fernsehen.'

SCHULZ, Günter: 'Die Volksbühne und ihre Forderungen an das Theater', VB Spiegel (October 1970), p. 1.

NOTES

PROLOGUE

1   <u>H</u>, pp. 11-12.
2   <u>S</u>, p. 185.
3   Schlieper, p. 198.
4   Two years later, in 1871, six months after the establishment of the German empire, Bismarck was to begin his <u>Kulturkampf</u> against the supra-national pretensions of the Catholic Church.
5   Taylor, pp. 129-30.
6   <u>F</u>, p. 64.
7   Cf. Sartre's use of a classical subject in <u>Les Mouches</u>.
8   <u>S</u>, p. 18.
9   1845-1909.
10 Even some months after the founding of the Freie Volksbühne in August 1890, came the Association for Popular Entertainment (Verein für Volksunterhaltung) whose chief aim was to try to prevent Social Democracy from monopolising theatrical movements. It planned to give seven performances in its first year, including two plays by Schiller and two by Charlotte Birch-Pfeiffer (1800-1868), a popular purveyor of other people's goods — e.g. her play <u>Die Waise von Lowood</u> (<u>Jane Eyre</u>). The admission charge was to be 40 Pfennigs and the deficit covered by wealthy patrons. This never came to life.
11 <u>S</u>, p. 26.
12 Osborne, p. 2.
13 <u>Frankfurter Zeitung</u>, 10 May 1904.
14 <u>Neue Rundschau</u> (1913), p. 328.
15 <u>Frankfurter Zeitung</u>, 12 January 1887.
16 Conrad Schmidt, editor of the <u>Berliner Volkstribüne</u>.

ACT I / 1 The first decade

1 <u>Deutsche Illustrierte Zeitung</u>, 13 June 1885.
2 <u>Freie Bühne für modernes Leben</u>, Jahrgang 1, Heft 3.
3 Some sources omit Stockhausen and mention others.
4 Schley.
5 <u>Die Nation</u>, 26 October 1889 (in Brahm, pp. 298-9).
6 Schley, p. 52.
7 Brahm, p. 299.
8 He did not hurl them on to the stage (see Schley, p. 46 and note 134).
9 Schley, p. 46.
10 <u>Die Gesellschaft</u>, Jahrgang 1893, Heft 2.
11 All these citations from <u>S</u>, p. 185.
12 <u>Die Kunst dem Volke</u>, Nr 6, quoted in <u>G</u>, p. 11.
13 Cf. his reference in the 'Appeal' to 'the cheap seats'.
14 <u>G</u>, p. 17.
15 See Appendix A.
16 The ultimate exclusion of the first two may have been on account of their large casts.
17 <u>G</u>, p. 18.
18 <u>S</u>, p. 106.
19 Türk, quoted in <u>S</u>, p. 106.
20 <u>G</u>, pp. 46-7.
21 Namely: <u>Vor Sonnenaufgang</u>, <u>Doppelselbstmord</u>, <u>Thérèse Raquin</u>, <u>Ghosts</u>.
22 <u>G</u>, p. 45.
23 <u>G</u>, p. 34.
24 Bernhard von Richthofen (1836-1895) was a relative of Frieda, wife of D. H. Lawrence. His comment on the theatrical developments of this time was: 'Die ganze Richtung passt uns nicht!' (see Robert Lucas, <u>Frieda Lawrence</u>, English translation, 1973, p. 19).
25 <u>F</u>, p. 39.
26 <u>S</u>, <u>passim</u>.
27 <u>G</u>, p. 68.
28 List of artistic experts: Bruno Wille, Wilhelm Bölsche, Julius Hart, O. E. Hartleben, the two Kampffmeyers, Fritz Mauthner, Leopold Schönhoff, Carl Wildberger (all of the 'old guard'); Gustav Landauer, Dr Albert Dresdner (historian), Adalbart von Hanstein (poet), Maximilian Harden (publisher of <u>Zukunft</u>), Wilhelm Hegeler (short-story writer), Max Marschalk (musicologist), Wilhelm von Polenz (a 'lord of the manor' turned novelist), Ernst von Wollzogen (a clever conversationalist), Victor Holländer (orchestral conductor), Emil Lessing (theatre director) (<u>G</u>, pp. 69-70). Nestriepke says there were twenty, but gives only these nineteen names.

29 Mehring, p. 291.
30 <u>S</u>, p. 73.
31 For example: Ibsen, <u>The Master Builder</u>; Hauptmann, <u>Hanneles Himmelfahrt</u> (<u>Hannele's Assumption</u>).
32 Mehring's socialist activities continued unabated after his leaving the Volksbühne. At the start of the First World War he was a member of the Opposition and later was one of the founders of the Spartakusbund. He died on 29 January 1919, physically broken through the harsh conditions so-called 'protective custody'.
33 1892-93: two sections (2,400 members).
    1893-94: five sections (5000-6000 members).
    1894: six sections (6,600 members).
    October 1894: seven sections (7,600 members).
    April 1895: eight sections (7,600 members).
34 See Appendix B.
35 This, however, could also have been due to the fact that the proposal involved having evening performances as well as those on Sunday afternoons. The idea was to have been presented to an extraordinary general meeting, but because of police action this never happened.
36 <u>Bildungsschwindel</u>. Said in 1892 by party secretary Auer in relation to the Freie Volksbühne and the Arbeiterbildungsschule.
37 The Freie Bühne was revived for single plays in 1893, 1895, 1897, 1898, 1899 and 1901. In November 1909 it was resurrected for the last time to present a memorial performance of <u>Vor Sonnenaufgang</u>.
38 In a letter of 1 August 1893 (see Osborne, p. 131, note 1).
39 Schwab-Felisch, p. 195.
40 <u>Ibid</u>.
41 Wille (quoted in <u>G</u>, p. 119).
42 List given in <u>G</u>, pp. 122-3.
43 <u>G</u>, p. 111.
44 Other places where attempts were made to found Volksbühne associations even as early as this were Cologne, Frankfurt am Main and Leipzig. Interested persons in Vienna, Zürich and even Milan were in contact with the Berlin leaders.
45 <u>G</u>, p. 133.
46 This is clearly the view of Heinz Selo.

ACT I / 2 Into the twentieth century

1 <u>S</u>, p. 78.
2 See Appendix B.
3 Lists in <u>G</u>, pp. 179-81 and 229-31.
4 <u>G</u>, p. 234.
5 <u>G</u>, p. 170.
6 See Appendix B.

7   Lists in <u>G</u>, pp. 207-9.

8   In 1898 he volunteered to write one thousand addresses every month in order to enable the periodical to be sent to members by post at a cheap rate.

9   Löhr became worse in health and died in April 1902.

10 <u>G</u>, p. 263.

11 Melchinger, p. 8.

12 Particularly in plays by Strindberg, Wilde and Wedekind at the Kleines Theater.

13 Tape-recorded interview with the author, 10 May 1974.

14 Julius Bab, <u>Volksbühne</u>. In <u>Literarische Welt</u>, Berlin, Heft 26 (30 June 1927), p. 6. Reprinted in Bab/Bergholz, p. 305.

15 Bab/Bergholz, p. 307.

16 These quotations from <u>G</u>, 289-91.

17 <u>G</u>, p. 246.

18 Later it was decided that the interest on single shares (10 Marks) would be added to the capital, but that interest on blocks of five shares would be payable yearly on 1 October. All share capital was ultimately to be repayable, either after two years from the opening of the theatre (with six months' notice), or gradually, through amortisation; also if the holder were ill, unemployed, no longer living in Greater Berlin, or deceased.

19 'Immer strebe zum Ganzen! Und kannst du selber kein Ganzes werden, als dienendes Glied schliess an ein Ganzes dich an!' (<u>G</u>, p. 342).

20 Lists in <u>G</u>, pp. 327-8, 387-9.

21 'O Schutzgeist alles Schönen, steig hernieder.'

22 <u>G</u>, p. 353.

FIRST INTERMISSION War and revolution

1 <u>H</u>, p. 349.

2 L. Löb in <u>Penguin Companion to Literature</u>, vol. 2, p. 390.

ACT II / 1 To 1923

1 Oschilewski, p. 51.

2 <u>Ibid</u>.

3 'eingetragener Verein': a 'registered society', for legal purposes.

4 'The author to the producer, October 1921', translated by Vera Mendel in <u>Masses and Man</u>, Nonesuch Press, 1923, pp. ix-x.

5 Translated by Vera Mendel (see note 4).

6 <u>Masses and Man</u>, pp. ix and x.

7 Jürgen Fehling, 'Note on the production of <u>Masses and Man</u>', translated by Vera Mendel, pp. 57-8.

8 <u>Masses and Man</u>, p. x.

9 According to Piscator — not a reliable witness in this matter — the executive bore Nestriepke a grudge on account of this for a long time.

ACT II / 2 The Piscator affair

1 Even this, alleges Rühle, was 'because the Volksbühne had remained spiritually untouched by the revolution and had not found the way back to the social commitment of its origins' (Rühle, p. 198).

2 Piscator's theatre supported the actors' strike, and the actors' union authorised the theatre to play; then Gorter, the actual concessionaire, dismissed the company; but Piscator re-engaged them half an hour later.

3 PT, p. 60.

4 PT, p. 40.

5 Maria Ley-Piscator, p. 72.

6 PT, p. 60.

7 Maria Ley-Piscator, p. 74.

8 Piscator says 1880, but this is typical of the slips in Das politische Theater.

9 Fifty-six actors are needed.

10 Oddly enough, Piscator does not claim credit for this, but gives it to the author: 'The author has expressed the events in an objective manner and without poetic pretensions, in a kind of scenic illustration. Not for nothing does the piece bear the sub-title: An Epic Drama' (PT, p. 61).

11 Quoted in PT, p. 62.

12 I, p. 17.

13 Innes says that Piscator 'experimented with a formal prologue in Flags, in which the play was declared to be a puppet show' (I, p. 105).

14 PT, p. 63.

15 PT, p. 85.

16 PT, p. 78. Piscator misnames Umnitsch 'Umeitet' and Sawin 'Ssarin'. He is obviously writing from memory.

17 Arthur Eloesser in Das blaue Heft, 15 March 1926. In Rühle, p. 694.

18 PT, p. 79.

19 PT, p. 81.

20 PT, p. 82.

21 Paquet, Sturmflut. Volksbühne Verlag, Berlin, 1926, p. 7.

22 Sturmflut, p. 110.

23 PT, p. 80.

24 Rühle, p. 693.

25 Rühle, p. 692.

26 Rühle, p. 695.

27 PT, p. 84.

28 Ibid.

29   Staatliches Schauspielhaus, 4 December 1924, directed, by Jürgen
     Fehling — his only close contact with Brecht. They disagreed
     strongly over the production (see Hanser, p. 36).
30   Company of the Deutsches Theater in the Lessing Theater, 27
     February 1925. Brecht regarded this as a decisive attempt at
     epic Theatre (see Hanser, p. 37).
31   See PT pp. 88 ff.; Rühle, pp. 721 ff.; Bab/Bergholz, pp. 163 ff.
32   Bernhard Diebold in Tod der Klassiker. Quoted in PT, p. 91.
33   Bela Balász. Quoted in PT, p. 95.
34   'The strongest propaganda that can be devised arises simply out
     of objective, unretouched, raw reality' (PT, p. 80).
35   H, p. 359.
36   Quoted in PT, p. 99.
37   PT, p. 97.
38   Holitscher must mean the Bühnenvolksbund, the 'Christian Volks-
     bühne' founded in 1919 (see Appendix D).
39   PT, p. 97-8.
40   PT, p. 100.
41   PT, pp. 100-1.
42   In Rühle, p. 785.
43   PT, pp. 101-2.
44   PT, p. 103.
45   Ibid.
46   Rühle, p. 788.
47   Rühle, p. 789
48   'Owing to lack of time, neither Herr Welk, nor Herr Holl, the
     director, nor I myself, saw a finished dress rehearsal, with the
     result that the night before, I disclaimed responsibility' (!)
     (PT, p. 109).
49   H, pp. 134-5.
50   See also Tilla Durieux' own account of this: 'In 1927 I saw a pro-
     duction of Schiller's The Robbers in the Staatstheater and thereby
     became acquainted with a — for me — new man: Erwin Piscator.
     His manner of production pleased me so much that I sought his
     personal acquaintance. He told me his plans, which so enthralled
     me that I determined to provide him with the money for a theatre.
     I gave him 400,000 gold marks and he rented the Theater am
     Nollendorfplatz, one of the largest in Berlin. It was opened on 3
     September 1927 with Hoppla, wir leben! by Ernst Toller. I played
     a role in the following production, that of the Czarina in the play
     Rasputin. Piscator's talent is indisputable. He was the first to
     follow Max Reinhardt in new ways of staging. He tried to combine
     film and live theatre, and achieved thereby astonishing results.
     And when in the epic satire, The Adventures of the Good Soldier
     Schwejk, he had Pallenberg marching on the 'treadmill', and land-
     scapes and artificial people passed him by, it gave an effect that

was new and enthralling.... But these contrivances cost so much
money that it could not be covered by the box-office receipts from
the audiences that streamed in in great numbers. After a brief
existence the theatre had to close'. (Durieux, pp. 317-18.)

51   Oschilewski, p. 36.
52   Kreuz-Zeitung, 14 July 1927.
53   Piscator admitted some truth in Alfred Kerr's description of this
     as 'a creepy-crawly tortoise of grey tent-cloth'.
54   Tape-recorded interview with the author, 10 May 1974.
55   Quoted in Oschilewski, p. 58.
56   Oschilewski, p. 39.

SECOND INTERMISSION   The Nazis

1   Chronik, p. 28.
2   Chronik, p. 29.
3   Chronik, p. 30.
4   Bochow, pp. 17-18.
5   Protokolle der Hauptversammlung vom 19. 12. 33. In: Volks-
    bühne e. V. (2), Materialien des Berliner Stadtarchivs. Quoted in
    Braulich.
6   'Seven sub-chambers were established to guide and control every
    sphere of cultural life: the Reich chambers of fine arts, music,
    the theatre, literature, the press, radio and the film. All persons
    engaged in these fields were obligated to join their respective
    chambers, whose decisions and directives had the validity of law.
    Among other powers, the chambers could expel — or refuse to
    accept— members for "political unreliability", which meant that
    those who were even lukewarm about National Socialism could be,
    and usually were, excluded from practicing [sic] their profession
    or art and thus deprived of a livelihood'. (Shirer, pp. 241-2.)
7   Neft, who had been pensioned in 1932, continued under the Nazis
    to receive a pension of 700 RM.
8   NB, p. 13.

ACT III / 1   In Berlin

1   Luft, p. 10.
2   Only the Russians occupied Berlin at this time. The American and
    British troops moved into their appointed sectors of the city on
    4 July 1945; the first session of the Allied Kommandatura was on
    11 July 1945. The French troops occupied their sector on 12
    August 1945. (In Brief, p. 33.)
3   Howley, p. 141.
4   Howley, p. 142.
5   Howley, p. 143.
6   Ist die Welt nicht schön? by Alec Dyer, the pen-name of a German
    living in London.

7   From the weekly periodical, sie. Quoted in NB, p. 126.
8   Oschilewski, p. 50.
9   Piscator, extempore speech to the Volksbühne conference in
    Kassel, 1962. Quoted in Oschilewski, p. 59.
10 Oschilewski, p. 60.
11 Oschilewski, p. 50.
12 22. Volksbühnentag, p. 22.
13 22. Volksbühnentag, pp. 29-30.
14 Luft, p. 7.
15 Quoted in I, p. 175.
16 Piscator's introduction to the rororo edition of the play.
17 22. Volksbühnentag, p. 31.
18 21. Volksbühnentag, p. 117.
19 Ibid.
20 22. Volksbühnentag, p. 31.
21 22. Volksbühnentag, p. 33.
22 22. Volksbühnentag, p. 32.
23 22. Volksbühnentag, p. 34.
24 Piscator's other FVB Productions include: The Merchant of
    Venice, Androcles and the Lion, Fuhrmann Henschell (Hauptmann).
    Other productions during his directorship include: Osborne,
    Luther (Peter Zadek), Arden, Workhouse Donkey (Ulrich Erfurth),
    Walser, Überlebensgross Herr Krott (The larger than life Mr
    Krott) (Peter Palitzch), Sartre, Nekrassov (Robert Freytag).
25 22. Volksbühnentag, p. 40.
26 Ibid.
27 Richard Voigt (21. Volksbühnentag, p. 65).
28 23. Volksbühnentag, p. 102 and 24. Volksbühnentag, p. 142.
29 22. Volksbühnentag, p. 110.
30 24. Volksbühnentag, p. 133-4.
31 See Appendix B.
32 Bochow, p. 76.

ACT III / 2 Developments outside Berlin

1   21. Volksbühnentag, p. 20. The Spielplan is the plan, fixed months
    in advance, of which work in the repertoire is being performed
    each day.
2   Bochow. See List of Sources.
3   During the 1970s the TAT has suffered vicissitudes. An unsuccess-
    ful attempt at a collective directorship was followed by the
    appointment of Rainer-Werner Fassbinder as director in 1974. His
    brief period of office was stormy, though some productions, notably
    his Uncle Vanya, were outstanding. He resigned without notice in
    June 1975.   In December 1976 the city took over the TAT and Frankfurt
    Volksbühne as a municipal limited company, the former becoming a
    Children's and Youth Theatre.

APPENDICES

From S, pp. 187 ff. Reprinted from Berliner Volksblatt, 10 August 1890

1 The Freie Volksbühne Association sets itself the task of bringing before the people poetry in its modern sense, and particularly to to present, read in public and explain through lectures up-to-date works executed with truthfulness.

2 Membership is acquired by payment of the registration fee (11). It lapses automatically if the minimum contribution (11 & 12) is unpaid by the 7th of any one month.

3 An Ordinary General Meeting is held every April and August.

4 Notice of each General Meeting and its agenda is given at least four days in advance through an insertion in a workers' daily newspaper published in Berlin and to be decided by the Executive, and by street posters on the day of the meeting.

5 The August General Meeting elects the Chairman, Treasurer and Secretary, the six ordinary committee members, the Organisers and the three Auditors.

6 The form of election is decided by the meeting before each election.

7 The Chairman, Treasurer and Secretary together constitute the Executive.

8 The Executive manages the business of the Association, represents it publicly, is authorised to conclude binding agreements, enter into engagements, acquire and dispose of property on behalf of the Association. It is responsible for choosing and appointing an artistic director [Regisseur], it selects the actors, readers and lecturers. If the Association's means permit, it is empowered to engage a permanent acting company. If the number of elected

organisers is inadequate, it may nominate organisers to make up
the full number.

9 The Committee consists of the three members of the Executive
   and six ordinary members [5]. It has the right of co-option to fill
   vacancies caused by individual resignations during the working
   year. If, however, the number of the Committee falls at any time
   to four, or the Executive is reduced to one, a General Meeting must
   be called within fourteen days for supplementary elections.

10 The Executive decides the plays to be produced, the subject of
   lectures and readings, and decides in all questions, what is author-
   itative for the literary character of the Association.

11 The size of the registration fee and the regular monthly contributions is decided by self-assessment, but the registration fee must
   amount to at least 1 Mark and the contribution for the months
   October to March inclusive to at least 50 Pfennigs per month, for
   the remainder of the year at least 25 Pfennigs per month.

12 The Executive is empowered, if the expenses are covered, to
   decide that the contributions for the months of March and September
   remain unlevied, and if the normal income does not suffice to cover
   the expenses, to levy supplements to the contributions of up to 10
   Pfennigs per month.

13 The Treasurer sets up collection offices in all parts of the city
   according to need, whose occupiers receive the contributions and
   registrations of members. The membership card is issued on
   payment of the registration fee. It bears on the first page the name,
   status and permanent address of the member and is valid for the
   named member only. The monthly contributions can be paid at any
   chosen collection office. The receipt is given by sticking a voucher
   to the value of the contribution paid on the appropriate monthly col-
   umn on the card. Only a member who can prove by producing his
   card that he has paid the statutory contributions has the right to
   attend performances and general meetings.

14 The Treasurer administers the property of the Association. He is
   bound and empowered to deposit amounts of over 300 Marks in a
   place of safety. For drawing deposited money a cheque is required
   signed by all three members of the Executive. The Treasurer must
   present a statement of accounts to each ordinary general meeting.

15 The auditors are empowered to inspect the account books jointly at
   any time, and are required to do this at least once a quarter.

16 In each month from October to March at least one performance
   takes place for each member.

17 If necessary the membership is divided into sections by the Executive. The performances for each section are the same.

18 Seats are allocated at performances by the organisers by means of
   a lottery.

19 The organisers choose a chairman and two committee members
    from among their number. These put the tickets in the urns and
    decide which seats are to be excluded from the lottery when the
    number of seats available is greater than the number of members
    who should obtain seats at the performance.
20 The lottery must be prepared in time for members to be able to
    draw their tickets one hour before the beginning of the performance
    at latest.
21 Each member who has produced his card at the theatre entrance,
    goes to the lottery tables on which urns with the duplicate tickets
    stand and draws from the urn a ticket on which the name and number
    of the seat is indicated. Each urn is superintended by one organiser.
22 The Association's working year runs from 1 September to 31
    August.
23 Resolutions concerning alterations to the statutes or winding up the
    association must be delivered to the Executive at least fourteen
    days before the particular general meeting at which they are to be
    debated.
24 A two-thirds majority of those present is required to alter the
    statutes or wind up the Association.
25 In the event of the Association's being wound up the assets in hand
    are to be disposed of according to the decision of the last general
    meeting.

[For the many modifications made to these articles in the early years,
see S, pp. 187 ff.]

APPENDIX B

Membership statistics of the Freie Volksbühne, 1893-94 (From G,
p. 89)

    Total membership: 6,312
    Men: 3,272
    Women: 3,040

Occupations	Men	Wives
Carpenters	448	144
Not certain	269	79
Locksmiths	217	66
Shop assistants	204	29
Stonemasons	193	58
Painters	154	46
Bookbinders	144	34
Shopkeepers	134	42
Compositors	124	33

Occupations	Men	Wives
Tailors	121	—
Beltmakers	113	28
Mechanics	102	28
Printers	94	24
Lathe operators [Dreher]	88	28
Tinkers	95	34
Upholsterers	76	27
Woodturners [Drechsler]	71	24
Shoemakers	76	11
Lithographers	64	26
Engravers	63	19
Moulders	63	19
Domestic servants	57	17
Saddlers	50	15
Civil servants and teachers	27	9
Engineers and technicians	22	8
Draughtsmen	10	3
Manufacturers	9	4
Drivers	6	3
Editors	5	2
Students	10	—

Women in employment

Tailoresses		290
Unskilled female workers		246
Female shop assistants		67
Women teachers		4

Occupation unknown	259	1,132

Membership statistics of the Freie Volksbühne at the turn of the century (from G, p. 156).

4,921 members, male and female, gave their occupations.

Men

Joiners	357
'Workers'	252
In commerce [Kaufleute]	238
Printers	230
Tailors	142
Stonemasons	122
Mechanics	110
Machine-minders	110

Men

Turners	102
Belt-makers	96
Bookbinders	86
Tinsmiths	78
Painters	77
Paperhangers	70
Builders	63
Moulders	62
Wood-turners	60
Leatherworkers, etc.	58
Civil servants	20
Writers	14
Private means	12
Doctors	6

Women

'Women workers'	405
Needlewomen	276
Tailoresses	270
Saleswomen	74
Bookkeepers	41
Dressmakers	30
Ironers	25

The Neue Freie Volksbühne: Census of occupations, October 1900 (from G, p. 193)

548 men answered the questionnaire and a few hundred women. Details of women's answers are not available.

Cabinet makers	55
Printers	41
'In trade'	38
Fitters	30
Tailors	24
Mechanics	20
Shoemakers	18
Turners	15

The Neue Freie Volksbühne: Census of occupations, winter 1902-03
(from G, p. 251)

1,022 answered the questionnaire.

Men

Cabinetmakers	98
Printers	69
Retail trade	51
Fitters	39
Tailors	33
'Workers'	31
Turners	24
Glass-workers	24
Upholsterers	23
Builders	22
Shoemakers	22
Painters	21
Bookbinders, etc.	20
Writers	6
Manufacturers	3
Editors	2
Dairy owner	1
Engineer	1

Women

Tailoresses	53
Sempstresses	35
Female workers	27
Shop assistants	26
(and others in smaller numbers)	

Membership statistics of the Freie Volksbühne Berlin, 1952-53

75,000 copies of questionnaire issued.
32,000 completed: 67.1 per cent from West Berlin; 32.9 per cent
from East Berlin.

A.

Professions	17,998	55.9%
Out of work	1,417	4.4%
Pensioners	5,087	4.4%
Housewives, daughters, school children, students without income	7,695	23.9%

<u>B.</u>

Occupations of the 19,415 who gave a profession (whether or not in work):

Self-employed	2,019	10.4%
Helping in family business	116	0.6%
Commercial and administrative employees in leading positions	466	2.4%
Commercial and administrative employees <u>not</u> in leading positions	8,524	43.9%
Other salaried employees	5,534	28.5%
Manual workers	2,757	14.2%

<u>C.</u>

Category <u>Self-employed</u> (2,019) included:

Lawyers, economic advisers, doctors, dentists, chemists   434

Others: cabinet makers, tailors, electricians, hairdressers, agents and masseurs, etc., approximately   300

That is, out of 2,019, there were about seven hundred with secure positions and incomes.

<u>D.</u>

Category <u>Other salaried employees</u> (5,534) included:

Magistrates, State lawyers, salaried doctors and dentists, high school and Oberschule teachers, engineers, architects   652

Others: technicians, foremen, elementary school teachers, librarians, nurses, kindergarten teachers, etc., approximately   250

That is, out of 5,534, there were about nine hundred with above average incomes.

<u>E.</u>

Self-employed with secure positions and income	700
Salaried employees with secure positions and income	900
Commercial and administrative employees in leading positions	466

Approximate total of those with secure positions and income 2,000

Age-groups and occupations of new members of FVB, 1965-6

Total number of new members asked: approximately one thousand

A. Occupations (%)

Salaried employees	35.0
Housewives	21.4
No information	18.4
Craftsmen and manual workers	15.0
Academics	4.0
School-children and apprentices	3.0
Pensioners and those of private means	3.0
Own business	0.3

B. Comparison of these with population of West Berlin as a whole (%) (Figures available in four categories only)

	New members	Population
Salaried employees	64.0	34.0
Manual workers	28.0	51.0
School/Apprentices	7.5	5.0
Self-employed	0.6	10.0

C. Ages of new members, compared with whole population of West Berlin (%)

Year of birth	New members	Population
1880-1899	4.0	23.0
1900-1919	21.0	37.0
1920-1939	51.0	27.0
1940-1949	24.0	13.0

i.e. 75% members under 45 years of age, against 40% in West Berlin as a whole.

Reasons for resignations from FVB (results of two enquiries) (%)

	1962	1965
Dissatisfaction	28.0	33.0
Age or illness	25.0	26.0
Professional or family reasons	15.0	15.0
Change of address	15.0	13.0
Financial reasons	4.0	3.0
Other reasons	–	0.9

APPENDIX C   THE SIXTEEN DISTRICTS OF THE FEDERATION IN
1930 (from H)

Saxony (Free State)   Forty-one Volksbühne societies, served by nineteen theatres in eleven towns and two touring companies,
Saxony (Province) and Anhalt   Twenty-five Volksbühne societies,
served by ten theatres in nine towns and two touring companies.
Thuringia   Sixteen Volksbühne societies, served by nine theatres in
nine towns.
Lower Silesia   Nineteen Volksbühne societies, served by ten theatres
in eight towns and two touring companies.
Upper Silesia   Six Volksbühne societies, served by four theatres in four
towns and one touring company.
Brandenburg   Twenty-three Volksbühne societies, served by seven
theatres in seven towns (omitting Berlin) and seven touring companies.
East Prussia, Free City of Danzig, Memel Territory   Twenty-two
Volksbühne societies, served by six theatres in five towns and three
touring companies.
Pomerania   Seven Volksbühne societies, served by five theatres in
five towns and two touring companies.
Nordmark   Twenty-six Volksbühne societies, served by seventeen
theatres in 9 towns and two touring companies.
Lower Saxony   Twenty-three Volksbühne societies, served by eighteen
theatres in twelve towns and four touring companies.
Westphalia   Seventeen Volksbühne societies, served by six theatres in
five towns and three touring companies.
Rheinland   Twenty-three Volksbühne societies, served by seventeen
theatres in thirteen towns and four touring companies.
Hessen, Hessen-Nassau, Saargebiet   Seventeen Volksbühne societies,
served by ten theatres in seven towns and three touring companies.
Baden, Pfalz   Twelve Volksbühne societies, served by eight theatres
in eight towns, and two touring companies.
Württemburg   Eight Volksbühne societies, served by four theatres in
three towns and one touring company.
Bavaria   Twelve Volksbühne societies, served by sixteen theatres in
nine towns and one touring company.

APPENDIX D   THE CHRISTIAN 'VOLKSBÜHNE' MOVEMENT

1   Der Bühnenvolksbund (The National Theatre Union)

Following the tendency in the early years of the twentieth century known
as the re-encounter of culture and Church (Wiederbegegnung von Kultur
und Kirche) a journalist, Wilhelm Karl Gerst, founded in 1916 in

Hildesheim a broadly based Union for the promotion of German Theatrical Culture (Verband zur Förderung deutscher Theaterkultur), united
under the motto 'Cultural theatre instead of showbusiness' (Kulturthe-
ater statt Geschäftstheaters). This soon saw the Berlin Volksbühne as
its organisational model, and at a conference held in Frankfurt am
Main in April 1919 the Bühnenvolksbund was founded with Gerst as
general secretary and a head office in Frankfurt (later moved to
Berlin). It described itself as 'an alliance for the encouragement of
the theatre in a Christian German National spirit'. Closely modelled
on the Volksbühne and with an impressive list of publications to its
credit, the Bühnenvolksbund, starting from the Christian-National
rather than the Socialist-International position, achieved work comparable with that of its prototype and rival, until Nazi measures in
1933 brought it to an end.

2   Der Bund der Theatergemeinden (Union of Theatre Societies)

After 1949 organisations formerly associated with the Bühnenvolksbund
began to revive, especially in the Augsburg-Munich and Cologne-
Düsseldorf areas. In February 1951, chiefly through the initiative of
Max Hohenester and Karl Fürst, both of Augsburg, a conference held
in Frankfurt decided unanimously to found a successor to the Bühnenvolksbund: Der Bund der Theatergemeinden. A steering committee
was set up under the chairmanship of Dr Rudolf Reuter, a library
director of Cologne, who later became the 'Grand Old Man' of the
movement, and whose professional and voluntary interests were bound
up with literature, theatre and adult education. Though not the first
chairman (that was Hohenester until his death in 1956), he became
vice-chairman in 1954, succeeding to the chair in 1956, a position he
held for seventeen years, resigning at the 21st Annual Conference at
Mainz in 1973.

Conflict with the Volksbühne came quickly. Dr Benecke, Managing
Director of the Deutscher Bühnenverein, welcomed the formation of a
Christian theatre audience organisation. Nestriepke replied in an open
letter: the formation of such an organisation was mistaken; 'Christian'
audience organisations could only exist to draw attention to, or produce,
works of their own persuasion. In response, Dr Reuter pointed out the
historical roots of his movement and its independence from party or
confessional ties; he suggested that the two organisations had many
common aims and ought to co-operate, but that the new body could
make contacts inaccessible to the Volksbühne.

The themes of the annual conferences express a wide spectrum of
interest in the theatre. The monthly periodical, Theater Rundshau,
published since 1955 carries serious reviews and articles. Information
sheets, brochures and booklets are also published.

Since 1955, the Bund, its headquarters now in Bonn, has been affiliated to the International Theatre Institute, and its general manager, Dr Weizel, was vice-president of the German section of the ITI from 1964 to 1971. It is strongly represented at the international meetings of IATO where, as elsewhere, a friendly relationship with the Volksbühne is now well established.

By 1975 the Bund had a membership of about 140,000 persons in thirty local societies with about three hundred 'feeder' groups. On the whole this 'Christian' organisation flourishes best where the 'Social Democratic' one has less success. The following is a list of the largest affiliated bodies of the Bund der Theatergemeinden (1971) with the Volksbühne figures (1969) in those places for comparison:

Place	Theatergemeinde (1971)	Volksbühne (1969)
Munich	50,000	1,650*
Berlin	17,000	83,780
Düsseldorf	13,000	13,500
Cologne	13,000	10,000
Bonn	11,500	2,790
Augsburg	5,000	2,275
Wurzburg (including Youth Organisation)	4,600	716
Wiesbaden	2,800	639
Münster	2,500	833
Mönchengladbach	2,000	—
Wuppertal	2,000	11,750
Bamberg	1,250	347
Frankfurt	1,000	18,232
Totals (thirteen places)	127,650	146,566
Total (omitting Berlin)	110,650	62,786
Total (omitting Berlin and Munich)	60,650	61,136

*There is also a larger 'breakaway' Volksbühne in Munich, whose constitution excludes it from the Federation.

APPENDIX E   OTHER AUDIENCE ORGANISATIONS

Germany

A number of audience organisations are now run commercially, with
popular programmes, often arranging bus groups through local voluntary organisers who are given free tickets. These organisations
sometimes serve small towns and villages more effectively than can
the Volksbühne.

One of the most important is the Besucherring Dr Otto Kasten.
Founded in Lübeck, when the Volksbühne there was at low ebb, this
organisation now has many branches. Its headquarters are at Wiesbaden.

Austria

In Graz two organisations, the Grazer Theatergemeinschaft and the
Theaterringgemeinde work in close co-operation with each other and
with the Graz United Theatres. First-night, fixed-day, and flexible
season tickets can be bought with differing price reductions. In 1972-3
the numbers of these were:

Fixed-day seasons: 1,369   (cf. 220 in 1950)
Flexible seasons: 3,500
First-night seasons: 1,000

The periodical Theater in Graz appears three times a month during the
ten-month season and is a joint publication of the municipal theatres
and the two audience organisations, an arrangement unique in the
German-speaking world.

In Vienna, the Theater der Jugend arranges a whole series of
season tickets for schoolchildren (and teachers), and a series of music
cycles for children and young people.

For young people of sixteen-plus a Jugendabonnement gives admission to nine theatre performances and one concert, free admission
to certain art galleries, the Vienna planetarium and certain folk high
school courses; also a 50 per cent reduction in all Vienna studio
theatres.

Switzerland

Organisation is dominated by the Federalism of the Swiss state. There
are eleven different organisations, all with different structures and
different sources of income. All seek to be more than mere ticket-
agencies and to work in partnership with theatres and audiences. All
are fully neutral, politically and ideologically. The total membership
is about 14,500, and membership of individual organisations varies
from 190 to 4,100 (in Berne). Affiliation is to the umbrella organisation,
the Swiss Theatre Associations (Theatervereine der Schweiz). All organisations have youth sections; in 1974 there were 8,750 youth members.

Scandinavia

Denmark, Norway and Sweden all have strong audience organisations in their capital cities.

ARTE, in Copenhagen grew tenfold between 1970-1 and 1973-4 because of a subsidised rescue operation which was mounted to save several private theatres. In 1973-4, ARTE distributed half a million theatre tickets in the city. As a result of pressure from ARTE Danish theatre law has been amended so that by 1975-6 a system of half-price season tickets is extended from Copenhagen to the whole country.

Oslo has a Theatre Centre closely associated with the trade union movement and with much in common with the Volksbühne. The lively and long-established Swedish organisation Skådebanen (The Theatre) is very active, especially in Stockholm.

IATO

International Association of theatre-public organisations (Internationale Arbeitsgemeinschaft der Theaterbesucherorganisationen). A kind of standing conference of theatre audience organisations on an international level, meeting bi- or tri-ennially in different countries (e. g. 1972: Graz. 1974: Oslo). There is regular representation from the non-German organisations already mentioned, and representatives of experimental organisations or youth organisations in other countries have been present from time to time (e. g. France, Holland, Yugoslavia). The present author has attended the 1972 and 1974 conferences as a British contact. To some extent the conferences are dominated by the two great German organisations, and Gerard Schmid, manager of the Federation of the Volksbühne Societies, is general secretary of IATO, the Federation office providing IATO's secretariat.

Between conferences an executive committee meets at least once a year.

The conference can pass resolutions to be sent to governments or elsewhere. The 1974 conference passed a resolution calling for greater financial support from governments for audience-organisations.

Great Britain

The Federation of Playgoers' Societies was set up by the Council of Repertory Theatres (CORT) in 1957 to link audience support organisations and to provide a forum for exchange of ideas and methods of supporting theatres. Its annual conference is the most important event of its year. The Scottish Federation and the Young Playgoers' Federation are offshoots. It has some sixty affiliated societies. It is not affiliated to IATO and has comparatively little in common with the Volksbühne and related organisations.

INDEX

Theatres, concert halls etc. are listed under appropriate place-names.
Plays are listed under their authors' names. References to the Volksbühne, its constituent bodies and the principal sources are not indexed.

Abendroth, Günther, 135
Academic Dramatic Association, 51
Adler, Georg, 9
Agrell, see Anzengruber
Alberti (-Sittendfeld), Conrad, 25; Brot, 24
Allgemeine Arbeiter-Union, 96
Allgemeiner Deutscher Arbeiter-verein (ADAV), 3
Alte Tante, 4, 19
Altona, 53, 139
Antoine, André, 10, 14, 52
Anouilh, Jean: La Grotte, 134
Anzengruber, Ludwig, 13, 46, 70; Der Pfarrer von Kirchfeld, 33, 49; Das vierte Gebot, 18; Doppelselbstmord, 31, 33, 150; Einsam, 53
Arbeiterbildungsschule, 37, 55, 151
Arbeitersängerchor, 73
Arden, John: The Workhouse Donkey, 156
ARTE, 169
Association for Popular Entertainment, see Verein für Volksunterhaltung
Association for the Founding of People's Theatres, see Verein zur Begründung von Volksbühnen
Auber, D. F. E.: Fra Diavolo, 70
Augier, Émile, 46
Auer (party secretary), 151
Augsburg, 11, 166ff
Augsburger Allgemeine Zeitung, 13

Baake, Curt, 23, 25, 27, 38, 62f, 73, 75, 115
Bab, Julius, 71f, 84, 104, 123, 139
Bach, J. S., 117
Baden-Pfalz, 140, 165
Baginski, Richard, 27
Balázs, Bela, 36, 104, 154
Bamberg, 167
Barlach, Ernst: Der tote Tag, 94
Barlog, Boleslaw, 118f
Barmen, 60

Barnay, Ludwig, 6, 9
Bartenstein, 88
Barthelmann, Fritz, 120ff
Bauhaus, 110
Baum, Bruno, 120
Bavaria, 92, 139, 165
Bayreuth, 6
Bebel, August, 38
Bechmann, Walter, 128
Becker, Maria, 128
Beethoven, 61, 82, 111
Benecke, Dr, 166
Berg, Leo, 20
Berger, Hermann, 52
Berisch (theatre director), 94
Berlin, vii, 13f, 19, 23, 43, 52f, 56, 60, 88, 92, 114ff, 117-38, 141, 167
Alexanderplatz-Theater, 54
Belle-Alliance Theater, 6, 32f, 51, 54
Berliner Ensemble, see Theater am Schiffbauerdamm
Berliner Theater, 6, 9, 60
Böhmisches Brauhaus, 24, 27, 33, 41
Bürgerliches-Schauspielhaus, see Ostend Theater
Carl-Weiss Theater, see Ostend Theater
Colosseum, 126
Deutsches Künstler-Theater, 86
Deutsches Theater, 6, 47, 51, 58, 60, 63f, 67, 69, 71, 84, 117, 126f, 154
Fortuna Festsälen, 41
Freie Volksbühne, 131-8
Friedrich Wilhelmstädtisches Theater, 60
Grosses Schauspielhaus, 68
Hebbel-Theater, 78f, 123
Herrenhaus, 108
Kammerspiele, 70
Kastanienallee, see Prater Theater
Kleines Theater, 68f, 70, 152
Königliches Theater (Royal), 6ff
Krollschen Oper (Krolloper), 91
Lessing Theater, 6, 16, 30, 46, 60, 84, 86, 154

Lortzing Theater, 70
Luxemburgplatz, see Theater am
  Bülowplatz
Metropol Theater, 60
Municipal Opera, 124, 129
National Theater, see Ostend
  Theater
Neues Operetten-Theater, see
  Theater am Schiffbauerdamm
Neues Operntheater, see Kroll-
  schen Oper (Krolloper)
Neues Theater, 69f
Neues Volkstheater, 78, 91f, 94,
  129
Neue Welt, 75
Oberschöneweide Accumulator
  Works, 126
Ostend Theater, 6, 8, 28f, 31ff,
  46ff, 53f, 60
Prater Theater, 119, 121, 126
Proletarian Theatre, 95f
Rehberge (open-air theatre), 124
Residenz Theater, 6, 16
Sans Souci (concert hall), 29, 40f
Schiller-Theater, 45, 54, 69, 70,
  80, 124
Schiller-Theater Company, 69
Schiller-Theater East, 69
Schiller-Theater North, 69
Schlosspark Theater, 118
Staatliches Schauspielhaus
  (Staatstheater), 94, 103f, 154
Thalia Theater, 110
Theater am Bülowplatz, 79-86,
  90f, 94f, 111f, 114ff, 119f,
  125ff
Theater am Kurfürstendamm,
  125, 127-134
Theater am Nollendorfplatz (Pis-
  cator-Bühne), 97, 110f, 115
Theater am Schiffbauerdamm, 84,
  91, 110, 126, 135
Theater an der Schaperstrasse,
  see Freie Volksbühne
Theater in der Köpenicker
  Strasse, see Neues Volkstheater
Titania-Palast, Steglitz, 123
Tribüne, 95, 130
Viktoria Theater, 47
Volksbühne theatre, see Theater
  am Bülowplatz
Wallner Theater, 6
Weinstube bei Kempinski, 14

Zentral Theater, 6, 51, 53, 76,
  96f, 100
Zirkus Schumann ('theatre of a
  thousand'), 82f
Berlin Commission for Claims on
  Property, 125
Berliner Morgenpost, 99
Berliner Neueste Nachricht, 9
Berliner Volksblatt, 21, 38, 157
Berliner Volkstribüne, 149
Berliner Volkszeitung, 43
Berne, 168
Bersarin, Colonel-General, 118
Besucherring Dr Otto Kasten, 168
Bethmann-Hollweg, 104
Bielefeld, 139
Birch-Pfeiffer, Charlotte, 149;
  Die Waise von Lowood (Jane
  Eyre), 149
Bismarck, 2ff, 98, 149
Björnson, Björnstjerne, 13, 46,
  70, 79; Bankruptcy, 11; Beyond
  Our Power II, 64f; New System,
  64; Paul Lange and Tora Pars-
  berg, 64; The Glove, 18; When
  the Vineyards are in Blossom,
  84
Blaue Heft, Das, 153
Bleibtreu, Karl, 24
Blum, Victor, 108
Blumenthal, Oscar, 6, 16, 30, 60;
  Abu Seid, 62
Bölsche, Wilhelm, 20, 22, 25, 27,
  29f, 33, 150
Bond, Edward: Saved, 137
Bonn, 19, 167
Borchardt, Bruno, 56
Bornemann, Fritz, 131f
Börsen-Courier (Berliner Börsen-
  Courier), 58, 102
Brahm, Otto, 10ff, 13-19, 25ff,
  30, 37, 47, 49, 60, 64, 67f, 71,
  84
Brandenburg, 165; Touring Theatre
  of the March of Brandenburg, 140
Braunsdorf, Bruno, 123
Brecht, Bertolt, vii, 98, 154;
  Edward II (Marlowe), 104
Bremen, 88; Kammerspiele, 127
Breslau, 3, 16, 75, 120
Brod, M. see Hašek, Jaroslav
Brüsseler Deutscher Arbeiterver-
  ein, 5

Brussels, 2, 14
Brussels German Workers'
  Association, see Brüsseler
  Deutscher Arbeiterverein
Bucharest, 20
Büchner, Georg: Dantons Tod,
  24, 27, 64, 98, 112
Buckle, H. T.: History of Civ-
  ilisation in England, 7
Bühnenvolksbund, 105, 114, 140,
  154, 165f
Bund der Geächteten, 2
Bund der Gerechten, 2
Bund der Kommunisten, 2
Bund der Theatergemeinden, 166f
Buschold, Max, 57, 63

Calderón, Pedro, 46, 70
Central Administration for Educa-
  tion, 118
Charlottenburg, 63, 69, 139
Chekhov, Anton: Seagull, 17, 70,
  129; Uncle Vanya, 156
Chicago, 97
Choral Speaking Group, see Sprech-
  chor
Christian Democratic Union (CDU),
  131
Chronegk, Ludwig, 10, 13
Cohen, Hermann, 89
Cohn, Julius, 57, 63
Cologne, 60, 129, 151, 166f
Commercial Salaried Employee,
  The, 89
Committee of Allied Theatre
  Officers, 120f
Committee for Popular Lectures,
  139
Communist Correspondence Com-
  mittee, see Kommunistische
  Korrespondenzkomitee
Communist Manifesto, 2
Communist Party, see Kommun-
  istische Partei Deutschlands
  (KPD) and Sozialistische Einheits-
  partei Deutschlands (SED)
Conrad, C. F., 18
Copenhagen, 169
Cottbus, 55
Council of Repertory Theatres
  (CORT), 169
Courteline, Georges, 70

Danzig, 165
Davidson, Hans, 63
Dehmel, Richard, 29f
Demmer, Friedrich, 125
Democratic Union, see Demokrat-
  ische Vereinigung
Demokratische Vereinigung, 89
Denmark, 169
Deutsche Bühne (1890), 16
Deutsche Bühne (1933), 113ff
Deutsche Freie Studentenschaft, 89
Deutsche Illustrierte Zeitung, 150
Deutsche Monatsblätter, 10
Deutscher Arbeitersängerbund, 61
Deutscher Bühnenverein, 166
Diebold, Bernhard: Tod der Klass-
  iker, 154
Döblin, Alfred, 98
Dortmund, 133
Dostoyevsky, Fyodor, 2, 21;
  Crime and Punishment, 12
Dramaturgische Blätter, 141
Dresdner, Albert, 150
Dreyer, Max, 66
Dumas, Alexandre (fils), 7
Dumont, Louise, 68
Dupont, Paul, 40f, 55f, 63
Durch, 18, 20
Durieux, Tilla, 109, 154
Düsseldorf, 166f; Düsseldorfer
  Schauspielhaus, 92; Kammer-
  spiele, 137
Dyer, Alec: Ist die Welt nicht
  schön?, 155
Dymschitz, Major, 120

East Prussia, 165
Ebert, Carl, 117
Ebert, Friedrich, 87, 91
Eggers, Paul, 120, 123, 126
Eisner, Kurt, 63, 92
Eloesser, Arthur, 102, 153
Elster, Ernst, 89
Engel, Erich, 104
Engels, Friedrich, 2, 5
Eisenach, 3
Erfurt, 39, 62
Erfurth, Ulrich, 156
Ettlinger, Joseph, 66f, 70, 72ff,
  77f
Euripides: Medea, 79

Fassbinder, Rainer-Werner, 156
Fechter, Paul, 108
Federation of Playgoers' Societies, 169
Fehdmer, Helene, 94
Fehling, Jürgen, 78, 92ff, 152, 154
Feuchtwanger, Lion: Jew Süss, 128
Fischer, Samuel, 15f
Fitger, Arthur: Von Gottes Gnaden, 18
Florath, A., 111
Fontane, Theodor, 13, 15, 17
Forster, Karl, 121
Fraenkel, Victor, 63
France, 169
Frankfurt-am-Main, 72, 75, 117, 129, 139, 142, 151, 166f; Neues Theater, 92; Theater-am-Turm (TAT), 142, 156
Frankfurt Artists' Theatre for Rhine and Main, 140
Frankfurter Zeitung, 11, 72, 149
Frankfurt Federation for Popular Education, 142
Freie Bühne, 11, 13-21, 24, 28f, 34, 38, 46f, 67, 151
Freie Bühne für modernes Leben, 150
Freier Deutscher Gewerkschaftsbund (FDGB), 118ff, 126f
Freie Volksbühne, 33, 61
Frenzel (critic), 17ff
Freytag, Robert, 156
Friedrich, E., 28
Friedrichshagen, 20
Fugger, Karl, 120f
Fulda, Ludwig, 15; Das verlorene Paradies, 31; Die Sklavin, 33
Fürst, Karl, 166

Gaulke, Johannes, 62
Geilgens, Hubert, 123
General German Workers' Association, see Allgemeiner Deutscher Arbeiterverein
George (actor), 108
Gerlach, Helmuth von, 89
Gerlach, Schutzmann, 45
Gerst, Wilhelm Karl, 165f
Gesellschaft, 66, 150
Gladstone, W. E., 4
Goebbels, Joseph, 115

Goethe, J. W., 24, 46, 85, 102, 113; Faust I, 51; Götz von Berlichingen, 5, 84
Gogol, N. V.: Government Inspector, 33; Marriage, 92
Goncourt, Edmond and Jules de: Henriette Maréchal, 17
Goldberg, Heinz, 94
Goll, Ywan, 99
Gorky, Maxim: Lower Depths, 61, 67f, 70f, 103; Suburbans, 96
Gorter (theatre concessionaire), 153
Granach, Alexander, 111
Graz, 168f
Great Britain, 169
Greater German Theatre Society, see Grossdeutsche Theatergemeinschaft
Griepenkerl: Robespierre, 24
Grillparzer, Franz, 46, 70
Gröber, Hedwig, 27
Gropius, Walter, 110
Grossdeutsche Theatergemeinschaft, 104
Grosz, George, 103
Günther, Paul, 94

Hachmann, Cord, 29, 33, 47
Halbe, Max: Der Eisgang, 33
Halle, 54
Hamburg, 13, 25, 27, 53, 113f, 119, 128, 139, 141f; State Opera, 128
Hammacher, Rudolf, 127f
Hannover, 54, 119, 123, 140, 142
Hanstein, Adalbart von, 150
Harden, Maximilian, 14, 150
Hart, Heinrich, 10, 15f, 20, 33
Hart, Julius, 10, 15f, 20, 23, 27, 47, 50, 150; Der Sumpf, 16, 24
Hartleben, Otto Erich, 29f, 37, 39, 79, 150
Hašek, Jaroslav: The Good Soldier Schweik (M. Brod and H. Reimann), 111, 154
Hauptmann, Carl, 20; Marianne, 70
Hauptmann, Gerhart, vii, 15f, 20, 45, 48, 70, 75, 94, 112; Atrides Tetralogy, 134; Das Friedenfest, 18; Der Biberpelz, 46;

[Hauptmann, Gerhart,]
Die Ratten, 94; Die Weber, 2,
6, 46ff, 50ff, 98, 121, 134
Fuhrmann Henschel, 128, 156
Hanneles Himmelfahrt, 151
Herbert Engelmann, 128
Vor Sonnenaufgang, 17ff, 24, 27,
29f, 32, 35, 49, 150f
Hebbel, C. F.: Julia, 73; Maria
Magdalena, 33, 54, 64; Nibel-
ungen Parts I and II, 70
Heartfield, John, see Herzfelde,
Helmut
Hegeler, Wilhelm, 150
Heidelberg, 13
Heijermans, Herman, 73f;
Armour, 58; No. 80, 58; Ora
et Labora, 58; The Good Hope,
58
Heine, Heinrich, 61
Heine, Wolfgang, 35
Heinemann (lawyer), 75
Henckell, Karl, 31
Henckels, Paul, 99
Henschel, Bruno, 118
Herzfelde, Helmut, 95
Herzog, see Rehfisch
Herzoglich-Meiningensches Hof-
theater, 9ff, 17
Hessen, 165
Hessen-Nassau, 165
Heyse, Paul, 13, 46
Hildesheim, 166
Hilpert, Heinz, 112, 127
Hindenburg, President, 113
Hitler, Adolf, 4, 113, 136
Hochhuth, Rolf: Der Stellvertreter,
134f; Soldaten, 137
Hochmann, Vasa, 127
Hofmannsthal, Hugo von: Jeder-
mann, 68
Hohenester, Max, 166
Holitscher, Arthur, 105, 108
Holl, Fritz, 95, 97, 99, 111, 154
Holland, 169
Holländer, Felix, 67, 94
Holländer, Victor, 150
Holz, Arno, 20, 51, 70; Die Fam-
ilie Selicke (with Schlaf), 18, 24,
27
Horvath, Ödön von: Bergbahn, 112

Howley, Brigadier-General Frank,
122
Hülsen, Botho von, 8

Ibsen, Henrik, vii, 2, 6, 12f, 20f,
30, 45ff, 70f, 94; A Doll's House,
10ff, 24, 33; An Enemy of the
People, 10f, 27, 30, 35; Ghosts,
10f, 14, 17f, 24, 27, 33, 150;
John Gabriel Borkman, 128;
Lady Inger, 11; Pillars of Soc-
iety, 10f, 24, 29, 78; Rosmers-
holme, 10f; The Lady from the
Sea, 11; The League of Youth, 33;
The Master Builder, 151; The
Pretenders, 10; The Wild Duck,
10f
Ibsen Society (Berlin), 11
Ihering, Herbert, 100, 102, 106f,
110, 112, 121, 126; The Betrayal
of the Volksbühne, 97
Immermann, K. L., 87; Merlin,
87
Independent German Trades Union
Federation, see Freier Deutscher
Gewerkschaftsbund (FDGB)
Independent Social Democratic
Party, 39
Internationale Arbeiterassoziation,
3
Internationale Arbeitsgemein-
schaft Theaterbesucherorgan-
isationen (IATO), 142, 167, 169
International Theatre Institute
(ITI), 167
International Working Men's
Association, see Internationale
Arbeiterassoziation

Jacobs, Monty, 99f
Jacobsohn, Siegfried, 94
Jagow, von, Police President, 75
Jahnke, see Reuter, Fritz
Jakobowski, Ludwig, 66f
Jena, 13, 43, 114, 139
Jessner, Leopold, 83, 94, 103f
Jonas, Paul, 15

Kainz (actor), 68
Kaiser, Georg, 92, 100; Gas, 91
Kalser, Erwin, 108

Kampffmeyer, Bernhard, 40f, 150
Kampffmeyer, Paul, 150
Karchow, Ernst, 127f
Karlsruhe, 140
Kassel, 130, 132, 156
Kastan, Isidor, 19
Kauffmann (lawyer), 54
Kaufmann, Oscar, 79f, 82, 91, 127
Kautsky (editor), 38
Kayssler, Friedrich, 70, 87, 91f, 94f, 97
Kean, Charles, 9
Kerr, Alfred, 76, 136, 155
Kestenberg, Leo, 86
Kiel, 139
Kielland, Alexander, 2, 21; On the Way Home, 18
Kipphardt, Heinar: In der Sache J. Robert Oppenheimer, 135
Kirst, Hans Hellmut: Der Aufstand der Offiziere, 135f
Kleist, Heinrich von, 10, 46
Klöpfer, Eugen, 115
Knina (engineer), 84
Kölnische Zeitung, 22
Kommunistische Arbeiter-Partei, 96
Kommunistische Korrespondenzkomitee, 2
Kommunistische Partei Deutschlands, 96, 105, 110
Königsberg: Das Tribunal, 95
Körber, Hilde, 121
Korpsstudententum, 89
Kotikov, Major-General, 122
Krauss, Werner, 128
Kreutzberg, Harald, 111
Kreuz-Zeitung, 155
Kühl, Gustav, 63
Kulterbund, 118f
Kunst dem Volke, Die, 150
Kurth, Otto, 128
Kurz (Ostend Theater), 8, 28
Kuznetsov, General, 122

Land, Hans, 72
Landau, J., 17f
Landauer, Gustav, 66, 81, 87, 150
Landenberg (Minister), 7
Langen, Alfred, 64
Langhoff, Walter, 126

Lania, Leo, 98
L'Arronge, Adolf, 6
Lassalle, Ferdinand, 3, 5; Franz von Sickingen, 5; System of Acquired Rights, 3
Laubinger (National Chamber of Theatre), 115
Lautenburg, Siegmund, 16
Lautenberg, 23
League of Communists, see Bund der Kommunisten
League of Outlaws, see Bund der Geächteten
League of the Just, see Bund der Gerechten
Lehmann, John, 82
Leipzig, 3, 54, 151
Leonhard, Rudolf, 100; Segel am Horizont (Towarischtsch), 100f
Lessing, Emil, 50f, 66, 84, 86, 150
Lessing, G. E., vii, 46, 70; Minna von Barnhelm, 69f; Nathan der Weise, 64
Ley-Piscator, Maria, see Piscator, Maria Ley-
Licho, Adolf Edgar, 78, 83
Liebknecht, Karl, 87
Liebknecht, Wilhelm, 37
Lindau, Paul, 58, 60, 69
Lindemann, Alfred, 120-3, 126
Literarisches Echo, 67
Litten, Heinz W., 120, 122, 126
Löhr, Adolf, 55, 65f, 152
London, 2, 129; Princess Theatre, 9
Lortzing, G. A.: Zar und Zimmermann, 70
Lothar, Frank, 130
Löwenfeld, Raphael, 45, 57
Lower Saxony, 165
Lübeck, 140, 168
Ludwig, Hermann, 129
Ludwig, Otto, 13; Der Erbforster, 33
Luft, Friedrich, 117, 130
Lüttgenau, Franz, 30
Luzynski, Julius, 75

Maass, Benno, 62f
Magazin für Literatur, 29
Magdeburg, 19, 54, 139

Mainz, 166
Malzahn, Baron von, 8f
Mannheim, 75, 83, 140
Marburg, 88f
Marschalk, Max, 150
Martersteig, Max, 66
Martin, Karl-Heinz, 95, 108, 112,
  119-122, 126
Marx, Karl, 2f, 5, 20, 89; Cap-
  ital, 3
Mauthner, Fritz, 15f, 66, 150
May, Walter, 122f, 125f
Meery, Hans, 17
Mehring, Franz, 37ff, 41, 43ff,
  48, 50, 55ff, 59, 62, 76, 79
Meiningen Court Theatre, see
  Herzoglich-Meiningensches
  Hoftheater
Memel Territory, 165
Mendel, Vera, 152
Merscheidt-Hüllessem, 63
Milan, 151
Miller, Arthur: Death of a Sales-
  man, 132
Möest, Friedrich, 69
Molière, 46; La Malade imagi-
  naire, 64
Möller, Eduard, 65
Mönchengladbach, 167
Moraller (Reichskulturamtsleiter),
  115f
Moscow, 10
Mostar, Hermann: Der Zimmer-
  herr, 126
Mozart, W. A., 61: Marriage of
  Figaro, 70; Zauberflöte, 70
Müller, August, 65
Müller, Julius, 52
Müller, Traugott, 101, 108
Munich, 87, 92, 139, 166f
Münster, 167

Nation, Die, 11, 13, 17f, 150
National Chamber of Literature,
  116
National Chamber of Theatre, 115
National Women's Circle, 104
National-Zeitung, 13
Neft, Heinrich, 65f, 69, 76ff,
  81ff, 84, 99, 155
Nestriepke, Siegfried, 88ff, 94f,
  97, 111f, 114ff, 118-123, 127ff,
  133, 137, 141f, 150, 152, 166;

[Nestriepke, Siegfried,]
  The Theory of Trades Unionism,
  90; The Trade Union Movement,
  90
Nestroy, Johann, 70
Neue Rundschau, 149
Neue Zeit, Die, 38, 44, 73, 76
Neumann-Hofer, Otto, 9
New York, 10, 72, 132
Nicolai, K. O. E.: Merry Wives
  of Windsor, 70
Niederschönenfeld, 92
1984, 114
Noelte, Rudolf, 129
Nordmark, 165
Norway, 169
Nuremburg, 104

Old Aunt, see Alte Tante
O'Neill, Eugene, 100; A Touch of
  the Poet, 129; Under the Car-
  ibbean Moon, 100
Osborn, Max, 99
Osborne, John: Luther, 156
Oschilewski, Walther G., 137
Oslo, 169
Ostrovsky, A. N.: The Storm, 52
Otto, Erich, 121

Pahl, Rudolf, 115
Palitzch, Peter, 156
Pallenberg (actor), 154
Palucca, Gret, 111
Papproth, Walter, 129
Paquet, Alfons: Fahnen, 96-101,
  153; Sturmflut, 101ff, 153
Paris, 14, 52, 132
Pirandello, Luigi: Six Characters
  in Search of an Author, 128
Piscator, Erwin, viii, 34, 80, 94,
  95-112, 132-9, 152f, 156; Das
  Politische Theater, 95, 100, 153
Piscator, Maria Ley-, 97
Pissemski: Der Leibeigene, 31
Poelzig (architect), 68
Pohlmann (Nazi), 114
Polenz, Wilhelm von, 150
Pomerania, 140, 165
Potsdam, 116
Pravda, 110
Prussian Provincial Theatre, Ltd.,
  140

Raimund, Ferdinand: Der Bauer als Millionär, 92; Der Verschwender, 94
Recklinghausen, 129
Redlich, Gerda, 68, 111
Rehfisch, Hans José, 96, 100; Dreyfus Affair (with Herzog), 112; Wer weint um Juckenack?, 100
Reicher, Emanuel, 65
Reicke, Dr, 80
Reimann, H., see Hašek, Jaroslav
Reinhardt, Max, 59f, 63, 67f, 70, 72, 79, 86, 94, 97, 127, 154; Miracle, 69; World Theatre, 69
Reinhold, Conny, 142
Reuter, Ernst, 125
Reuter, Fritz: Kein Hüsung (Jahnke and Schirmer), 31
Reuter, Rudolf, 166
Rheinland, 165
Rhine-Main Federation for Popular Education, 140
Rhine-Main Federation Theatre, 140
Richter, Paul, 23f
Richthofen, Bernhard von, 35ff, 150
Richthofen, Frieda von, 150
Rickelt, Gustav, 82
Rimbeau, Arthur, 103
Robert, Emmerich, 17
Rolland, Romain: Le Temps viendra, 96; Robespierre, 136
Rosenov: Die im Schatten leben, 75
Ross, Rudolf, 113
Rote Fahne, 96
Ruhr, 140

Saargebiet, 165
Sachsen-Anhalt, see Saxony
Sächsische Arbeiterzeitung, 25
Sahm (auditor), 63
Salzburg, 67f, 128f
Samst, Max, 28f, 31f, 54, 60
Sardou, V., 7
Sartre, Jean-Paul: Iron in the Soul, 136; Les Mouches, 149; Nekrassov, 156
Sassenbach, Johann, 61
Saxe-Meiningen, Duke George II of, 9-10

Saxony, 59, 119, 139, 165
Scandinavia, 169
Schaubühne, Die, 71
Scheidemann, Philipp, 87, 90
Schikowski, John, 63
Schiller, Friedrich, vii, 7, 10, 24, 46, 49, 61, 77, 82, 113, 149; Die Braut von Messina, 70; Die Räuber, 5, 31, 61, 103f, 110, 154; Kabale und Liebe, 30, 61 Piccolomini, 70; Wallensteins Lager, 70; Wilhelm Tell, 109
Schirmer, see Reuter, Fritz
Schlaf, Johannes: Die Familie Selicke (with Holz), 18, 24, 27; Meister Oelze, 51
Schlaikjer, Erich, 63; Des Pastors Rieke, 63
Schlawe (Pomerania), 43
Schlenther, Paul, 10f, 15f
Schleupner (monumental mason), 19f
Schlösser (National dramaturge), 115
Schmid, Gerard, 142, 169
Schmidt, Conrad, 23, 25, 27, 29, 34f, 38, 56ff, 62f, 74, 81f
Schmidt, Erich, 13
Schmidt, Robert, 55
Schmidtbonn: Mutter Landstrasse, 70
Schmoller, Gustav, 88
Schnabel, Arthur, 72
Schönhoff, Leopold, 62, 150
School for Workers' Education, see Arbeiterbildungsschule
Schubart, C. F. D., 89
Schuh, Oscar Fritz, 88, 128f, 131
Schulz, Günter, 133ff
Schulz, Heinrich, 57, 62
Schwerin, Count, 8
Scottish Federation of Playgoers' Societies, 169
Scribe, Eugène, 7
Selo, Heinz, 44, 56f
Shakespeare, William: Comedy of Errors, 92; Coriolanus, 104; Hamlet, 103f, 127; Julius Caesar, 10; King Lear, 94; Merchant of Venice, 70, 156; Midsummer Night's Dream, 70; Twelfth Night, 70; The Winter's Tale, 10, 70
Shaw, G. B., 58f, 70, 94;

[Shaw, G. B. ,]
Androcles and the Lion, 156;
Arms and the Man, 58; Captain
Brassbound's Conversion, 92;
Mrs Warren's Profession, 58;
The Devil's Disciple, 58; Wid-
owers' Houses, 58
Siebenmark (printer), 65
Silesia, 59, 139, 165
Sinsheimer, Hermann, 83
Skådebanen, 169
Skopnik, Günter, 129, 132
Social Democratic Party, 3ff, 11,
23ff, 33ff, 46, 55, 57, 76, 83,
87, 89f, 105, 119ff, 126, 131
Solms, Graf, 115
Sonnenburg, 23
Sophocles: Antigone, 92
Sorma, Agnes, 51, 70
Soviet Central Command, 118
Sozialdemokrat, 120
Sozialdemokratische Arbeiter-
partei, see Social Democratic
Party
Sozialist, Der, 39, 65
Sozialistische Einheitspartei
Deutschlands (SED), 119, 126
Spartakusbund, 151
Sperber, Heinz, see Heijermans,
Hermann
Spohr, Wilhelm, 109
Sprechchor, 111
Springer, Georg, 72, 76ff, 81f,
84, 91, 105
Staar, Fritz, 116
Stampfer, Friedrich, 73f
Stanislavsky, Constantin, 17
Stauffenberg, Klaus von, 136
Steckel, Leonard, 129
Stehl (Third Volksbühne), 52
Stein, Ludwig, 78
Steinert, Adolf, 60, 76
Sternheim, Carl, 95
Stettenheim, Julius, 15f
Stockhausen (theatre agent), 15
Stockholm, 169
Stollberg, George, 33
Stoltzenburg, Peter, 137
Strassburg, 13
Strindberg, August, 95, 152; A
Dream Play, 129; Miss Julie,
47; The Father, 10, 18
Ströbel, Heinrich, 73
Stuttgart, 71, 140, 142; Württem-
burg Landestheater, 95

Sudermann, Hermann, 30, 46; Die
Ehre, 30
Sweden, 169
Swiss Theatre Associations, see
Theatervereine der Schweiz
Switzerland, 59, 168

Tag, Der, 106f
Tägliche Rundschau, 48, 119
Telegraf, 120f
Tesch, Carl, 142
Tettenborn: Perspektiven, 130
Theater der Jugend, 168
Theater in Graz, 168
Theater Rundschau, 166
Theatervereine der Schweiz, 168
Théâtre Libre, 10, 14, 52
Thuringia, 139, 165
Tieck, Ludwig: Der gestiefelte
Kater, 92
Tiburtius, Joachim, 121
Toller, Ernst, 108; Die Wandlung,
95; Hoppla, wir leben!, 111, 154;
Masse-Mensch, 92f, 152
Tolstoy, Alexei: Rasputin, 111, 154
Tolstoy, Leo, 2, 12, 21, 57, 70;
Power of Darkness, 10, 17, 24,
27, 57, 96; War and Peace, 136
Trade Union 17, 120
Tribüne, 119
Troeltsch, Walter, 89
Tschirikow: The Jews, 58
Türk, Julius, 21ff, 25, 27f, 30,
34f, 39ff, 44, 54, 57, 59, 62,
150
Türk, Moritz, 23

Union for the promotion of German
Theatrical Culture, see Verband
zur Förderung deutscher Theater-
kultur
Union of German Workers' Asso-
ciations, see Verband der
deutschen Arbeitervereine
(VDAV)
Union of Non-commercial Touring
Companies, 141
Union of Theatre Societies, see
Bund der Theatergemeinden
USSR, 124, 132
Utzerath, Hansjörg, 137

Vallentin, Richard, 68
Verband der deutschen Arbeitervereine (VDAV), 3

Verband zur Förderung deutscher Theaterkultur, 166
Verdi, Giuseppe: Aida, 124
Verein für Volksunterhaltung, 149
Verein zur Begründung von Volks- bühnen, 9
Verga, Giovanni, 46
Verlaine, Paul, 103
Versuchsbühne, Die, 51
Vienna, 16, 92, 127, 129, 139, 151, 168; Burgtheater, 17; Opera, 128; Volksbühne, 92
Voigt, Richard, 137, 156
Volksblatt, Das, 23
Volksbühne, Die, 91, 140f
Volksbühnenbund, see Bühnen- volksbund
Volksbühnenchor, see Volkschor
Volkschor, 61, 73
Volkstribüne, 23, 30, 34
Vorwärts, 40, 54ff, 62f, 73f, 89, 99
Voss, J. H.: Eva, 51
Vossische Zeitung, 13, 99

Wach, Willi, 19f
Wagner, Adolf, 88
Wagner, Anton, 91
Wagner, Heinrich Leopold: Die Kindesmörderin, 70
Waldow, Carl, 60
Wallner, Franz, 17
Walser, Martin: Überlebensgross Herr Krott, 156
Wedekind, Frank, 95, 152; Früh- lings Erwachen, 70, 112
Weisenborn: U-Boot S.4, 112
Weiss, Peter: Die Ermittlung, 135f
Welk, Elm, 154; Gewitter über Gottland, 103, 106-9, 112; Kreuzabnahme, 112
Weltbühne, 105
Welzel, Gotthard, 167
Westphalia, 165
Wibker, Heinrich, 20

Wiener Arbeiterzeitung, 98
Wiesbaden, 129, 167f
Wigman, Mary, 111
Wildangel (deputy head of education), 122
Wildberger, Carl, 23, 25, 27, 39ff, 43, 150
Wilde, Oscar, 152
Wildenbruch, Ernst von, 8, 13; Das neue Gebot, 8
Wilhelm II, 104
Wilhelmshagen, 20
Wille, Bruno, 2, 7, 19-43, 49, 50ff, 55, 60, 62, 66ff, 77, 81f, 84, 136, 150; Durch Kampf zur Freiheit, 31
Wilmersdorf, 123
Winkler, Gustav, 57, 61ff, 81
Winzer, Otto, 118f
Witte-Wild, Fritz, 8, 28, 60
Wolff, Theodor, 14
Wollzogen, Ernst von, 150
Workers' Educational Association, vii
Wuppertal, 60
Wurm: May Festival Marseillaise, 31
Württemburg, 140, 165
Wurzburg, 167

Young Playgoers' Federation, 169
Yugoslavia, 169

Zadek, Peter, 137, 156
Zander, Ernst, 61
Zech, Paul: Das trunkene Schiff, 103
Zickel (theatre director), 96
Zola, Émile, 2, 6, 10, 20f; Thérèse Raquin, 27, 33, 150
Zuckmayer, Carl, 123; Herbert Engelmann, see Hauptmann, Gerhart
Zukunft, 150
Zürich, 47, 56, 151